Evaluating Teaching and Learning

Every semester, colleges and universities ask students to complete innumerable questionnaires to evaluate the learning and teaching in courses they have taken. For many universities it is a requirement that all courses be evaluated every semester. The laudable rationale is that the feedback provided will enable instructors to improve their teaching and the curriculum, thus enhancing the quality of student learning.

In spite of this there is little evidence that it does improve the quality of teaching and learning. Ratings only improve if the instruments and the presentation of results are sufficiently diagnostic to identify potential improvements and there is effective counselling. *Evaluating Teaching and Learning* explains how evaluation can be more effective in enhancing the quality of teaching and learning, and introduces broader and more diverse forms of evaluation.

This guide explains how to develop questionnaires and protocols that are valid, reliable and diagnostic. It also contains proven instruments that have undergone appropriate testing procedures, together with a substantial item bank. The book looks at the specific national frameworks for the evaluation of teaching in use in the USA, UK and Australasia.

It caters for diverse methodologies, both quantitative and qualitative, and offers solutions that allow evaluation at a wide range of levels, from classrooms to programmes to departments and entire institutions. With detail on all aspects of the main evaluation techniques and instruments, the authors show how effective evaluation can make use of a variety of approaches and combine them into an effective project.

With a companion website that has listings of the questionnaires and item bank, this book will be of interest to those concerned with organising and conducting evaluation in a college, university, faculty or department. It will also appeal to those engaged in the scholarship of teaching and learning.

David Kember is Professor in Higher Education, University of Hong Kong.

Paul Ginns is Senior Lecturer in Educational Psychology, University of Sydney, Australia.

Evaluating Teaching and Learning

A practical handbook for colleges, universities and the scholarship of teaching

David Kember and Paul Ginns

Routledge
Taylor & Francis Group

LONDON AND NEW YORK

First published 2012
by Routledge
2 Park Square, Milton Park, Abingdon, Oxon OX14 4RN

Simultaneously published in the USA and Canada
by Routledge
711 Third Avenue, New York, NY 10017

Routledge is an imprint of the Taylor & Francis Group, an informa business

British Library Cataloguing in Publication Data
A catalogue record for this book is available from the British Library

Library of Congress Cataloging in Publication Data
Kember, David.
Evaluating teaching and learning : a practical handbook for colleges, universities and the scholarship of teaching / by David Kember and Paul Ginns.
p. cm.
Includes bibliographical references and index.
1. College teaching—Evaluation. 2. Effective teaching—Evaluation. I. Ginns, Paul.
II. Title.
LB2331.K386 2012
378.1'25—dc23
2011028579

ISBN: 978–0–415–59884–2 (hbk)
ISBN: 978–0–415–59885–9 (pbk)
ISBN: 978–0–203–81757–5 (ebk)

Typeset in Galliard
by FiSH Books, Enfield

Printed and bound in Great Britain by the MPG Books Group

Contents

Acknowledgements

Copyright ownership of the questionnaires listed in Chapter 3 is given below. Purchasers of the book have permission to use the questionnaires for purposes of evaluation or research, provided there is no financial gain. In any resulting publication, there should be citation to both this book and the original publications.

Exemplary teacher course questionnaire   David Kember and Doris Y.P. Leung
Revised study process questionnaire   John Biggs and David Kember
Reflection questionnaire   David Kember and Doris Y.P. Leung
Student engagement questionnaire   David Kember, Doris Y.P. Leung and Carmel McNaught
Taught postgraduate experience questionnaire   David Kember
Blended learning environment questionnaire   Taylor & Francis
E-Learning Scale   John Wiley and Sons

Table 5.1 is reproduced with permission from John Wiley and Sons.

Abbreviations

3P	presage–process–product
ACER	Australian Council for Educational Research
AGS	Australian Graduate Survey
ATAR	Australian Tertiary Admission Rank
AUQA	Australian Universities Quality Assurance Agency
AUSSE	Australasian Survey of Student Engagement
BCSSE	Beginning College Survey of Student Engagement
CEQ	Course Experience Questionnaire
CFA	confirmatory factor analysis
CFI	comparative fit index
CLASSE	Classroom Survey of Student Engagement
CPQ	Course Perceptions Questionnaire
CPR	Center for Postsecondary Research, Indiana University School of Education
CTEQ	course and teaching evaluation questionnaires
CUHK	Chinese University of Hong Kong
DEL	Department for Employment and Learning, Northern Ireland
EFA	exploratory factor analysis
ETCQ	exemplary teacher course questionnaire
FCI	force concept inventory
FEC	further education colleges
FSSE	Faculty Survey of Student Engagement
GDS	Graduate Destination Survey
GSS	Generic Skills Scale
GTS	Good Teaching Scale
HEFCE	Higher Education Funding Council for England
HEFCW	Higher Education Funding Council for Wales
HEI	higher education institution
HSC	Higher School Certificate
ICT	information and communication technology
IRA	inter-rater agreement
IRR	inter-rater reliability
MDT	mechanics diagnostic test
MLR	robust maximum likelihood estimator
NHST	null hypothesis significance test
NSS	National Student Survey (UK)

NSSE	National Survey of Student Engagement
OSI	Overall Satisfaction Indicator
PB	personal best
PBL	problem-based learning
QAA	Quality Assurance Agency for Higher Education
RMSEA	root mean square error of approximation
R-SPQ	revised study process questionnaire
SAL	students' approaches to learning
SCEQ	Student Course Experience Questionnaire
SEM	structural equation modelling
SEQ	student engagement questionnaire
SLT	student learning theory
SOLO	structure of observed learning outcome
SoTL	scholarship of teaching and learning
SPQ	study process questionnaire
SRMR	standardised root mean squared residual
STEM	science, technology, engineering and mathematics
TPg	taught postgraduate
USE	Unit of Study Evaluation
VSA	Voluntary System of Accountability
WAM	weighted average mark

Figures and tables

Figures

Tables

Chapter 1

Evaluation principles

What is evaluation?

Evaluation is introduced as the collection and analysis of data for the purpose of informing decision-making. In general, it is commonly thought of as a process of obtaining feedback from stakeholders or clients to assess their satisfaction with a service provided. The aim should be one of identifying strengths, which can be built upon, and indicating aspects that have the potential for improvement.

If the evaluation data is properly utilised, the process of evaluation will be incorporated within a set of procedures for making use of the information to improve the service. In developing a new product, the process is normally referred to as a development and testing cycle. Data from the tests are used to improve the product. With respect to services or social systems, the cyclical process is more commonly thought of as a version of the action research cycle. Each cycle includes steps of planning, action, evaluation or observation and reflection. One cycle leads into another, thus facilitating iterative improvement.

With respect to learning and teaching, the evaluation is informing decisions, design, development, revisions and actions with respect to teaching and learning. The aim or purpose should be improving the quality of teaching, providing a better learning and teaching environment, and improving the chances that desired learning outcomes will be attained. If this is to happen, the gathering of the evaluation data needs to be a part of a system for making use of the data to make changes, so that there is improvement.

Why evaluate learning and teaching?

The most common form of evaluation is that for courses and/or teachers and instructors. Every semester colleges ask students to complete innumerable course and teaching evaluation questionnaires (CTEQ) to evaluate the learning and teaching in courses they have taken. For many universities it is a requirement that all courses be evaluated every semester. The practice has become so pervasive that for many students evaluation has become synonymous with the completion of CTEQ forms at the end of every semester. Many teachers envisage evaluation purely in terms of the (often dreaded) results sheets they receive shortly after.

At this point we will introduce a terminology convention used throughout the book. A degree taken by a student will be referred to as a programme. Programmes are made up of courses (also referred to in some settings as subjects, or units of study);

so a full-time student might take around four courses per semester. Apologies to those who use different terms or attribute different meanings to these terms.

The laudable rationale for the mammoth undertaking of collecting such a huge body of CTEQ data is that the feedback provided will enable instructors to improve their teaching and the curriculum, thus enhancing the quality of student learning. The theory is that teachers will use the results to diagnose aspects of their teaching that are susceptible to improvement. Over time, the quality of teaching will rise as individual teachers perform better.

In spite of the supposed justification for this vast CTEQ enterprise, there is little evidence that it does improve the quality of teaching and learning. Reviews of studies into changes in teachers' ratings suggest they are remarkably stable (Marsh, 1987), indicating little sign of improvement over time. This finding applies both at the individual teacher level (Marsh, 2007) and the whole college (Kember, Leung, & Kwan, 2002). Research evidence suggests that ratings only improve if the instruments and the presentation of results are sufficiently diagnostic to identify potential improvements and the feedback is accompanied by effective counselling (Marsh & Roche, 1993).

Staff appraisal

There is another less salubrious justification, which is the use of CTEQ data for personnel decisions. The pressures of being seen to take teaching seriously are such that CTEQ scores and other evidence of teaching effectiveness are normally required in tenure and promotion applications, and, if most universities policies are to be believed, do inform personnel decisions. However, in most institutions there is a perception that the number of publications counts more.

There is often a tension between the use of evaluation to provide feedback and its function within staff appraisal. It is rare for appraisers or appraisees to enjoy the experience of appraisal. More seriously, appraisees commonly complain that the outcomes are unfair. A common reason for this is that teaching is not given enough weight compared to research.

Another commonly aired grievance is that the exercise does not provide constructive feedback. One possible reason for this is that there is evidence that CTEQ ratings are effective in improving teaching quality only if accompanied by effective counselling. We suspect that appraisals rarely involve discussions of CTEQ data in a diagnostic way.

Reviews

It is commonplace nowadays for universities to be reviewed or audited, particularly in British Commonwealth countries. For this exercise they normally have to produce a self-evaluation document showing that they have in place effective quality assurance and enhancement procedures. These need to include evaluation processes that gather feedback about a wide range of aspects of teaching and learning from appropriate stakeholders. The audit panel will try to ascertain whether the feedback obtained is capable of informing teaching and learning practices and is incorporated within processes that can lead to improvements.

At the programme level, professional programmes are commonly audited by professional bodies. These audits normally follow a similar format to the reviews of universities. Reviews and audits normally take an outcomes-based approach, by which a college or programme is asked to specify the goals, aims or learning outcomes they are striving towards. They are then asked to provide evidence that there is in place a teaching and learning environment consistent with students achieving the stated learning outcomes. The evidence obviously comes from evaluation procedures and needs to be focused on stated learning outcomes if it is to be pertinent to this exercise.

These reviews and audits imply a need to gather evaluation data other than that from CTEQ instruments. If a university or programme is to be properly reviewed, there needs to be evaluation at the level of the institution or programme. These cannot be properly evaluated solely by conflating CTEQ data, as higher-level constructs become relevant, thus needing evaluation with an alternative focus. This implies different forms of evaluation seeking answers to alternative questions.

Stakeholders

Another factor which has diversified assessment is the need to consult a wider range of stakeholders. It is recognised that it is not just those taking a particular course who need to be asked questions. New students, first-year students, fresh graduates, alumni, part-time students, mature students, post-graduate students, employers and even teachers can be seen as having relevant opinions and able to give useful feedback on teaching and learning. Each of these stakeholder groups has different perspectives, and therefore needs to be asked different questions.

There are then a range of needs for evaluation at universities. As the expectations of colleges have grown and their roles have become more diverse, the forms of necessary evaluations have expanded, and seem set to grow further. It is widely accepted that triangulation against multiple sources of data is desirable, which places additional demands. The lack of improvement resulting from much of the CTEQ exercise, though, suggests that there is a need, in many cases, for these evaluation practices to be improved. Hopefully, this book will be of assistance in this process.

Scholarship of teaching

A further area that requires evaluation is the growing number of teachers heeding the call to engage in the scholarship of teaching (Boyer, 1990). These teachers are normally introducing some form of innovation into their own teaching. They need evaluation or research data to enable them to fine-tune their innovation and hopefully to provide evidence of its effectiveness.

One motivation to engage in the scholarship of teaching is the growing number of new teachers enrolling in courses in teaching in higher education, to prepare themselves for the teaching component of academic careers. Many of the longer courses include a project requirement.

The evaluation strategies need to be tailored to the nature and intended outcomes of the innovation if they are to provide useful information. In a mega-project that supported 90 action research projects practising the scholarship of teaching (Kember, 2000b), virtually none found any value in CTEQ data. These were too general, so they did not provide evidence specific to the aims of the project or the nature of the innovation introduced.

The most common form of advice or help sought from the project's supporting team was help in devising appropriate forms of evaluation. In this book we aim to provide this type of advice, so that those engaged in scholarship in teaching will be able to devise suitable evaluation instruments and designs.

Evidence of improvements from award-winning teachers

Evidence that properly used evaluation data can lead to enhancement in the quality of teaching and learning comes from interviews with award-winning teachers (Kember with McNaught, 2007). Many of the interviewed teachers admitted that their teaching had not always been of award-winning quality, including over half of the Chinese University of Hong Kong (CUHK) interviewees. Indeed, some had to make consider-able progress to reach their current standard.

> I think what I used to do was poor teaching. I would write on the blackboard for fifty-five minutes and the students would diligently copy it down and occasionally there would be some brave soul who would ask a question – usually, 'Can I go to the toilet, sir?' – and I would think 'a job well done'. (I'd feel quite tired after writ-ing for fifty-five minutes.) There would be no assignments, just a formal exam, and at the end of that there'd be a mark. And then I'd wonder why the vast majority of students weren't able to answer any of the questions in the exam. To my mind, that is ineffective teaching.
> (Michael Morgan, Monash, Physics, quoted in Kember with McNaught, 2007, p. 135)

Interestingly, the change commonly followed a similar pattern. At the start of their careers teaching tended to be didactic and concentrated on covering content. Over time, the focus shifted towards aiming to ensure that students actually learned what was important.

> When I first started teaching, I did my best to stuff students with as much content as possible. I realise that this is not the right thing to do. On the contrary, I don't need to teach so much, and I should pace my teaching so that students can truly absorb what is being taught. There is knowledge of the world that can never all be taught.
> (John Lui, CUHK, Computer Science and Engineering, quoted in Kember with McNaught, 2007, p. 136)

Reflection and action research cycle

What was common to the award-winning teachers was reflection upon practice. Gathering evaluation data and making observations are only of value if accompanied by reflection.

> My teaching is improving continuously. I reflect upon my practice as I go along. Personally, I constantly reflect upon my teaching and seek to improve my skills almost daily. I think of ways to enhance students' learning so that they can retain

the knowledge and skills for a long time and apply them appropriately. It will be great if I can make the learning process enjoyable.

(Leung Sing Fai, CUHK, Clinical Oncology, quoted in Kember with McNaught, 2007, p. 143)

Iterative improvement of teaching in this way can be seen as an application of the action learning cycle – planning, action, observation and reflection. It is also akin to the developmental testing cycle used in business and engineering.

Learning is an internalisation experience. I think action learning is important in the context of education. Reflection is also important. … Application of action learning is important.

(John Chi Kin Lee, CUHK, Curriculum and Instruction, quoted in Kember with McNaught, 2007, p. 144)

Another way of putting this is learning from mistakes. If something doesn't work, either determine how to improve it or try something else. You can also learn from your successes, of course. If you learn from your successes and failures you will find that, over time, you start having more of the former.

You learn from your mistakes as much as you learn from your successes – in fact you learn more from mistakes. I've made some monumental cock-ups in my experience as a teacher, but you've got to embrace your mistakes and enjoy them and learn from them. You've got to cherish and love your mistakes. That's what it's about, isn't it – learning from experience.

(Jim McKnight, UWS, Psychology, quoted in Kember with McNaught, 2007, p. 144)

Roadmap for two audiences

This book caters for two main audiences. The first is those concerned with organising and conducting evaluation in a college, university, faculty or department. Many colleges have designated offices and staff appointed specifically for this role. The information for these will also be useful to the vice-presidents, deans and heads of department who have to ensure that evaluation is properly conducted and the best use made of the data.

The other audience is those engaged in the scholarship of teaching and learning (SoTL). This growing body conduct research on teaching and learning in their own discipline, and often on courses they teach. To properly conduct projects, evaluation evidence is needed.

These two audiences have somewhat different aims and needs. To help readers efficiently get what they need from the book, the table below provides a roadmap through the book, showing how the two audiences might make use of each chapter.

Table 1.1 Roadmap through the chapters for the two audiences

Chapter	Institutional evaluation	SoTL
1. Evaluation principles	Provides an introduction to both	
2. Questionnaire design	Vital for institutional evaluation. If questionnaires are not well designed, valid, reliable and possessing diagnostic power, the evaluation exercise will be seriously undermined.	Projects normally need questionnaires related to the aims and desired outcomes of the initiative. This implies tailoring the questionnaire to the project, so design principles are important.
3. Questionnaires	Provides standard questionnaires at course, programme and graduate level and for taught postgraduate programmes and blended learning environments.	Questionnaires for approaches to learning, reflection and blended learning are ideal for SoTL.
4. Item bank	The item bank will be useful if questionnaires are needed for specialised purposes.	The item bank will be helpful in designing questionnaires tailored for a project.
5. Collecting and processing questionnaire data	Very important if data are to be collected and processed efficiently across an institution.	The basic ideas of collecting and processing data are needed. A complete sample is normally collected.
6. Collection of qualitative data	An argument is made that institutional evaluation should make more use of qualitative work, in which case Chapters 6 and 7 are relevant.	A high proportion of SoTL projects collect qualitative data. Chapter 6 deals with the basics of planning qualitative projects and collecting data.
7. Analysis of qualitative data		Analysis of qualitative data is often not well explained, so this chapter gives a straightforward explanation, based on the main elements or steps in analysis. Many examples are given.
8. Observation	Not applicable	Reflective checklists for small and large classes are given, to promote systematic observation and reflection.
9. Use of assessment for evaluation	May be useful for educational developers, as it gives three well-utilised examples of standards-based assessment.	Promotes the use of assessment as evidence in SoTL projects by showing how well developed protocols can give reliable results. Concept inventories are explained.
10. Using evaluation data for the scholarship of teaching	Evaluation officers are often asked for advice by those engaged in SoTL. This chapter deals with project design and has useful examples.	Deals with project design from a paradigmatic perspective. Uses examples to illustrate good practice.
11. International perspectives on teaching evaluation	A number of countries have moved towards required or recommended instruments, so it is necessary to be aware of international practices.	Unlikely to be useful, as the instruments focus at the institutional or programme level.

Table 1.1 (continued)

Chapter	Institutional evaluation	SoTL
12. Institutional use of teaching evaluation data	Deals with how to design questionnaires, present results and provide counselling in order to achieve quality enhancement across an institution.	The section on presenting results will be useful for writing up the project.
13. Conclusion	Revisits some important principles, including: • The purpose of evaluation • A focus on enhancing the quality of teaching and learning • A focus on the aims or desired learning outcomes • Multiple perspectives • Multiple methods	
Appendix.	Advanced statistical methods for teaching evaluation data. The appendix provides a brief treatment of statistical methods that are particularly important for evaluation. The orientation is towards the application of the statistics in projects, so those engaged in SoTL should find the appendix particularly valuable. Institutional researchers may also find it useful, as the focus is different to that of most conventional statistics courses.	

Triangulation

Triangulation of multiple sources of data is accepted as a good principle in evaluation. Table 1.2 acts as an advance organiser for the remainder of the book by introducing the more significant forms of evaluation covered in subsequent chapters. These are classified by type of evaluation technique: observation, dialogue/qualitative data, questionnaires and reflection/mentoring. Cross-categorisation indicates the appropriate level: class, course, programme and graduates.

Table 1.2 Principal evaluation techniques and instruments

	Class	Course	Programme	Graduates
Observation	Class observation	Assessment		
Dialogue Qualitative data	End of class	Focus group Course website Open-ended questions	Staff–student committee Open-ended questions	Alumni meetings Employer meetings
Questionnaire	Post-it notes	Course questionnaire Knowledge questionnaire Skills questionnaire R-SPQ-2F Blended learning questionnaire	Student engagement questionnaire R-SPQ-2F TPg questionnaire	Tailored survey Employer survey
Mentoring Reflection	Large class checklist Small class checklist Mentoring	Reflection protocol Reflection questionnaire Mentoring	Review	

Accompanying website

Accompanying the book is a website (www.routledge.com/9780415598859) with downloadable Word files containing questionnaire items for each questionnaire given in Chapter 3 of the book. This enables readers to form versions of the questionnaire in their own format either on paper or online. In addition, there is a substantial item bank, listed in Chapter 4, on the website as a Word file, which will enable you to form your own questionnaires.

Chapter 2

Questionnaire design

There was an inter-institutional project in Hong Kong that aimed to gather question-naires from the universities, test them and make them available in the form of complete or partial instruments and an item bank. It seemed likely to be a worthwhile project. However, when the team started soliciting questionnaires, they were disappointed to find that, with a few exceptions, they were given lots and lots of course and teaching evaluation questionnaires (CTEQs). What was even more disappointing, and rather shocking, was the poor quality of the questionnaires, even though many had been used for some time and quite widely within the departments, faculties and universities. A significant number of questionnaire items had the sort of basic errors described in a later section of this chapter. The examples of what to avoid mostly came from this proj-ect. Not surprisingly, the psychometric properties of the instruments mostly left a lot to be desired.

International confirmation that undue confidence is placed in the design of CTEQs comes from the work of Onwuegbuzie, Daniel, and Collins (2009). They argue that instruments, which have used the traditional approaches to validity, may still be weak in content- and construct-related validity, because of limitations in the commonly used approaches. This suggests that instruments designed by committees or administrators, without expertise in instrument design, have little chance of possessing adequate psychometric properties.

It seems, then, that there is a need for guidelines in designing good questionnaires. For many purposes it is possible to make use of tried and tested instruments, such as those included with this book. In other cases, though, it is desirable to have all or part of questionnaires focusing on the intended learning outcomes of a course or on the aims of teaching innovation. Clearly these need to be designed specifically for the course or innovation in question. This is therefore an important chapter.

In this chapter there are guidelines for writing good items. The value of forming items into coherent scales is explained. The concepts of reliability and validity are discussed, since these are the two criteria most widely used to determine whether an instrument is viable. The ability of a questionnaire to fulfil its intended purpose of providing useful feedback and information relating to its intended application is also considered. This is important in evaluation questionnaires, as it enables relative strengths and weaknesses to be identified, which makes it possible to advise on reme-dial action. For this purpose, the concept of diagnostic power is introduced as the ability of an instrument to distinguish between related constructs.

Examples given in this chapter mostly concentrate on CTEQs, which are the most widely used instruments in higher education. It is important that they are well designed, since they are often the most widely used (and sometimes the only) quality assurance procedure to ensure that teaching and learning is of a reputable standard. They also find an increasing use in personnel decisions, as an integral component of staff appraisal procedures.

Open/closed questions

Questionnaires contain either open or closed questions, or often a combination of the two. Open questions invite a written response. If well designed, they will be sufficiently open to permit respondents to raise issues that they feel are pertinent, but which may not have been encompassed by closed-response questions. Typical open questions are:

> What were the best aspects of this course?
> Which aspects were most in need of improvement?

Closed questions give respondents a choice of a limited number of responses. These can be a choice of categories, such as male/female, or School of Arts/Engineering/ Science/Social Science, etc. They more commonly use a response scale, which asks respondents to rate their response to a statement in the item by choosing one of a number of possible responses. In this book the most commonly used closed response scale is a five-point Likert scale consisting of the following response anchors: strongly disagree (1), disagree (2), neither agree nor disagree (3), agree (4) and strongly agree (5). Vagias (2006) provides 37 different examples of Likert-type response anchors with different foci (e.g. agreement, importance, priority level, frequency), ranging from 4 to 7 anchors.

This chapter will just deal with closed questions. As open questions gather qualitative data, they will be dealt with in Chapter 6, and to a lesser extent in Chapter 7.

Writing items

This section deals with writing questionnaire items. It introduces six basic principles that need to be adhered to if items are to give useful unambiguous feedback. Each principle is illustrated by giving examples of what to avoid. Most of these were taken from existing questionnaires, many of which had been extensively used. If questionnaires are used and completed over and over again without anyone taking action to deal with basic errors, it would seem to suggest either that these basic principles are not well understood or that insufficient care and attention is given to item design. The common practice of appointing a representative working group to design questionnaires may also be a contributing factor. All too often this seems to result in awkwardly worded compromises.

For each of the example items in this section, it can be assumed that the students are asked to use a five item response scale of strongly disagree (SD), disagree (D), neither agree nor disagree (N), agree (A) or strongly agree (SA).

Single question

It is only possible to give an adequate answer to an item if it asks just a single question. If two or more constructs are asked about, respondents are uncertain which quality to respond to. The item below contains no less than four questions.

> The lecturer was helpful, patient, encouraging and easy to approach.

Presumably the designer intended to shorten the length of the questionnaire by including four similar constructs in one item. However, most lecturers exhibit the four qualities to different degrees, so respondents probably pick a neutral response unless one or more quality is extreme. If all four qualities are important, there should be four items. If that makes the questionnaire too long, pick the one or two most important and have an item for each.

The item below contains not just two questions, but also two conditions.

> The lecturer returned students' assignments promptly and with constructive comments, considering the size of the class and the nature of the assignment.

Even a single condition makes a question hard to respond to, as judgments about them are not easy for students to make. It is better to omit the condition and make a judgment on the context when interpreting the results, rather than relying on absolute values.

Simple language

Simply worded items are the clearest and least ambiguous. Therefore, avoid complex sentence structures, like the double (or even triple) negative in the item below.

> It was not unusual to have too little feedback in this course.

Also avoid jargon or technical terms which respondents may not be familiar with.

> The lecturer had adopted the principles of andragogy in his teaching, which promoted an active cognitive engagement in the learning process among students.

The following item would have lawyers leaping up and objecting that it is a leading question.

> I prefer the practical, down-to-earth method of learning in this course to the abstract and theoretical learning in the conventional lecture-based method.

It is, though, the type of question asked by those introducing an innovation into courses they teach. Comparisons are hard to make as they assume uniformity in 'conventional' teaching, which is an unreasonable assumption.

Generality

The problems with the following items are the words *never*, *always* and *each*. It means, for example, that even if a lecturer was just one minute late for one class, they could legitimately get a response of *disagree*.

> The lecturer was never late for class.
> The lecturer was always considerate.
> The lecturer explained the objectives of each lesson to us.

It is not difficult to re-word these items to remove the problem. Just removing a word or two could make a big difference to the response.

> The lecturer was punctual.
> The lecturer was considerate.
> The lecturer explained the objectives to us.

Credible for respondent to answer

It is important to avoid questions that respondents cannot reasonably be expected to give a considered answer to. This applies particularly to items that would normally be considered beyond the expertise of the respondents. For example, undergraduate students are not normally asked about the subject knowledge of their teachers. This could, however, be a legitimate question to students in a taught post-graduate course, with an enrolment of professionals in the field.

> The lecturer seemed to have an up-to-date knowledge of the subject matter.

Consistency with response scale

The introductory paragraph to this section stated that a SA, A, N, D and SD response scale should be assumed. The questions below are quite inconsistent with this response scale as they demand yes/no answers.

> Were the teaching assistants well prepared to answer questions about the lab classes?
> Did you have adequate time to write up laboratory reports?

Notice again that it is easy to re-word the questions to fit the response scale.

> The teaching assistants were well prepared to answer questions about the lab classes.
> Adequate time was given to write up laboratory reports.

Indicating direction of disagreement

The problem with the two items below is apparent if you think about the meaning of a response of disagree. Does it mean the workload was too heavy or too light? Was the course too easy or too difficult?

The workload for this course was reasonable.
The subject was taught at the right level of difficulty.

There are two ways to rectify the problem. One is to use a different response scale, such as too difficult to too easy. The alternative is to retain the response scale but re-word the item to something like:

The workload for this course did not cause undue stress.

Scales

There are two quite different types of scale that will be dealt with under this heading. First, there are a few issues concerned with response scales. Second, a scale also refers to the concept of grouping related items together to represent an overall construct.

Response scales

The most commonly used response scale in this book is the five-point Likert scale below. It is also one of the most commonly used response scales in research instruments – possibly the most common.

5	SA	strongly agree
4	A	agree
3	N	only to be used if a definite answer is not possible
2	D	disagree
1	SD	strongly disagree

There are advocates of response scales with more or less than five points. An argument for four- or six-point scales, without a neutral point, is that it forces respondents to commit themselves, rather than sit on the fence. There are also those who favour seven-point scales, claiming that they permit greater discrimination. Practical experience suggests that whether four-, five-, six- or seven-point scales are used makes little difference to the results. Good teaching still gets a higher rating than poor teaching.

What is important is that a scale should be balanced. Positive responses should be balanced against an equal number of negative ones, and the wording of them should be matching opposites. To illustrate this point, I show below a response scale used in a short customer comment card I found in a restaurant. Obviously the staff wanted to report high levels of customer satisfaction to management!

excellent   good   average   poor

It is important to be consistent about the use of response scales. Within a questionnaire, try to use as few as possible. You will notice that the questionnaires in this book rarely use more than one. It is not difficult to arrange this – it is just an issue of thinking carefully about the wording of items. However, it is common to see questionnaires with many different response scales – some with a different one for each question. Questionnaires like this are harder to complete and take longer to fill in. They also tend to be less compact. This can reduce return rates as the longer a questionnaire, the less likely it is to be completed.

Grouping items into scales

When experts design a questionnaire, they normally start by deciding which constructs need to be included. They then write several items for each construct to denote pertinent characteristics of the construct. The items for each construct then constitute a scale within the questionnaire. Sometimes scales are formed by factor analysis of items to see which belong together.

The rationale for having scales in questionnaires about teaching and learning is that teaching is a multidimensional construct. A well-designed questionnaire will have a scale for each important dimension. It is common for CTEQs to have no explicit scale structure. Factor analysis of such instruments often produces just one overall impression factor. As will be explained below, this limits the diagnostic ability of the instrument.

For evaluation questionnaires with scale structures, it is common to arrange the instrument by the scales and give the name of the scale or construct above the items. The purpose is to provide extra clarity to respondents as to what they are being asked about. For research instruments the scale names are not normally given and items are not normally grouped together in scales.

Reliability

Scales within questionnaires can be tested for reliability. The most commonly used measure of reliability is Cronbach's coefficient alpha (e.g. Raykov & Shrout, 2002). This gives a measure of the accuracy or consistency with which a set of items measures a single construct (Miller, 1995). When instruments are described in journal articles, figures for Cronbach's alpha are normally given. Computing these is straightforward. SPSS, for example, has a procedure called 'reliability' (Norusis, 2002). Note that it is the scales within questionnaires that are tested for reliability. It serves no useful purpose to report the reliability for the whole instrument.

For a scale to be considered reliable Cronbach's alpha needs to exceed a cut-off value. Nunnally (1978) argued that reliability estimates of around 0.70 were acceptable for basic research, and that efforts to increase reliability substantially from that level (e.g. beyond 0.80) 'is often wasteful of time and funds' (p. 245). In contrast, he argued that research in applied settings required considerably more reliable tests, and when important decisions are to be made about individuals, very reliable tests (at least 0.90, but up to 0.95) are needed. Schmitt (1996) discussed the value of alpha that should be acceptable and noted that a number of sources recommended the 0.70 level, but argued that values of criterion reliability as low as 0.50 would not seriously attenuate validity estimates.

It might be thought that there would be little left to discuss about a statistic that was invented a long time ago (Cronbach, 1951) and is very widely used. However, papers are still being written about Cronbach's alpha. There are two issues that concern the design of evaluation questionnaires which will be raised here.

The first is that Cronbach's alpha values are a function of the number of items in a scale (see, for example, Miller, 1995; Nunnally, 1978). Adding more items to a scale tends to increase alpha. The problem is that students can be asked to complete so many questionnaires nowadays that many have become reluctant to complete lengthy ones. Questionnaire design, therefore, has to compromise between reliability and length (Scriven, 1994).

Cronbach's alpha is also a function of the average inter-correlation between items (Green, Lissitz, & Mulaik, 1977). This means that higher alpha values are obtained if it is assumed that the construct being measured is unidimensional. However, education and the social sciences generally deal with constructs that are complex. There can then be a tension between fully describing a construct and achieving reliable measurements. Including all pertinent facets of a construct in a scale will result in multidimensionality, which will reduce alpha values. Restricting the number of dimensions in a scale will increase alpha values, but will mean that the scale no longer addresses the complexity of the construct. The dichotomy is between measurement and validity.

The most common practice with verification of questionnaires, of restricting analysis and reporting to Cronbach's alpha values, masks this issue because the statistic does not reveal the dimensionality of the scale (Hattie, 1985; McDonald, 1981). Structural equation modelling can address this issue as it can reveal the underlying dimensionality of a scale (Noar, 2003; Rubio, Berg-Weber, & Tegg, 2001). In the development of a revised version of the learning process questionnaire (Kember, Biggs, & Leung, 2004), the use of structural equation modelling proved to be vital because of the hierarchical multidimensional character of the learning approach scales. An additional caveat is that instrument reliability should not simply be assumed because of previous demonstrations of reliability in other samples; researchers should test whether an instrument's psychometric functioning is suitable when used with a new sample (Thompson & Vacha-Haase, 2000).

While internal consistency measures of reliability are a common focus in CTEQ development, inter-rater reliability (IRR) – the consistency of results across multiple raters – should also be tested. Inter-rater reliability is a function of the number of participant ratings, with high reliabilities ranging from 0.70 to 0.90 usually resulting when ratings from at least 20 to 25 respondents are averaged (Feldman, 1977). One-way analyses of variance using the focus of evaluation (e.g. lecturer, course) as the 'level' of the independent variable can be used to calculate IRR, by dividing the mean square between minus mean square within by mean square between, or $(F-1)/F$ (Gillmore, 2000).

Morley (2009) provides SPSS macros to automate the calculation of another measure of inter-rater reliability, Krippendorf's alpha, across large numbers of teaching evaluations. Unlike the $(F-1)/F$ IRR method, Krippendorf's alpha provides an IRR estimate for ratings of a particular course or teacher; providing such analyses to teachers should allow them to judge the reliability of a particular set of feedback based on an objective index.

Inter-rater agreement (IRA) is of concern when researchers wish to aggregate ratings made at one level (e.g. quality of teaching in a programme) to represent the same construct at a higher level (e.g. quality of teaching in the faculty responsible for a number of programmes). IRA evaluates the degree to which multiple raters rate dimensions of an organisation's climate or culture similarly (Chan, 1998). For example, Barrie and Ginns (2007), based on suitable levels of IRA for teaching quality constructs measured by related CTEQ and programme-level instruments, investigated the correlations between faculty-level measures of these constructs. LeBreton and Senter (2008) provide a comprehensive review of both IRA and IRR, as well as SPSS syntax for performing these analyses.

Validity

Validity is established if an instrument or scale actually provides a measure of what it claims to measure. An invalid questionnaire or scale measures something other than that which it purports to measure, or does not adequately characterise the construct in question. The concept is quite simple, but establishing validity with any degree of certainty is very hard.

Two examples might help to illustrate the issues involved. First, take the single construct of critical thinking. As education has come to accept the importance of graduates developing a range of generic capabilities like critical thinking, it becomes important to seek feedback on the extent to which students feel that it has been nurtured during their programme. Finding a way to do this which will be widely accepted as valid is far from straightforward.

There has been considerable discussion, which implies disagreement, over the definition of critical thinking in general terms (Moon, 2008). It can be even more difficult to find a way of defining it which is acceptable across a range of disciplines. Also, even if any agreement on definition can be reached, it is not easy to establish that questions will adequately relate to the agreed definition of critical thinking. For example, there are paper and pencil tests which purport to measure critical thinking (see King & Kitchener, 1994 for a review). However, most assess responses to well-defined problems, which is inconsistent with the most widely accepted visions of critical thinking.

The second example is that of a course questionnaire. To be valid, the instrument must provide a measure of good teaching and learning, and be capable of distinguishing it from poor teaching and learning. It needs to contain constructs that have been shown to be consistent with teaching of high quality, which implies being based upon a valid model of quality in education.

This then poses a fundamental issue, because arriving at an agreed definition of quality in education which is useable in practice has been like the search for the Holy Grail. Just about the only agreement is that the topic is complex and that many formulations of quality are possible. Marsh (1987) starts the chapter on validity in his review of research into students' evaluations of university teaching by noting that 'Student ratings, which constitute one measure of teaching effectiveness, are difficult to validate since there is no single criterion of effective teaching' (p. 285). The edited collection in Green (1994), with the title *What is Quality in Higher Education?*, presents a variety of formulations of quality used for quality assurance purposes.

Approaches to establishing validity

Published articles introducing questionnaires commonly deal with reliability, but often fail to mention validity at all. There are readily available statistics to measure reliability. However, there is no simply computed statistic that establishes validity. Indeed, validity does not even get a mention in the extensive index of the SPSS manual (Norusis, 2002).

While the issue of validity is often ducked, there are several approaches which are used. Non-specialists often rely on face validity, in which the wording of items makes some reference to what is being measured. Content validity goes somewhat further by seeking to include the range of facets of a construct and do it in a balanced way (Moser & Kalton, 1979). The obvious problem here is the criterion for accepting that it does so. One approach has been the use of expert panels; Hinkin and Tracey (1999) describe a quantitative method to analyse such panel data using analysis of variance, in which expert respondents rate how consistent each of a set of draft items is with its hypothesised construct. The limitation of these methods is that instrument designers tend to pick professional colleagues with similar paradigmatic beliefs to their own, so alternative views are unlikely to be considered.

Marsh (1987) argues that construct validity is the best practical method available for validating course evaluation instruments and reviews a number of methods which have been employed with the aim of showing construct validity. The most common designs compare students' evaluation ratings with other measures of teaching, such as instructor self-evaluation, peer rating, rating by external observers and ratings with other instruments.

The danger with this approach to construct validity lies in cross-validation of instruments or measures based upon similar theoretical origins. For example, course evaluation questionnaires have frequently been validated against other measures emanating from behavioural research with teacher-centred models of good teaching. Many of the course evaluation instruments most often cited in the literature have been criticised as being consistent with teacher-centred models of teaching (e.g. Centra, 1993; d'Apollonia & Abrami, 1997; McKeachie, 1997), and quite inconsistent with learner-centred forms (Kolitch & Dean, 1999). This arises because they were often based on early work on instructor evaluation, which had largely positivist origins.

As they are based on related theoretical origins, correlations between measures are inevitably high; so claims of validity are made. The instruments and what they are compared to all measure the same teacher-centred model of good teaching. However, if the teacher-centred model of good teaching is rejected – and there are compelling grounds for doing so – the procedures establish that the measures compared are equally valid measures of poor teaching. Alternatively, neither are valid measures of good teaching.

Onwuegbuzie, Daniel, and Collins (2009) build on Messick's (1989, 1995) conceptualisation of validity to develop a meta-validity model, which argues that instruments ought to be able to provide evidence of validity for the main types of validity. They argue that, by these demanding standards, CTEQs in general show evidence of criterion-referenced validity, but limited evidence of content- or construct-related validity.

Establishing validity by deriving constructs from naturalistic research

A form of construct validation that avoids the problems which can arise from cross-validation is that of deriving constructs in an open way from the perspectives of the participants by using qualitative data. The method eschews hypothesis-based or top-down generation of the theory underpinning the design of an instrument. Essentially, it moves the origins of questionnaire design from a positivist paradigm to a naturalistic base. Rather than designing a questionnaire from the theory of the researcher, the instrument is grounded in the beliefs and practices of participants similar to those who will eventually be included in the sample from which data will be gathered.

This approach to establishing validity is consistent with Messick's (1996) argument that directness and authenticity are important constructs which should be taken into account when validity is considered. Messick (1992) further asserted that validity is an integrated evaluative judgement of the extent to which evidence supports the appropriateness of both interpretations and actions.

This approach to validating instruments does not appear to have been widely utilised, possibly because many researchers lack confidence in using combinations of qualitative and quantitative research. One research area in which questionnaire design has been informed by qualitative research from a naturalistic perspective is student approaches to learning. The process has not been described as a strategy for validating questionnaires, however. Entwistle and Ramsden (1983) used both quantitative and qualitative methods to study approaches to learning. Interpretations from the two methods appear to have influenced each other; so the design of the approaches to studying inventory and the course perceptions questionnaire can be said to have both been informed by interviews with students.

In developing the exemplary teacher course questionnaire (ETCQ) included in Chapter 3 (Kember & Leung, 2008), the issue of validity was tackled by basing the design on research into the practices of teachers who were judged to be exemplary. Award-winning teachers were interviewed on the topic of their beliefs and practices as a teacher (Kember with McNaught, 2007). Analysis of the transcripts using grounded theory (Glaser & Strauss, 1967; Lincoln & Guber, 1985) and the constant comparative method (Strauss & Corbin, 1990) found a set of common principles of what constitutes excellence in teaching (Kember with McNaught, 2007). While there was variety in the way these were applied, there was a very high degree of consistency in holding to the principles.

Nine principles were then used to derive a set of dimensions of good teaching. In a questionnaire, each dimension becomes a scale, made up of a number of items which deal with important facets of the dimension. In this case the principles serve to identify scales and provide guidance in wording the items. By following this path the questionnaire becomes grounded in the constructs derived from the interviews. If these are accepted as forming a valid model of good teaching in the university, then it follows that the questionnaire has the same construct validity. Authenticity and applicability are also dealt with since the base data was gathered from exemplary teachers from a wide variety of disciplines and teachers in a range of universities.

Pilot testing

It is normal to pilot test new questionnaires before using them on the intended sample. An initial test of the meaning of items is often valuable. The appropriate number for this test is small – four to five is about right. Those selected must be typical of the intended sample for the instrument. Ask the pilot sample to go through the questions slowly, commenting out loud on what they think each question means. Giving their interpretation enables the designer to check perceived meaning against that intended. In particular, they should be asked to point out any question with an uncertain meaning or ones that might be difficult to respond to for any reason.

It is then necessary to perform a larger pilot test on a sample of at least 200, typical of the intended respondents. The reason for the 200 is that the statistical tests performed on the pilot survey do not work properly with smaller samples. Many questionnaire designers employ multiple pilot tests, but this can often be avoided by careful initial design and by the strategy of including eventually redundant items in the pilot test.

When designing and pilot testing a new questionnaire, it is common to include more items in each scale than will be retained in the final version of the instrument. The rationale for this strategy is that less successful items can be removed after pilot testing, hopefully leaving a useable version of the questionnaire. If the initial tests were on an instrument of the intended final length, it would be necessary to do more pilot testing. After the first pilot test, unsatisfactory items would be removed. These would then have to be replaced and another pilot test performed. If any of the replacement items are not satisfactory, which is quite likely, yet more cycles of replacing and testing will be needed. Including eventually redundant items in the initial pilot versions of questions, therefore, can reduce the number of development cycles for new instruments.

Reducing the number of items in scales

Employing this strategy requires testing procedures to decide which items to remove and which can be retained. The process can be illustrated using the development of the ETCQ as a case study (Kember & Leung, 2008). An initial trial version of the ETCQ with 49 items was developed. Each of the nine scales contained between five and seven items. This was more than were likely to feature in the final version. The testing process could then be used to test which items had better psychometric properties with respect to a particular scale (Noar, 2003), so that less satisfactory items could be removed. Given the concern about the reluctance of students to complete questionnaires, the aim has to be to produce an instrument which is as short as possible, while at the same time including all relevant dimensions and providing a reliable measure of them.

The reduction of items was based on two sets of evidence: use of reliability statistics and a series of confirmatory factor analyses (see Appendix if necessary). Values for Cronbach's alpha for scales were produced with the 'reliability' procedure of SPSS (see Lei & Wu, 2007, for SPSS and SAS syntax for extended reliability analyses based on classical test theory). The analysis includes a value for alpha if an item were deleted, together with inter-item correlations. These statistics give useful guidance in deciding which items to delete.

Confirmatory factor analysis was performed to assess the dimensionality of each of the nine scales of ETCQ. The model tested was that of the scale as a latent factor with each item as an indicator. The results of the test show the degree of fit of the model to the data and show the loading of each item on the factor. Those items with higher loadings make a greater contribution to the scale and are therefore generally the better ones to retain. This type of testing can also test alternative relationships between items, subscales and scales. This is particularly helpful where multidimensionality is suspected, as the tests of reliability give little indication of this.

Both Gerbing and Anderson (1988) and Bentler (1995) suggested that the standardised residual matrix be examined, as large standardised residuals associated with specific items indicate that the model probably does not explain the covariances among the items adequately. Therefore, those items with large standardised residuals should generally be dropped. In this case, this procedure led to the same outcomes as examination of factor loadings, so the residual matrices were not used.

The questionnaire was reduced to three items in each scale. The items making the least reliable and least significant contribution to scales were eliminated. The items removed were those with the lowest factor loadings, associated with the largest standardised residuals, and the most detrimental effect on alpha values.

Diagnostic power

In carrying out practical tests on the ETCQ it became apparent that there was another criterion by which evaluation questionnaires ought to be assessed, which does not normally appear to be taken into consideration. We have called the criterion *diagnostic power*, which is the degree to which the questionnaire distinguishes between similar constructs in the questionnaire. For a course questionnaire, it is the capability of the instrument to distinguish strengths and weaknesses in a course or teacher. In other words, it is the degree of diagnosis and the extent to which results can be used to identify remedial action by pointing out which aspects of teaching need attention.

Results from course evaluation questionnaires are commonly reported in comparison with scores from the remainder of a university or faculty. This can be done by comparing course or teacher means to university or faculty means. A quantitative measure can be provided by using z-scores, which are the number of standard deviations from the mean.

The sample for the tests of the ETCQ had previously completed a committee-designed CTEQ to report on the teaching in the same courses. The internally developed instrument used 11 individual items for constructs, rather than the scales of a well-designed questionnaire. We had noticed that the z-scores for a course or teacher from this instrument were all very close. The instrument could rank teachers according to overall teaching quality, but provided little insight into which aspects of teaching might need attention.

This finding was not surprising in view of the factor structure of the instrument. A factor analysis was performed with the 11 items and only one factor was retained, with very similar factor loadings for each item. This evidence indicates that all the 11 items are measuring one single factor, with each item contributing to the factor to a similar extent. The students appear to have responded to the questionnaire by giving an overall judgement on teaching quality, rather than responding to specific facets of teaching. This seems to be a common problem with committee-designed CTEQs. For an instrument to be diagnostic, it seems to be important for it to have an explicit set of scales corresponding to the dimensions of teaching. We propose the use of the degree of variation of the z-scores among scales (or items) as a measure of the diagnostic power of an instrument.

Summary

The principles of designing good questionnaire items have been explained by noting some common faults to avoid. These were illustrated by showing some examples taken from quite widely used questionnaires, which suggest that questionnaire items are often poorly designed.

For a questionnaire to be valid, it needs to be based upon a relevant model of good teaching and learning. This is difficult because there is no universally agreed model of good teaching. A principle used here is that of a focus upon student learning outcomes, rather than on teacher performance, as there is evidence that teacher-centred forms of instruction are less effective. Establishing validity through prior qualitative research is introduced as a strategy.

Testing for reliability is straightforward, but the results are commonly misinterpreted. Diagnostic power is important in identifying strengths and weaknesses. Poorly designed evaluation instruments commonly have a single factor, which means that teachers get similar ratings on all scales or items. Better-designed instruments have multifactor structures with explicit scales for identified aspects of learning and teaching. This means that ratings for scales tend to show greater differences, enabling relative strengths and weaknesses to be identified.

Chapter 3

Questionnaires

Introduction

This chapter introduces some standard instruments and adaptable types of questionnaire, which collectively will cover many applications in both routine evaluations and the scholarship of teaching. There are generally applicable questionnaires for evaluating teaching and learning at course and programme level, and in taught post-graduate programmes. The revised study process questionnaire and the reflection questionnaire are research-based instruments that have both been used in the scholarship of teaching. A format is introduced that can be adapted to produce discipline-specific questionnaires for evaluating the understanding of key concepts, the mastery of skills and the attainment of designated learning outcomes. An experiential learning questionnaire is presented, and there is an explanation as to how it can be used as a model for the development of questionnaires for other forms of innovative teaching and learning.

In each case the purpose and typical usage of the questionnaire is explained. For the standard instruments, there are references to articles describing the development and testing of the questionnaire. Where necessary there is an explanation of how to process the results.

Unless otherwise indicated, the following standard response scale should be used.

A   strongly disagree
B   disagree
C   only to be used if a definite answer is not possible
D   agree
E   strongly agree

Exemplary teacher course questionnaire

The exemplary teacher course questionnaire (ETCQ) is a CTEQ-type instrument derived from a project that made use of interviews with award-winning teachers. From the interviews, nine principles of good teaching were derived (Kember with McNaught, 2007). These nine principles were used to formulate the nine scales in the questionnaire, each of which has three items. Chapter 2 (see also Kember & Leung, 2008) explains that this process of deriving questionnaire scales from qualitative research is a basis for validity claims. Kember and Leung (2008) deal with other psychometric properties, including reliability and diagnostic power.

Results should be presented to teachers as nine mean scores, one for each of the nine scales. These can be compared to those for other members of the university, faculty or department. The questionnaire is very diagnostic as it gives feedback on nine key facets of good teaching. It can therefore show teachers their strengths and areas for potential improvement. The book (Kember with McNaught, 2007) has sections or chapters corresponding with each of the nine principles or scales, which give advice based on a synthesis of the interviews with the award-winning teachers. The questionnaire and the book combined can therefore function as part of a counselling system.

The questionnaire is shown below. Each three-item scale is shown under a heading which is the name of both the scale and the principle.

Exemplary teacher course questionnaire

Understanding fundamental concepts

This course concentrated on fundamental concepts.
In each class the key points were made clear.
In this course I learned the key principles.

Relevance

Local examples were used to show the relevance of material.
I could see the relevance of material because real life examples were given.
Current issues were used to make the course interesting.

Challenging beliefs

After taking this course I have a better understanding of fundamental concepts.
I have become more flexible in my learning.
I am now more willing to change my views and accept new ideas.

Active learning

Students were given the chance to participate in class.
There was discussion between students in class.
The teaching staff promoted discussion in class.

Teacher–student relationships

There was a friendly relationship between teaching staff and students.
The communication between teaching staff and students is good.
Our teacher(s) knew the individuals in the class.

Motivation

The teacher(s) were enthusiastic.
I found the classes enjoyable.
This was an interesting course.

Organisation

This course was well organised.
This course was well planned.
The classes were well planned.

Flexibility

I found teaching staff helpful when I had difficulty understanding concepts.
The teaching staff were sensitive to student feedback.
The teacher(s) were helpful when asked questions.

Assessment

The type of assessment related closely to the expected learning outcomes.
The assessment tested our understanding of key concepts.
A variety of assessment methods were used.

What was the best aspect of your course?
Which aspect, if any, was most in need of change?

Knowledge questionnaire

Most teachers want to know about students' understanding of key concepts, but CTEQs do not give any relevant information. The knowledge questionnaire introduces a format for seeking feedback on students' understanding of key concepts. Concepts appropriate for the subject taught need to be specified by the teacher. The example given is for the mythical subject of cosmic palaeontology. This is almost certainly not what you teach, but it should not be too hard to adapt the format to your subject.

Knowledge questionnaire

For each of the topics please indicate your level of understanding by using the 5-point scale below.

5   Understand very well
4   Understand
3   Only to be used if a definite answer is not possible
2   Not understood
1   Have no idea about

Table 3.1 Example of a knowledge questionnaire

Topic	Understanding
Effect of cosmic radiation on fossils	
Xanthium dating techniques for outer-terrestrial bodies	
The importance of the Palaeolithic era in the Milky Way galaxy	
Theories of cosmic evolution in the pre-Cambrian period	

Skills questionnaire

This is similar to the knowledge questionnaire, but this time the focus is on skills. Again the example is from cosmic palaeontology, so you will need to adapt the skills to ones relevant to your own discipline.

Skills questionnaire

For each of the skills please indicate your level of ability in the skill by using the 5-point scale below.

5   Very good at
4   Good at
3   Only to be used if a definite answer is not possible
2   Not good at
1   Very poor at

Table 3.2 Example of a skills questionnaire

Skill	Level
Use of X-ray fluorescence imaging to analyse samples	
Writing analytical reports	
Formulating and testing hypotheses	
Gathering fossil data on cosmic field trips	

Experiential learning questionnaire

In the scholarship of teaching, it is common to evaluate innovative forms of teaching. In such cases the most insightful results are normally obtained if a questionnaire specific to the type of innovation is utilised. The reason is that questions can be asked about facets or constructs of teaching and learning specifically relevant to the form of innovation.

There are many forms of innovation, so questionnaires specific to each cannot be given here. An experiential learning questionnaire is given primarily because it is useful in itself for forms of learning like internships and work experience. It may need some adaptation for experiential learning in particular disciplines, such as the clinical practice for nursing or teaching practice for education. The main constructs of appropriateness of experience, preparation, supervision, assessment and outcomes are still likely to apply, though.

The second reason for including this questionnaire is that it shows the principles for designing instruments for other types of innovative teaching. The first step is to determine the factors that make for a successful implementation of the innovation. These are shown as the scale headings below. Next, items need to be devised to seek feedback on aspects of the factors which seem to be important. Guidance on design from qualitative studies is good practice.

Experiential learning questionnaire

Appropriateness of experience

The activities were related to my discipline.
I had to perform meaningful tasks.
I valued the experience I gained from the internship.
There was enough work to keep me occupied.

Preparation from taught curriculum

I was well prepared for the internship by the taught courses I had taken.

Supervision

There was good supervision from staff of the agency.
There was good supervision from staff of the university.

Assessment

The assessment was fair.
The assessment was appropriate for the nature of the internship.

Outcomes

I was able to use my initiative.
I feel that I made a contribution to the needs of society.
I had a chance to practise using skills I will need to use in my likely profession.
I was able to apply the knowledge I gained from taught courses I had taken.
The internship broadened my perspective.
I developed a better understanding of people in other cultures.

Revised study process questionnaire

The revised study process questionnaire (R-SPQ) gives a measure of a student's use of deep and surface approaches to learning. The development, testing, use and interpretation of data are described in Biggs, Kember, and Leung (2001).

Revised study process questionnaire

This questionnaire has a number of questions about your attitudes towards your studies and your usual way of studying.

There is no *right* way of studying. It depends on what suits your own style and the course you are studying. It is accordingly important that you answer each question as honestly as you can. If you think your answer to a question would depend on the subject being studied, give the answer that would apply to the subject(s) most important to you.

Please fill in the appropriate circle alongside the question number on the answer sheet. The letters alongside each number stand for the following response.

A   this item is *never* or only rarely true of me
B   this item is *sometimes* true of me
C   this item is true of me about *half the time*
D   this item is *frequently* true of me
E   this item is *always* or *almost always* true of me

Please choose the *one* most appropriate response to each question. Fill the oval on the answer sheet that best fits your immediate reaction. Do not spend a long time on each item: your first reaction is probably the best one. Please answer each item.

Do not worry about projecting a good image. Your answers are CONFIDENTIAL. Thank you for your cooperation.

1   I find that at times studying gives me a feeling of deep personal satisfaction.
2   I find that I have to do enough work on a topic so that I can form my own conclusions before I am satisfied.
3   My aim is to pass the course while doing as little work as possible.
4   I only study seriously what's given out in class or in the course outlines.
5   I feel that virtually any topic can be highly interesting once I get into it.
6   I find most new topics interesting and often spend extra time trying to obtain more information about them.
7   I do not find my course very interesting so I keep my work to the minimum.
8   I learn some things by rote, going over and over them until I know them by heart even if I do not understand them.
9   I find that studying academic topics can at times be as exciting as a good novel or movie.
10 I test myself on important topics until I understand them completely.
11 I find I can get by in most assessments by memorising key sections rather than trying to understand them.
12 I generally restrict my study to what is specifically set as I think it is unnecessary to do anything extra.
13 I work hard at my studies because I find the material interesting.
14 I spend a lot of my free time finding out more about interesting topics which have been discussed in different classes.
15 I find it is not helpful to study topics in depth. It confuses and wastes time, when all you need is a passing acquaintance with topics.
16 I believe that lecturers shouldn't expect students to spend significant amounts of time studying material everyone knows won't be examined.
17 I come to most classes with questions in mind that I want answering.
18 I make a point of looking at most of the suggested readings that go with the lectures.
19 I see no point in learning material which is not likely to be in the examination.
20 I find the best way to pass examinations is to try to remember answers to likely questions.

Analysing results

The questionnaire was principally designed as a two-factor deep and surface approach model. For use in evaluation this is the simplest and most appropriate use. The second column in Table 3.3 identifies items that contribute to deep and surface approach scores. The score for deep approach, for example, is obtained by adding a student's score for items 1, 2, 5, 6, 9, 10, 13, 14, 17 and 18.

The deep and surface approach scales both have subscales for motive and strategy. These may be useful for research purposes. The third column identifies which items contribute to the four subscales.

Table 3.3 Scoring key for the revised study process questionnaire

item	2F model	4F model
1	DA	DM
2	DA	DS
3	SA	SM
4	SA	SS
5	DA	DM
6	DA	DS
7	SA	SM
8	SA	SS
9	DA	DM
10	DA	DS
11	SA	SM
12	SA	SS
13	DA	DM
14	DA	DS
15	SA	SM
16	SA	SS
17	DA	DM
18	DA	DS
19	SA	SM
20	SA	SS

Reflection questionnaire

The reflection questionnaire contains four scales corresponding to four levels of reflective thinking:

1   habitual action/non-reflection;
2   understanding;
3   reflection; and
4   critical reflection.

Each of the four scales has four items, so the score for a scale is obtained by adding the scores for the respective items shown in the table below.

Table 3.4 Scoring key for the reflection questionnaire

Scale	Scores obtained by adding scores for following items			
Habitual action/non-reflection	1	5	9	13
Understanding	2	6	10	14
Reflection	3	7	11	15
Critical reflection	4	8	12	16

Chapter 9 includes a qualitative protocol for assessing the level of reflection into the same four categories. The protocol includes a detailed description of the four levels or categories.

The development and testing of the questionnaire was introduced in Kember, Leung Jones, Loke, McKay, Sinclair, Tse, Webb, Wong, F.K.Y., Wong, M.W.L. and Yeung (2000); see Leung and Kember (2003) for an investigation of associations between approaches to learning and reflection on practice.

Reflection questionnaire

Please fill in the appropriate circle to indicate your level of agreement with statements about your actions and thinking in this course.

A   definitely disagree
B   disagree with reservation
C   only to be used if a definite answer is not possible
D   agree with reservation
E   definitely agree

1   When I am working on some activities, I can do them without thinking about what I am doing.
2   This course requires us to understand concepts taught by the lecturer.
3   I sometimes question the way others do something and try to think of a better way.
4   As a result of this course I have changed the way I look at myself.
5   In this course we do things so many times that I started doing them without thinking about it.
6   To pass this course you need to understand the content.
7   I like to think over what I have been doing and consider alternative ways of doing it.
8   This course has challenged some of my firmly held ideas.
9   As long as I can remember handout material for examinations, I do not have to think too much.
10   I need to understand the material taught by the teacher in order to perform practical tasks.
11   I often reflect on my actions to see whether I could have improved on what I did.
12   As a result of this course I have changed my normal way of doing things.
13   If I follow what the lecturer says, I do not have to think too much on this course.
14   In this course you have to continually think about the material you are being taught.

15 I often re-appraise my experience so I can learn from it and improve for my next performance.
16 During this course I discovered faults in what I had previously believed to be right.

Student engagement questionnaire

The student engagement questionnaire (SEQ) is a programme-level instrument. It was originally administered to students towards the end of their first and final years. It would also be suitable for administration to fresh graduates.

The development and testing of the instrument is described by Kember and Leung (2009). The questionnaire contains scales for eight generic graduate attributes and nine scales which together measure a broadly-based teaching and learning environment. The instrument is based on a model of the teaching and learning environment nurturing the generic attributes. SEM tests of this model of attribute development are given in Kember and Leung (2009), Kember, Leung and Ma (2007) and Leung and Kember (2006).

The questionnaire can be used as the principal diagnostic measure in a system for programme quality enhancement. Use for this purpose is described in Chapter 12 and also in Kember and Leung (2009). Another relevant article is Kember (2009), which describes a campaign to enhance teaching quality across a university by encouraging active learning approaches. Results from the student engagement questionnaire were used both to diagnose programmes which needed attention and to demonstrate that there had been improvements, through longitudinal data, at the institutional level, which showed increases in scores on relevant scales.

Results should be reported as scale scores. Forms of reporting which facilitate use in quality enhancement procedures are shown in Chapter 12.

Student engagement questionnaire

Please indicate your level of agreement with the statements below. Please choose the one most appropriate response to each question.

1   strongly disagree   2   disagree
3   only to be used if a definite answer is not possible
4   agree   5   strongly agree

Critical thinking

1   I have developed my ability to make judgements about alternative perspectives.
2   I have become more willing to consider different points of view.

Creative thinking

3   I have been encouraged to use my own initiative.
4   I have been challenged to come up with new ideas.

Self-managed learning

5   I feel that I can take responsibility for my own learning.
6   I have become more confident of my ability to pursue further learning.

Adaptability

7   During my time at university I have learned how to be more adaptable.
8   I have become more willing to change my views and accept new ideas.

Problem solving

9   I have improved my ability to use knowledge to solve problems in my field of study.
10   I am able to bring information and different ideas together to solve problems.

Communication skills

11   I have developed my ability to communicate effectively with others.
12   In my time at university I have improved my ability to convey ideas.

Interpersonal skills and groupwork

13   I have learned to become an effective team or group member.
14   I feel confident in dealing with a wide range of people.

Computer literacy

15   I feel confident in using computer applications when necessary.
16   I have learned more about using computers for presenting information.

Active learning

17   Our teaching staff use a variety of teaching methods.
18   Students are given the chance to participate in classes.

Teaching for understanding

19   The teaching staff try hard to help us understand the course material.
20   The course design helps students understand the course content.

Feedback to assist learning

21   When I have difficulty with learning materials, I find the explanations provided by the teaching staff useful.
22   There is sufficient feedback on activities and assignments to ensure that we learn from the work we do.

Assessment

23   The programme uses a variety of assessment methods.
24   To do well in assessment in this programme you need to have good analytical skills.
25   The assessment tested our understanding of key concepts in this programme.

Relationship between teachers and students

26   The communication between teaching staff and students is good.
27   I find teaching staff helpful when asked questions.

Workload

28 I manage to complete the requirements of the programme without feeling unduly stressed.
29 The amount of work we are expected to do is quite reasonable.

Relationship with other students

30 I feel a strong sense of belonging to my class group.
31 I frequently work together with others in my classes.

Cooperative learning

32 I have frequently discussed ideas from courses with other students out of class.
33 I have found that discussing course material with other students outside classes has helped me to reach a better understanding of the material.

Coherence of curriculum

34 I can see how courses fitted together to make a coherent programme of study for my major.
35 The programme of study for my major was well integrated.

Taught post-graduate experience questionnaire

The questionnaire is based on a project on the motivation of taught postgraduate (TPg) students. It also drew on work in an inter-institutional project on 'Evaluating the Part-Time Student Experience'. These studies indicated that there were characteristics of TPg programmes and their students that should inform the design of the questionnaire and which, to a degree at least, distinguished them from undergraduate degrees. Using the same questionnaire for undergraduate and TPg programmes is not good practice.

Students normally enrol in TPg programmes to acquire advanced specialist knowledge and skills of a relatively narrow field within a profession or discipline. The students could typically be characterised as mature students, commonly working within the field of study, with the majority being part-time. In interviews for the motivation project, the students were able to clearly articulate the type of advanced specialist knowledge and skills they expected to acquire through the programme. They could (and did) comment on whether the curriculum and content enabled them to develop the anticipated knowledge and skills. Teachers were expected to possess relevant expertise and to design a curriculum appropriate for the field of specialisation. As the students were mature, and often working in the field, they expected interaction with the teacher and to contribute to discussion.

These characteristics led to a model, on which the questionnaire is based, in which there are three domains: curriculum and content, teaching and learning environment, and learning outcomes. In the model, the first two serve to develop the latter.

Taught post-graduate experience questionnaire

Curriculum and content

Knowledge

The programme has provided me with the specialised knowledge I needed.
The content is appropriate for my needs.
The content is appropriate for this area of advanced study.

Skill development

The programme has helped me develop specialised skills I needed.
The programme has helped in the development of skills needed by professionals in the field.

Curriculum

The curriculum is designed well.
The curriculum is coherent.
The curriculum design is appropriate for the needs of students.

Teaching and learning environment

Assessment

The assessment was fair.
The assessment was appropriate for the nature of the advanced specialisation.
The assessment tested skills appropriate for professionals in the field.

Active learning

My teachers used a variety of relevant teaching and learning activities.
I was given the chance to participate in a variety of useful activities in class.
My teachers provided opportunities for meaningful interaction in class.
The teachers encouraged students to contribute their own knowledge and experience through class discussion.

Relevance

The teachers related material to practical applications.
The teachers were knowledgeable about this area of specialisation.
Local examples were used to show the relevance of material.

Teacher–student relationships

There was a friendly relationship between teaching staff and students.
The communication between teaching staff and students is good.
Teachers knew the background and needs of students.
The teaching staff were helpful when asked questions.

Feedback

Teachers gave me helpful feedback on my progress.
The teachers made a real effort to understand difficulties I may be having with my work.
The teachers put a lot of time into commenting on my work.
Feedback was effective and timely.

Teaching for understanding

Teachers tried to ensure that we had a good understanding of key concepts.
As a result of taking this programme, I now have a good mastery of important topics in this field.

Organisation

The programme as a whole was well organised.
Courses were planned well.

Learning outcomes

Career-related

The programme results in a qualification needed for my profession.
The programme has been of benefit to my current career.
I expect that taking this programme will benefit my career in the future.

Interest

I have found the material interesting
I enjoy studying
I have developed my network of professional and social contacts

Critical intellectual inquiry

My analytical skills have been sharpened.
I am able to look at things from different perspectives.

Lifelong learning

My enthusiasm for further learning has been stimulated.
I have developed skills which will enable me to engage in lifelong learning.

Tackling novel situations and ill-defined problems

I feel confident about tackling unfamiliar problems.
I have learned how to identify a problem and tackle it.
I feel confident when I am put in a new situation.

Communication

My communication skills have improved.
I feel able to communicate my ideas professionally with people.

Collaboration

I have improved my ability to collaborate with other people in completing tasks.
I have improved my ability to negotiate with others in coming to a decision.

Overall satisfaction

The programme was good value for the fees paid.
I would recommend this programme to others.

What were the best aspects of this programme?
How could the programme have been improved?

Graduate capabilities survey

To gain feedback from a comprehensive set of stakeholders, it is necessary to include graduates. In Australia, the national institutional- or programme-level questionnaire – the CEQ – is administered to fresh graduates. This is a debatable policy, as it would be easier to obtain acceptable return rates if the data were collected shortly before the end of the final year. Whether questionnaires are administered shortly before or shortly after a degree is completed appears unlikely to materially affect the results.

Continuing with the example of the CEQ in Australia, it is also hard to classify this as a true graduate survey. The aim is to gather information about student satisfaction with teaching and learning in their undergraduate degree. On this basis it should surely be classified as programme-level survey, serving a similar purpose to the student engagement questionnaire given earlier in this chapter.

For a survey to obtain data relevant to graduates as a stakeholder category, the questions surely need to relate to issues pertinent to graduates in their capacity as graduates, rather than their recollection of perceptions when they were undergraduates. The obvious questions are about whether their education has equipped them with the abilities they needed for employment.

The graduate capabilities survey is a very short instrument which seeks graduates' perceptions about whether they possess the sort of capabilities normally considered essential for employment. The instrument was developed in Hong Kong, which explains the inclusion of scales for communication skills in Chinese and English. It would not be difficult to substitute other languages for those in multilingual contexts. For those in a monolingual environment, delete the 'communication skills in Chinese' scale, and delete 'in English' from the title and items in the other communications skills scale.

The questionnaire is short because it was commonly used in conjunction with a tailored outcomes-based questionnaire asking about desired outcomes specific to the programme investigated. These tailored questionnaires are described in the next section.

If you intend to use a graduate survey on a stand-alone basis, you might consider adding other relevant graduate attributes. Scales could be taken from the student engagement questionnaire, listed earlier in this chapter. The item bank in the next chapter also has relevant items.

Graduate capabilities survey

Critical thinking

I am able to make judgements about alternative perspectives.
I am willing to consider different points of view.

Ability to pursue lifelong learning

I have found that I can take responsibility for my own learning.
I am confident of my ability to pursue further learning.

Communication skills in Chinese

I am able to communicate effectively when writing in Chinese to clients and colleagues.
I can speak effectively in Cantonese when communicating with clients and colleagues.
I can speak effectively in Putonghua when communicating with clients and colleagues.

Communication skills in English

I am able to communicate effectively when writing in English to clients and colleagues.
I can speak effectively in English when communicating with clients and colleagues.

Interpersonal skills and groupwork

I am able to perform as an effective team or group member.
I feel confident in dealing with a wide range of people.

Readiness for employment

I have found that I possess the skills needed in order to perform activities required in my job.
I am able to complete assigned tasks on schedule.

Tailored outcomes-based graduate surveys

Taking an outcomes-based approach to teaching and learning has become common. Many programmes have specified desired outcomes as the knowledge, skills and values graduates are expected to have developed by the completion of the degree. If outcomes have been stated, it seems logical to ask graduates if they feel they have developed them.

For those who have not specified outcomes, the QAA in the UK has developed benchmark statements for major disciplines. These include statements of graduate outcomes. The statements can be accessed from http://www.qaa.ac.uk/Assuring StandardsAndQuality/subject-guidance/Pages/Subject-benchmark-statements.aspx.

Where desired outcomes have been stated it is usually not too difficult to convert the outcomes statements to questionnaire items.

Two examples of tailored outcomes-based surveys are given below, from the very different disciplines of English and a branch of engineering. Only a part of the engineering outcomes-based survey is shown. Just one item for each of the main sections is shown.

English graduate survey

I have learned to understand and appreciate poetry in English.
I have learned to understand and appreciate fiction in English.
I have learned to understand and appreciate drama in English.
I understand how to study language systematically.
I understand the local dimensions of English.
I have developed an appreciation of the global dimensions of English.
I can produce creative and scholarly work in high quality written English.
I can produce creative and scholarly work using a variety of styles.
I am able to communicate effectively in spoken English in a manner appropriate to the communicative and cultural context.
I can make effective oral presentations using appropriate technology.
I am equipped to continue building upon my knowledge and skills after graduation.
I feel committed to learning as a lifelong process.

Engineering outcomes-based survey

Fundamental knowledge

I have a good understanding of the fundamentals of software.

Knowledge of specialisation

I have in-depth knowledge of the following Engineering specialisations.
Optical communication.

Application of knowledge

I am able to lead interdisciplinary engineering projects.

Capabilities

I have well developed problem-solving skills.

Perspective

I understand the importance of environmental, health and safety issues.

Blended learning surveys

It is increasingly common for colleges and universities to support face-to-face learning with online learning and teaching materials. Such *blended learning* is distinct from distance education, which typically involves little or no face-to-face contact with students or staff. This relatively new and evolving use of information and communication technologies for learning poses new challenges for teaching evaluation; thus, Jochems, van Merriënboer, and Koper (2004, p. 5) called for 'a variety of coherent measures at the pedagogical, organisational and technical levels for the successful implementation of e-learning in combination with more conventional methods'.

Ginns and Ellis (2007) and Ellis, Ginns, and Piggott (2009) investigated the core sources of variation in students' perceptions of the blended learning environments at the course level, and the associations between these perceptions, students' approaches to study and student grades. The scales below are drawn from the version given in Ellis, Ginns, and Piggott (2009).

Blended learning environment questionnaire

E-Teaching

The teacher helped to guide online discussions between students.
The teacher's responses online motivated me to learn more deeply.
The teacher's interactivity with me online encouraged me to get the most out of my learning.
I didn't receive enough helpful online feedback from my teacher. (reversed)
The teacher helped to focus online discussions.

Design

The online activities helped me to understand the face-to face activities in this course.
The online learning materials helped me to learn during the face-to-face situations in this course.
The online activities are designed to get the best out of students.
The design of the website (online experiences in this course) helped my learning.
The design of the website in this course made me want to explore the issues more.

Workload

The sheer volume of work for the online component of this course means it can't all be thoroughly comprehended. (reversed)
The workload for the online component of this course is too heavy. (reversed)
I generally had enough time to understand the things I had to learn online.

Interactivity

Other students' online submissions helped me understand my ideas from a new perspective.
I interacted with students' online postings/submissions even if they weren't assessed.
The submissions from other students helped develop my understanding of particular topics.
I felt my submissions to the course website were valued by other students.

The quality of blended learning provisions can also be assessed at the programme level. Ginns and Ellis (2009) developed a scale for this purpose, validating it against a form of the course experience questionnaire for currently enrolled students (Ginns, Prosser, & Barrie, 2007). The psychometric properties of a short form of this scale, consisting of the last two items, are discussed in Chapter 10.

E-learning Scale

Where it was used, information technology helped me to learn.
Resources on [*institution name*] (e.g. WebCT, Blackboard, degree course sites, faculty sites, etc.) websites supported my learning.
Communicating online with students and staff helped my learning.
The online learning experiences of my degree course were well-integrated with my face-to-face learning.
My online experiences helped me engage actively in my learning.

Chapter 4

Item bank

Rationale for the item bank

For those who wish to evaluate the effectiveness of innovations introduced into their teaching, it is important to use instruments that focus on the type of teaching employed and the learning outcomes intended. However, many people seem to find it hard to design good questionnaire items. For this reason a large item bank is included. The intention is to enable you to build questionnaires with an alternative focus to the general questionnaires in the previous chapter.

The first part of the data bank takes an outcomes-based approach, as innovations are commonly introduced to promote particular attributes. There are questions about student experiences. Many of these are particularly suited to the growing sectors of part-time students and those in taught post-graduate programmes. Such students can be neglected when it comes to evaluation, so the item bank is designed to help put this right.

There are questions related to general or common types of teaching. There are also items specific to types of teaching in particular disciplines, such as laboratory teaching or fieldwork.

Feel free to adapt items so that the focus is appropriate to the goals and teaching approach of your course. Also, change the terminology to that used in your institution. For example, many items refer to a 'teacher'. Your students may be more used to 'lecturer' or 'professor'.

Suggestions for how to use it

The item bank is printed below in this chapter. The items are also included in a Word document downloadable from www.routledge.com/9780415598859. This is organised following the same hierarchical structure below.

In designing a questionnaire from the item bank, note the principles of good design introduced in Chapter 2. Think first of the types of construct you need information about. These should relate to the aims of your project or the nature of the innovation introduced into your teaching. You should then select items to form a scale for each construct.

Try to keep the questionnaire short, as students are reluctant to complete lengthy questionnaires. This means that there should not be too many constructs and the number of items in each scale should not be too many.

Student development

Promoting student learning

The course encouraged students to think critically.
The course encouraged and helped students to work independently.
The course helped students to develop the ability to solve problems.
The course enabled students to develop skills needed by professionals in this field.
The course stressed and clarified the relevance of this subject for my future profession.
The course encouraged students to apply general principles in new situations.

Promoting the development of knowledge and skills

The course encouraged students to apply theories and principles in new situations.
The course helped students to identify main points and central issues in the field.
The course encouraged students to take novel and creative approaches to set work.
The course helped students to develop the ability to communicate clearly about the subject.
The course helped students to develop the necessary skills for carrying out original research in the subject.
The course enabled students to evaluate new work in this field.
The course enabled students to develop new viewpoints and perspectives.
The course included learning activities that helped students develop decision-making skills.
The course organised learning activities that helped students to think rationally.
The course enabled students to understand and use the methodological processes introduced in this subject.
The course enabled students to learn a lot of factual material.

Promoting interest and curiosity

The course stimulated me to do a lot of outside reading on the subject.
The course stimulated me to discuss subject-related topics with my friends.
I became interested in the subject, and developed plans to take more related units in future.
The course enables students to develop a set of values relating to the profession.
The course stimulated my desire to be employed in this field.
The course encouraged and stimulated students to ask questions about issues and topics in this field.
The course stimulated me to work harder than usual on this subject.

Promoting the development of social skills and attitudes

The course encouraged students to develop a greater awareness of social problems.
The course encouraged students to value alternative viewpoints.
The course encouraged students to learn from each other.
The course promoted the development of a sense of social responsibility among students.
The course encouraged and supported students in the development of their leadership skills.

Promoting the development of self-concept

The course promoted the development of a sense of personal responsibility among students.
The course enabled me to become aware of my own interests and abilities.
The course helped me to develop confidence in myself.
The course enabled me to gain a better understanding of myself.
The course encouraged students to become self-reliant.

Promoting the development of vocational skills and attitudes

The course helped me to develop skills needed by professionals in the field.
The course made information about career opportunities available for students.
The course helped students to clarify what it means to be a professional in this field.
The course helped students to understand how professionals operate in terms of gaining new knowledge.
The course helped students to develop attitudes and values needed by professionals in this field.

Student experience

Reasons for enrolment

I could continue my professional development through my career by taking the course.
For me, part-time study is an alternative to mainstream/traditional education.
The course provides me with training for a future career switch.
The course provided me with professional knowledge for work.
I will be equipped with professional skills for work.
I will gain knowledge for training my juniors.
I took this course purely for interest.
By studying, I can climb the social ladder.
My quality of life should improve, as a result of taking this course.
Studying is a meaningful way of spending my leisure time.

Expectations

I expected to gain professional knowledge to be applied in my work.
I wanted to gain more theoretical information, which would be useful in my work.
I wished to gain professional knowledge for promotion.
It was my aim to gain professional knowledge so as to increase future competitiveness.
I would like to gain academic knowledge to be used in the future.
Enhancing my study skills was one of my expectations.
I expected to gain a recognised qualification.
I expected to achieve an academic level competitive with my colleagues.
The course matches with my expectations.

Sense of belonging

I did not study on campus so I could not develop a sense of belonging.
Part-time students have less chance of using the institution's facilities.
I had no time to participate in out-of-class activities, which hindered my development of a sense of belonging.
The institution usually give priorities to full-time students, thus part-time students have fewer opportunities.
I felt alone because there was no support from others.
I did not have any sense of belonging to the university.
I had a very weak sense of belonging to the university.
Using institutional facilities is a way of helping me to increase my sense of belonging.
I do not feel affiliated with a department.
I contacted staff of my department, which helped me to build up a sense of belonging.
I did not feel affiliated with teaching staff.
Part-time students have less chance to meet tutors.
There is not enough concern from teaching staff for part-time students.
Interacting with teaching staff out of class can build up a sense of belonging.
I interacted with teaching staff in class to build up a sense of belonging.
It is possible to build up a sense of belonging through contacting administrative staff.
Teaching staff were encouraging which helped students to build up a sense of belonging.
Teaching staff were motivating which helped me to establish a sense of belonging.
There was no sense of belonging between me and my fellow students.
I participated in class activities to become familiar with other students.
It is necessary to participate in out-of-class social activities to build up a sense of belonging.
Students can build up a sense of belonging by participating in out-of-class academic activities.
Attending the orientation program before the formal start of course helped in building a sense of belonging.

Teaching

General teaching skills

The teacher stressed important points.
The teacher showed enthusiasm in his/her teaching.
The teacher presented ideas in an interesting way.
The teacher showed that he/she enjoyed teaching.
The teacher appeared to have a thorough knowledge of the subject.
The teacher appeared to have an up-to-date knowledge of the subject.
The teacher explained difficult concepts clearly and understandably.
The teacher showed evidence of good planning in his/her teaching.
The teacher made clear to students how each topic fits into the subject as a whole.
The teacher meaningfully related material to practical, everyday experiences.
The teacher enhanced student interest by giving them opportunities to participate actively in the learning.
The teacher used concrete examples to illustrate new concepts.

The teacher explained abstract ideas and theories clearly.
The teacher has motivated me to do my best work.
The teacher gave students clear instructions about set work.
The teacher made good use of examples and illustrations to help his/her explanations.
All things considered, I think the teacher is an effective teacher.

Interaction with students

The teacher encouraged students to volunteer their own opinions.
The teacher encouraged students to ask questions.
The teacher allowed students to disagree with his/her view.
The teacher praised students for good ideas or useful contributions.
The teacher showed concern for students.
The teacher created a relaxed atmosphere in class.
The teacher respected other people's points of view.
The teacher did a good job of answering students' questions.
The teacher had a friendly and interested attitude towards students.
The teacher was open to students' opinions.
The teacher was willing to assist students when they had problems.
The teacher was available for consultation.
The teacher made me feel welcome to ask him/her questions outside the classroom.
The teacher was successful in getting shy students to participate.

Promoting student involvement

The teacher facilitated discussion in classes.
The teacher organised class activities that encouraged students to participate.
The teacher valued students' views.
The teacher challenged students to reconsider their points of view.
The teacher encouraged students to take responsibility for their own learning.
The teacher encouraged students to interact with each other and work cooperatively.

Presentation of material

The teacher presented material in an organised way.
The teacher structured the material systematically.
The teacher put sufficient stress on important points.
The teacher used class time well.
The teacher pointed out links of the material to other subjects.
The teacher communicated his/her enthusiasm for the subject.
The teacher demonstrated how the work should be tackled.
Lecture and laboratory classes were well integrated.
Lecture and tutorial classes were well integrated.
The teacher emphasised understanding rather than memorising of material.
The teacher was well prepared for tutorials/lectures.

Feedback

The teacher suggested ways for students to improve.
The teacher gave adequate feedback on my work.
Written work was handed back promptly.
The teacher informed us of our progress.
The teacher encouraged and praised good work.

Difficulty

In this subject there were high standards set for students.
This subject was sufficiently difficult to be challenging.
The subject matter was too difficult.
In this subject there was an appropriate amount of required work.

Workload

The teacher sets high standards.
I spent too long each week on this subject.
I could handle the work load of this subject.
I worked harder on this subject than most subjects I have taken.
The teacher did not consider the other demands on my time.
The pace of the subject was too slow.
The assignment load was too heavy.
The workload for this course has been heavier than expected.
The pace in this course has been so rapid I had trouble keeping up.
Compared with other courses at the same level, there has been a heavy workload.
This course seems to cover too many topics.
The heavy workload in this course causes a great deal of stress for me.
I feel under a lot of pressure because of the amount of work we are expected to do.

Tutorials

The tutorials challenged me.
The tutorials were well planned.
The tutorials were essential to effective learning.
The tutorials helped me to overcome the problems I had.
The tutorials were suited to my needs.
The tutorials were generally enjoyable.
The tutorials helped me understand the lecture material.
The tutorials gave me a feeling of being part of a scholarly discussion.

General questions

I would recommend this subject to other students.
The teacher encouraged students to perform up to their potential.
The teacher motivated me to do my best work.

The course was better than the majority of others I have taken.
This course lived up to my expectations.

Assessment procedures

Written assignments

Assignments were returned promptly.
Assignments were a valuable part of the course.
Assignments had realistic deadlines.
Assignments were enjoyable to do.
Assignments seemed to be carefully designed.
Assignments were interesting and stimulating.
Assignments made students think.
Assignments had clear and specific instructions.
Assignments were relevant to and integrated with what had been presented in the subject.
Assignments were assessed fairly and reasonably.
Assignments tied in with the course objectives.
Assignments gave me enough opportunity to demonstrate what I have learned in this subject.

Examinations

The examination was of the right length.
The examination questions were clearly worded.
The examination seemed to be a good measure of student knowledge and understanding.
The examination required original thought.
The examination was assessed carefully and fairly.
The examination has focused on the most important points and topics in the subject.
The examination seemed to have been carefully and conscientiously prepared.

Grades and results

Grades were assigned fairly and impartially.
The grading system was clearly explained to students.
The teacher has a realistic standard of good performance.
My result reflected my ability in the subject.

Specific disciplines

Practical sessions

Practicals were a useful learning experience.
The practical sessions had clearly defined objectives.
The practical sessions were assessed fairly.
The practical sessions were well integrated with the other components of the subject.

The practical sessions add significantly to my knowledge of the subject.
The practical sessions were interesting and stimulating.
The practical sessions had clear directions.

Clinical teaching

The teacher demonstrated the techniques of physical examination well.
The teacher encouraged me to play an active part in the clinical session.
The course enabled me to evaluate alternative treatment options.
The teacher spent sufficient time in demonstrating the treatment techniques.
The teacher demonstrated well the skills of interviewing and examining patients.
The clinical work integrated well with the material covered in lectures and/or seminars.
The teacher showed the important features of the case history.

Language teaching

The course related language to cultural and other issues.
The teacher adjusted readily to students' level of competence.
The teacher corrected errors without causing embarrassment.
The course helped students to develop confidence in speaking the target language.
The course encouraged students to use the target language in the classroom.
The teacher spoke the target language too fast.
Conversation classes were used properly to develop conversation skills.
The course used the language laboratory well.
The teacher explained grammatical and other points clearly.

Resources

Textbooks

The textbooks made a valuable contribution to my learning.
The textbooks were easy to read and understand.
The textbooks presented subject matter relevant to the subject.
The textbooks stimulated my intellectual curiosity.
The prescribed textbook was useful.
Required reading material was easily available.
Required reading was appropriate for the subject.

Laboratory resources

The necessary laboratory materials were available.
The laboratory manuals were clear and easy to follow.
The laboratory manual assisted my learning.

Computing resources

There was adequate access to computing facilities.

The computing exercises aided my understanding.
There was adequate assistance to help students with difficulties.
There is a lack of computer facilities.
The opening hours of the computer lab does not suit students.
I could use the computer centre of my institution.
I am able to collect information through the internet.

Library

The library is too small.
Books and references in the library were not sufficient for the demands of the course.
The library closing time was too early.
Students are able to make use of the library.
It is very helpful to have in access to electronic libraries.

Other resources

Handouts helped me to understand the material.
Learning experiences outside the classroom (e.g. fieldwork, clinical sessions) were carefully planned.
Learning experiences outside the classroom (e.g. fieldwork, clinical sessions) were rewarding.
Case studies and simulations were a valuable part of this subject.
The institution does not provide a suitable place for students to work together on assignments or projects.
I shared information with other students.
Students are able to make use of suitable study facilities.

Chapter 5

Collecting and processing questionnaire data

Administration

The form of administration of CTEQs has often depended on the focus of evaluation. Historically, CTEQs for evaluating courses have usually been conducted in class, while programme-level evaluations (e.g. by graduates) have been conducted through mailed surveys. The widespread adoption of email over the last decade has added a relatively cheap and fast means of contacting stakeholders for all types of surveys. However, this ease of contact will not automatically lead to good response rates. In this chapter, we discuss a range of administration strategies for maximising response rates.

In class

CTEQs focusing on courses or instructors are often conducted in class, particularly towards the end of a semester. One obvious benefit of conducting CTEQs at this point is that one has a 'captive audience', especially if the CTEQ is scheduled in a lecture or tutorial in which details of the final examination will be discussed.

Caulfield (2007) used Vroom's (1964) expectancy model of motivation to investigate students' motivation to provide anonymous feedback using a CTEQ. Students who considered it likely that their feedback would help future students taking the same class, and likely that their feedback would increase the value of the class, were more likely to be attracted to providing anonymous feedback.

Caulfield suggests several strategies for communicating with students about CTEQs. The most obvious is to emphasise to students that feedback will be used to improve the value of the current course and future versions. Making these points at the beginning of the semester, and throughout, should bolster willingness to give feedback, not only through CTEQs. A second strategy, consistent with the above results, is to share the results with students, which Caulfield argues serves several purposes. First, it demonstrates the teacher is serious about using feedback to improve teaching and learning. Second, it provides an opportunity to seek clarification about the feedback and any interpretations made. Third, and related to the second point, it provides the opportunity to check if a given issue was important for a majority of students, or only a small proportion. Fourth, suggestions for changes based on the feedback can be mooted, providing an opportunity for further feedback. Finally, teachers can explain why some issues raised in feedback may not lead to change, such as fundamental requirements of the course or programme, or external constraints related to staffing. Depending on the timing of the evaluation, providing such 'feedback on feedback' may be done during the same semester, or might be done through emails to currently enrolled students in the following semester.

Online

The perceived convenience and lower costs of online survey delivery, data collection and management, and report generation, have led many universities to adopt online CTEQ systems. However, response rates from online surveys are often disappointingly low, raising questions about the representativeness of the sample. When faced with a choice between a survey in class or online, teachers will often choose the latter, in order to save class time. This can be counter-productive, as some students will perceive that the teacher views her teaching time as more valuable than students' feedback.

One potential trade-off between these competing tensions is to schedule class time in a computer laboratory for feedback, maximising the response rates often seen with in-class surveys while retaining benefits related to online delivery and data collection. Such benefits can be substantial when student responses to open questions are desired for 'triangulation' of results; transcribing written comments will be time-consuming and expensive compared with extracting typed comments from a database.

Fortunately, there is a substantial body of research related to maximising response rates for both online and mailed surveys (Dillman, 2009; Edwards, Roberts, Clarke, DiGuiseppi, Pratap, Wentz, & Kwan, 2002). If you are planning on administering a CTEQ entirely online, the following steps are recommended:

1   'Pre-notify' students of the online survey, through an in-class announcement prior to sending out the initial email, or mentioning it in online discussions.
2   Communicate to students that their feedback is important, and that you will take it seriously (cf. Caulfield, 2007).
3   Personalise your contact with students (Heerwegh, 2005). A class list spreadsheet can be used to do a mail merge. This will allow you to insert the student's first name, rather than simply 'Dear Student'.
4   Use multiple contacts and reminders. The most important determinant of a good response rate is the number of contacts. If only one contact is used (e.g. a single email), you may get a response rate of only 20 per cent or so (possibly less). In the first email, it can help to explicitly mention that you'll be sending reminders to encourage students to complete the survey online (Green, 1996). This might take the form: 'Because a good response rate is so important in helping me improve my teaching, I'll be sending a couple of reminders about the survey over the next two weeks.' At least two email reminders (send the first 5–7 days after the initial contact) reminding students in class should also help, if possible.
5   Clearly specify the time period for which the survey will be available.

Over and above these steps, the 'evaluation culture' of your school, department or faculty may affect students' willingness to give feedback online. Bennett, Nair, and Wayland (2006) give a case study of a faculty which moved to entirely online CTEQ delivery. In collaboration with their university's academic development unit, the faculty developed a communication policy around evaluation, with a strong emphasis on communicating to students the importance of their feedback through multiple channels (e.g. emails, 'have your say' posters around the faculty). Overall response rates for the first two semesters following the move to online surveys were substantially higher than for other faculties that also used only online surveys, a result attributed to the impact of the communication policy.

By post

Many of the methods for improving online response rates also hold for maximising postal survey response rates. The following recommendations are based on Dillman's (2000, 2009) tailored design method for conducting surveys, as well as findings from Edwards *et al.* (2002) and other meta-analyses and studies as provided.

1   *First contact:* Pre-notify your target population that they will be contacted. This contact, and all subsequent contacts, should emphasise your affiliation with a university through the letterhead and survey, as surveys originating from universities generate higher response rates (Edwards *et al.*, 2002).
2   *Second contact:* The letter for the second contact (i.e. containing the actual survey) should be personalised (e.g. 'Dear Susan' rather than 'Dear Graduate'); it should be signed in a contrasting ink; it should include a token of appreciation (e.g. a ballpoint pen or fridge magnet; Church, 1993); and it should include a stamped return envelope rather than business reply (Green & Hutchinson, 1996). The letter should also include a warning that reminders will be sent (Green, 1996), and the envelope containing the questionnaire should include a printed 'teaser' statement (e.g. 'Have your say!') to engage recipients (Dommeyer, Elganayan, & Umans, 1991).

    Larger effects of enclosed tokens of appreciation have been found (Green & Hutchinson, 1996), but these are typically associated with enclosing monetary tokens (e.g. one or two dollar bills in the US). The use of coinage in some countries makes this a less viable option, as the nature of the enclosure will be obvious, making theft a possibility.

    The research on the effects of lottery prizes on response rates is not very supportive of this practice, compared with the inclusion in the mailout of a monetary or non-monetary incentive. Church (1993) estimated the effects on response rate of a monetary prize contingent on return, and a non-monetary prize contingent on return, as 4.5 and 1.2 per cent, respectively.
3   *Third contact:* postcard thank you/reminder. This should be sent one week after the second contact (Dillman, 2000, pp. 178–181). The postcard follow-up '…is written not to overcome resistance but rather to jog memories and re-arrange priorities. It is timed to arrive just after the original mailing has produced its major effect, but before each person's questionnaire had had time to be buried under more recent mail or thrown away' (p. 179).
4   *Fourth contact:* first replacement questionnaire (Dillman, 2000, pp. 181–184). This should be sent about 3 weeks after the first questionnaire. The cover letter used in this contact differs from that of the second contact in being more insistent, and in reinforcing messages from the previous contacts that the respondent is important to the success of the survey. As with the first questionnaire, the cover letter should be personalised and signed with a different-colour ink, and a stamped return envelope should be used.

It should be emphasised that maximising response rates can be achieved by using a variety of channels. Heberlein and Baumgartner (1978) found the number of contacts correlated strongly ($r = 0.63$) with response rate, so for some CTEQs – particularly those sent to graduates or employers – multiple contacts using a combination of initial email contacts, paper-based surveys, and phone and/or postcard reminders will be needed.

Sampling

There is a common perception that students are often over-surveyed with CTEQs, particularly when an institution's policy is to evaluate every course each time it is run. As noted above, aspects of a faculty's or school's 'evaluation culture' may moderate the extent to which students feel a large number of surveys are an imposition. Nonetheless, rather than always asking all students to evaluate all courses or teachers, carefully collecting CTEQ data from a sample rather than the whole population may still yield accurate, useable and cost-effective information.

First, some definitions. A *population* is 'the entire set of individuals to which findings of the survey are to be extrapolated' (Levy & Lemeshow, 2008, p. 11). Thus, if we were interested in students' perceptions of the quality of a particular degree, the population would be all students enrolled in that degree. In contrast, if we were interested in how students viewed the quality of our university's library, the population would be the entire cohort of students (on the assumption that we expect all students to use the library). If the entire set of individuals in a population of interest respond to a survey, researchers are able to calculate *parameters* of the responses (e.g. mean response, standard deviation of responses).

However, it is very unusual to have access to data from a complete population. When a survey is only given to a proportion of the whole population, that proportion is called a *sample*. Researchers then calculate *statistics* from that sample, with the goal of extrapolating population parameters from the sample (Levy & Lemeshow, 2008). Examples of such extrapolations are commonly seen in newspaper polls, with an appropriate margin of error (e.g. with a representative sample of 1000 individuals, the margin of error for an estimate of a population proportion – such as the proportion who intend to vote for a particular party – is roughly 3%).

The goal of many CTEQ surveys conducted by handing out surveys in class or contacting students by email is to gain a simple sample of the relevant population in that course. Franklin (2001, p. 92) argues that 'the higher the proportion of respondents to students enrolled, the more reliable the results will be, and, at the same time, the smaller the class enrolment, the higher that proportion will need to be to ensure that the sample is reasonably representative'. Table 5.1 gives some recommendations for assessing whether an adequate sample has been obtained. Franklin notes that, assuming students were not absent for any systematic reasons, the impact of absence on results is larger in smaller classes.

More complex sampling strategies may be worth considering under some circumstances. Kreiter and Lakshman (2005) describe a medical faculty that wished to evaluate the quality of lectures given by 140 lecturers across a single programme. Instead of asking all students to evaluate all lectures, random samples of 20–21 students were drawn from the population of 191 students, with the constraint that each student

Table 5.1 Recommended response rates

Class size	Recommended response
5–20	At least 80%; more recommended
20–30	At least 75%; more recommended
30–50	At least 66%; 75% or more recommended
50 or more	At least 60%; 75% or more recommended
100 or more	More than 50%; 75% or more recommended

Source: Franklin (2001)

would evaluate a total of 28 lectures across the year. The authors report an overall response rate of 89 per cent, with each lecturer receiving 18.2 evaluations per lecture. A decision study (Shavelson, Webb, & Rowley, 1989) found this number of evaluations per lecture was sufficient to ensure a suitable level of inter-rater reliability.

When a student population has a variety of demographic (e.g. gender, race) or institutional (e.g. faculty of enrolment, undergraduate vs. postgraduate, part-time vs. full-time, freshman vs. upper-level students, local vs. international students) characteristics that are considered important, more complex sampling frames might be used. For instance, a university might wish to evaluate the quality of its programmes. One way to conduct such an evaluation would be to send all students a survey; but in a large institution, this could be very expensive. A stratified random survey may be a useful alternative.

The University of Sydney evaluates the quality of its programmes using a stratified random sample of coursework students (Ginns, Prosser, & Barrie, 2007). The size of the sample was based on an initial survey of all undergraduate students in 1999, with estimates of the population variability at the faculty level being derived from this dataset. The top stratum is faculty, followed by 'aggregate degree' (i.e. collections of similar degrees within faculties). So that all aggregated degrees appear in a given faculty's sample, the target number of students from each degree to be surveyed is calculated based on the proportion of students from each degree present in the population of the faculty. Lastly, because the university is particularly interested in the experiences of first-year students, the random sample is further stratified so that a representative number of first-year students from each faculty are included. For an example of a teaching evaluation study using stratified sampling to ensure adequate representation by faculty and year of course, see Beran, Violato, Kline, and Frideres (2009).

Complex sampling frames can support a range of advanced research questions, as well as being more cost-efficient, but must be designed and implemented carefully. A full discussion of survey sampling is beyond the scope of this text, but Scheaffer, Wendenhall, and Lyman (1996) is a good introductory text. Levy and Lemeshow (2008) provides a more advanced discussion of a range of simple and complex survey designs.

Processing data

Scanning

Data collected using paper-based forms can be entered into a spreadsheet manually, but this quickly becomes very resource-intensive if a large number of items and/or participants are involved. Scannable paper-based forms are widely used to collect teaching evaluation data in higher education. Such systems vary in the extent to which a third party, responsible for the design of the form, is involved. Institutions wishing to have the option of ad hoc or personalised forms will require hardware, software, expertise and resources for developing, delivering and scanning such forms. In contrast, if only a small number of standardised forms are to be used, it may be more economical to use forms designed and printed by a third party.

Online

Collecting data online has the advantages of considerable cost advantages and speed of processing, with the main overhead being either in-house design costs, or purchasing online surveying software. Such systems can be designed so that student records can be used to generate and track responses, but clear provisions must be made to ensure anonymity of student responses. Although individual staff members may not have the option of using their institution's online surveying system for ad hoc surveys, such surveys may be created for little or no cost using web-based tools such as SurveyMonkey (www.surveymonkey.com) or LimeSurvey (www.limesurvey.org).

Summary

Given the prevalence of CTEQs, and the resulting cynicism many students feel, it is crucial to communicate to students what the purpose of the evaluation is, how you will communicate the results of the evaluation back to students, and how results of similar evaluations have been used in the past for improvement of teaching and learning. If students perceive CTEQ administration as merely a bureaucratic exercise, the quality of responses (particularly to open-ended questions) and the response rate are likely to suffer.

Chapter 6

Collection of qualitative data

Qualitative and quantitative research

This is the first of three chapters on qualitative research or evaluation. Routine evaluation in universities tends to be dominated by quantitative data from questionnaires. Qualitative evaluation ought to be more widely used, as it tends to provide more valuable insights if little is known about a topic. Higher education these days is characterised by change, which suggests that an exploratory approach to new issues should be employed more often. It is all too easy to slip into routine use of quantitative evaluation of courses or programmes, while new, more diverse, issues are not investigated.

Qualitative approaches are used often in the scholarship of teaching. The scholarship of teaching is often conducted in conjunction with innovation in teaching or when there are major changes of some sort. This means that there is bound to be some degree of uncertainty over the key issues involved. Qualitative research normally adopts an exploratory stance, so it is well equipped to handle innovation.

Qualitative research is also valuable in conjunction with quantitative data. Qualitative work can be used to explore a topic before a questionnaire is developed. Qualitative data can be valuable for adding depth and illumination to results from a survey.

In starting to look at qualitative research or evaluation, it is useful to compare it to quantitative work, to help in visualising the strengths of each. There are a number of approaches to qualitative research and considerable variations between projects, just as there are with quantitative work. The differences suggested here are therefore broad generalisations, which may not apply in every case. Many of the distinctions arise because qualitative methods are commonly used with naturalistic research and quantitative with more positivistic studies. The differences often arise more from the paradigm than the method.

Intensive nature of qualitative research

A difference between qualitative and quantitative research that does need to be addressed lies in the resources needed to gather and analyse a comparable amount of data. Table 6.1 suggests that qualitative research normally has smaller samples. This is mainly because qualitative work is more resource-intensive.

If an online administration system is used, it takes the same amount of work to administer a questionnaire to a list of 100,000 email addresses as to 100. The task of analysis is the same. However, for qualitative research, each additional interview might

Table 6.1 Characteristics of quantitative vs. qualitative research

Quantitative	Qualitative
Concerned with numbers	Concerned with words and observations
Collects data with questionnaires, tests and other measuring instruments	Collects data from interviews, observations, field studies, documents, etc.
Data may be gathered by survey or in experiments	Data usually collected in authentic or field setting
Collects data from a sample which is statistically representative of population	Data usually collected from smaller samples or limited number of case studies
Tests stated hypotheses	More open and exploratory
Aims to develop theory	Aims for in-depth understanding and identification of relevant constructs
Usually claims to be generalisable	Findings may be limited to cases studied
Usually sticks closely to original plan	Plans evolve as project develops
Analysis is step-by-step	Analysis is cyclical
Hard?	Soft?

take an extra hour or two to conduct and at least the same amount of time to arrange. There would then be a week or so to produce a summary or transcript. Analysis takes longer as the pile of paper increases. No wonder samples tend to be small.

As qualitative work is more resource-intensive, it makes sense to employ it when quantitative work is less likely to succeed. The strength of qualitative research is in novel or exploratory situations. Quantitative studies are often difficult in new situations or with innovations as the questions to be asked may not be obvious. What is important from the student perspective may not be related to the questions on a questionnaire.

The differences in nature between the two forms of research also imply a logical sequence for using them if a new scenario is being investigated. Explore first with qualitative work, to find out what the issues are. Then use quantitative techniques to gather data from a larger and more representative sample.

The other advantage of qualitative work is that it can yield more detailed and in-depth information. Questionnaires sometimes suggest that there is a problem, but do not pinpoint exactly what the problem is. In-depth investigation through interviews can pinpoint the issues.

Sources

This section considers several sources of qualitative data, mainly for evaluation purposes. The remainder of the chapter on data collection, and also the next one on analysis, concentrates on interviews. The rationale is twofold. First, interviews are probably the most common method for gathering qualitative data, particularly for the scholarship of teaching. Second, the same or similar principles for data collection and analysis apply to interviews and the other sources.

Open-ended questions on questionnaires

Most questionnaires have an open-ended question or two on the end. The rationale is that students can enlarge on anything that seems important or comment on issues not covered by the closed questions.

The rationale is fine. In practice, though, the outcomes are often disappointing. First, students often do not respond to the open-ended questions. As there are so many questionnaires to fill in, enthusiasm for completing them has declined, particularly the open-ended sections.

Second, even if there are any comments, they are often not used because they are hard to process and tedious to analyse. If questionnaires are completed on paper, central units do not normally process them for obvious reasons. At best, the forms are returned to the teacher for perusal, though this practice sometimes used to be questioned in case teachers recognise students' handwriting. As nothing much is handwritten these days, this is presumably no longer an issue.

Online administration makes processing easier, as comments can be automatically transferred to a text file. The file can then be sent to the relevant teacher.

A practical recommendation for dealing with open-ended questions when using paper administration is to make use of the information or to leave out the open-ended question. If the information is not going to be processed or the teacher will not act on the information, it is better not to include the question. Students become alienated if data are collected and not used. This should not, however, be interpreted as recommending the omission of open-ended questions. They can give valuable information, so are worth including – but if you do, make use of the data.

Post-it notes

Post-it notes are a good way of collecting information during (or at the end of) classes. It is a form of evaluation that can gather data about individual classes or several classes from a course. You give each student a Post-it note; ask an open-ended question and ask students to stick the notes on a wall as they leave. As the comments have to be brief to fit on a Post-it note, it is usually not too much work to identify common themes. It is a good idea to report back at the next class as to what these are.

Some suggestions for the types of question that might be asked are as follows.

- What do you like most about my teaching?
- What do you like least about my teaching?
- How useful is/are the handouts/textbook/course website/reading list?
- What was the most important thing you learned in today's class?
- What do you understand by (concept) X?

Note that the last two of these ask about understanding of content or concepts. This is something most academics would like to obtain feedback on, but evaluation rarely provides feedback on the understanding of content.

End-of-class or out-of-class conversations

This is the least formal way of gathering information. It is hardly a systematic method of data collection, but if informal conversation does take place between teacher and students, any feedback obtained might as well be used. It could guide the direction of more formal data gathering.

Staff–student forums

Staff–student forums have become common. They normally seem to be constituted as a formal committee with elected student representatives.

Staff–student forums can be valuable sources of information. They need to be handled well if they are to be effective sources of feedback. Many of the principles are similar to those below, which apply to interviews.

Establishing a positive and open relationship is important as both sides can feel uneasy. The conversation is best kept at the programme level, as it can be embarrassing if individual teachers are singled out. Staff should try not to be defensive, but this does not preclude explaining that some suggestions are either not feasible or undesirable.

Interviews

Interviews are the most common way of gathering qualitative data for research purposes, but are less commonly used for evaluation. The bulk of this chapter, and all of the next, refer to interview data, but the principles apply equally well to other data sources discussed in this section.

Websites

Course websites have become very common. They can provide useful feedback, as today's generation of students are used to conversing freely over the internet. However, all too often course websites prove disappointing as messages are confined to trivial requests for administrative information.

Online or distance education courses can have difficulty getting students to engage in meaningful discussion about course topics. There is therefore a literature on moderating or promoting online discussion (see e.g. Salmon, 2011). The principles relate to those for interview techniques in the section below. Teachers who want feedback can try seeding discussion by asking questions similar to the semi-structured questions prepared for interviews. If discussion starts it can be promoted by using prompting and probing questions.

Planning qualitative research

Framing the study

Qualitative research tends to be more open than quantitative. However, there does need to be some balance between open exploration and framing the study. There needs to be some definition of what is to be examined and what are the boundaries of the study. There will inevitably be some direction-setting based upon existing knowledge – and there should be.

Qualitative research tends to be framed in terms of research questions or aims rather than testable hypotheses. The research aims for the study of conceptions of teaching, which is frequently used as an example in the next chapter, are given below.

- To identify the conceptions of teaching held by university lecturers.
- To develop a classification scheme for describing identified conceptions.
- To investigate whether identified conceptions of teaching are related to the ways in which lecturers teach, their students' approaches to learning and other learning outcomes.

In this chapter, examples are also given from a current project looking at how students adapt study behaviour between school and university. The research questions for this project are as follows.

1 What were the study approaches and beliefs about knowledge students acquired at school?
2 What were the study approaches and beliefs about knowledge students had to adopt at university if they were to become successful graduates?
3 How could teaching and learning approaches and curriculum design aid in prompting students to successfully make the transition?

Samples

The sample for qualitative research is invariably smaller than that for quantitative work. It can be as small as a single case. Qualitative research is often aiming for the identification and understanding of important constructs rather than aiming to gather data that represent a whole population. In other words, it is looking to see what is important and how it can be best described, rather than how many or what proportion of the population are affected.

In determining the sample size for qualitative studies important questions are listed below.

1 How much data will give you the insight you need?
2 How much data can you analyse?
3 How much data will make the sample seem reasonably representative?
4 How much data can you collect?

Note that question 1 implies that analysis takes place as the data are collected. It is good practice to do at least some analysis of qualitative data while collection takes place. This ensures that questions asked are yielding something worthwhile. It also helps in avoiding collecting too much data, because if new insights do not come from extra interviews, it is time to stop doing any more.

It is a common mistake to collect more data than can be analysed. It tends to arise when projects proceed step by step.

interview and observation → producing transcripts → analysis

It is all too easy to collect a lot of interviews, only to discover that they could not possibly all be analysed, even if they did all contain useful material. Even worse is collecting lots of material only to find it is not particularly helpful in answering the research questions. Again, starting analysis early helps avoid the problem.

Making the sample representative

It is unusual for a qualitative sample to be representative of the population by the strictest statistical standard. First, it is often impractical as the number of interviews required would not be manageable. Second, the aim is not usually to discover information about the characteristics of a population. Rather, it is to gain insights into the nature of a phenomenon.

While quantitative studies usually claim to have representative samples, it is common to suggest that findings are applicable well beyond the population actually sampled. The majority of quantitative studies in higher education collect data from students in just one university. Strictly speaking, if data are collected from one university, the population is that one university. Yet it is common to infer, implicitly at least, that conclusions can be generalised to higher education generally, or at least to Western countries (assuming the study took place in a Western country). While such generalisations from quantitative data are rarely questioned, generalisations from qualitative data seem to be treated with suspicion.

Eisner (1991, ch. 9) argues persuasively that generalisation from qualitative analysis can take place through processes other than the formal inference of statistics. His argument is that in real life we use the processes of *attribute analysis* and *pattern matching* to draw conclusions from our experiences. Attribute analysis utilises attributes or characteristics of an object or phenomenon to identify it as a member of a class we have previously experienced. Pattern matching draws upon the relationship between parts of an image or phenomenon. If these appear to have a similar formation to one we have experienced before, we might conclude that it has similar properties. In both cases we commonly draw conclusions based on partial evidence. In daily life we draw on these processes to make deductions related to our previous experiences. Eisner argues that similar principles can be used to make useable generalisations from qualitative data. The conclusions may be more tentative than those from formal inference, but quantitative studies often exaggerate the extent to which they have followed the processes of formal inference.

While qualitative studies may not be representative of the population by statistical standards, they should aim to be as close to being representative as possible. When conducting a limited number of interviews or observations, try to ensure a reasonably even coverage based upon known variables that are likely to be relevant. The study of lecturers' conceptions of teaching, for example, tried to ensure that those interviewed came from a range of departments in different faculties and were representative of levels of appointment. Certainly, try to pick cases that are likely to be typical rather than unusual. Even with a single case study it is possible to pick a typical case.

An alternative approach is starting with cases that are most likely to be revealing. The adapting study approaches project started with interviews with students who seemed to be having the greatest difficulties in adapting to university study. These included disciplines in the arts and social sciences, which were a marked contrast to school as they dealt with contested knowledge. There were also interviews with students in courses which used problem-based learning (again because this was such a marked contrast to school). Later interviews brought more balance to the sample, but the final sample was probably somewhat biased towards students showing difficulties in adapting. This seems reasonable as the main purpose of the study was investigating the nature of an apparent problem. If there was a desire to find out the extent to which the issue of adaptation applied to each discipline, it would be better to do it quantitatively. Scales and items for an appropriate instrument could be derived from the qualitative data.

Interview technique

The first step in conducting a productive interview is establishing rapport. Students will only be open and frank if they feel comfortable with the interviewer. This does have implications for selecting interviewers. Someone without people skills is unlikely to be successful. Research assistants of about the same age as the students are often better at establishing a relationship and eliciting information than ageing professors.

The most common form of interview is semi-structured. In these a list of questions is prepared. However, sticking solely to the questions on the list and performing a mechanical interview is very poor technique. Instead, the interview should be more like a conversation. Interviewers need to use the strategies of prompting for more information and probing for greater depth.

Interview questions

Given the previous discussion about the nature of qualitative and quantitative research, and the relative advantages of each, it seems sensible to reserve interviews for topics or situations when exploration is needed. In which case, the interview questions need to be open to uncover the nature of issues from the student perspective.

Interviews are sometimes conducted with closed questions. The most common example is probably the telephone opinion survey. Presumably, the administrators resort to this approach when they expect the sample to be either unwilling or unable to complete a questionnaire. Students, though, are capable of completing a questionnaire, and acceptable returns can be achieved. If you want to ask closed questions it seems more sensible to use a questionnaire, rather than a resource-intensive interview.

When designing interview questions, the most important point is to make the questions specific to the aims of the study or the nature of the innovation. This may seem obvious, but it is a departure from the design of items in questionnaires, which are administered to students in many courses or programmes. For these the wording of items has to be at the general level, so as to apply to all the courses.

For example, if you have introduced problem-based learning (PBL) you need questions specific to PBL: questions about the cases used, the way the students work to deal with them, the facilitating by the tutors, the difficulty of adapting to the PBL method and the outcomes which result.

Qualitative studies are normally trying to find out about complex and abstract phenomena. However, it is usually best to avoid asking students directly about the phenomenon itself. Often they will not know anything about the construct, and, if they do, the interviewer will often be putting words into students' mouths, as they will respond by casting themselves in a good light and saying what they think the inter-viewer wants to hear.

Instead it is best to ask questions about concrete acts of study; commonly, these are assignments students have just completed or study tasks performed in class. Information about the abstract phenomena investigated is then inferred from the descriptions of how the tasks were tackled and/or the outcomes of them.

A good example is the work on approaches to learning by Marton and Säljö (1976). They did not ask students which approaches they used – the concepts of deep and surface approaches did not exist prior to the study. Instead students were asked to read an academic article. They were then asked questions about what they had learned from the article. The answers were judged to be in two categories, of surface features of the article or an understanding of the underlying message the author intended to convey. This gave rise to the notion of deep and surface approaches.

Another example is from the current adaptation from school to university project. A major finding was that students had to make a major adaptation to epistemological beliefs to successfully adapt to university study. However, questions were not asked about epistemological beliefs, as most students are not aware that they hold them, let alone are able to describe them. Instead questions such as the following were used, and epistemological beliefs were inferred from the data:

Approaches to learning

Think back to how you went about studying in your secondary school.

- How did you write an essay? How do you do it now?
- How did you revise for tests and examinations? How do you do it now?
- How would you have described a good secondary school student?
- How would you describe a good final year university student?

Perceptions of good teaching

- How would you have described a good teacher at secondary school?
- How does that compare to how you would describe a good teacher now?

Experiences of what has helped and hindered their transition

- Given the changes you have described, what sorts of things in your courses have helped you in these changes and what sorts of things have hindered them?
- Can you point to a particular course which helped you change?

Processing interview data

Once data are collected, the main task is to analyse it, and this is the topic of the next chapter. It is worth reiterating at this point, though, that doing all the analysis after data collection is complete is not wise. It is much more sensible to do some analysis as the data are collected.

Before doing any analysis there is usually a need for an intermediate step in which the audio-recorded interview is converted into a form that can be analysed. For research projects requiring detailed conceptual analysis, this means producing a full transcript. This is a labour-intensive process that takes a considerable amount of time. The time taken should not be underestimated in research plans or grant proposals.

Much of my (DK) research has taken place in Hong Kong. In that location there is an added complication in that most interviews are conducted in the mother tongue, Cantonese. It is then necessary to translate the interview into English to produce a transcript. Fortunately, I have been able to find very talented research assistants who are able to listen to a tape in Cantonese and type out a fluent accurate English translation.

As producing transcripts is so time-consuming and labour-intensive, consideration should be given to producing instead a summary of main themes, probably backed by some illustrative quotations. Where the qualitative data are collected for evaluation purposes or to gain insights into a teaching evaluation, a summary is perfectly adequate (and may, indeed, be more suitable than a full transcript as there is no need for further analysis).

Conclusion

Qualitative data are commonly gathered in projects associated with the scholarship of teaching. Use in evaluation or institutional research is less common, particularly compared to the volume of quantitative evaluation. The status of qualitative work in evaluation is worthy of challenge.

As we noted earlier in the chapter, qualitative work is particularly suited to exploring new phenomena about which little is known. As higher education seems to be in a state of constant and ever more rapid change, new scenarios and phenomena are with us just about all the time. Many colleges evaluate few, if any, of them, which means that their decision-making is ill-informed.

Others proceed straight to a questionnaire. Chapter 2 dealt with the difficulty of establishing the validity of a questionnaire. A questionnaire drawn up by university administrators, based on intuitive feelings about the issue, can have no claim to validity. The questions asked could completely miss important student concerns, in which case the questionnaire provides misinformation for the decision-making process.

The bottom line is to encourage the use of qualitative evaluation to provide valid information for management decision-making. It may be more expensive than quantitative evaluation or no evaluation at all. But making inappropriate policy decisions based on incorrect information or no information at all could be more expensive still.

Chapter 7

Analysis of qualitative data

The analysis of qualitative data is often not clearly explained. It is common to see statements like 'intense scrutiny of the data' and 'categories emerging from the data'. To those trying to learn how to do analysis, this must sound rather like the three witches in *Macbeth*. But what if, after all the hubble, bubble, toil and trouble, nothing seems to emerge from the cauldron? Another approach that is not informative is to claim that qualitative analysis is an art. There is some truth in this. However, the statement is no help to those who are not initiated into the art form.

In this chapter we try to take a pragmatic approach to analysis. We outline steps to be taken, so the method seems systematic. However, we stress that the approach needs to be followed flexibly. Good qualitative research does not result from following a recipe step by step.

Analysis is a process of reducing a large amount of data to a form that can be communicated to a potential audience. In the data-reduction process, the aim is to distil out the important elements of the topic studied.

The method outlined here is consistent with standard grounded theory (Glaser & Strauss, 1967; Lincoln & Guber, 1985). This is probably the most commonly used approach to the analysis of qualitative data, and is related to several other forms of qualitative analysis.

Quantitative data are usually analysed using a step-by-step approach, which was often specified in the research design. By contrast, analysis of qualitative data tends to proceed in a cyclical or iterative manner. There is often a lot of to-ing and fro-ing, and steps are often omitted.

There can also be an overlap between data collection and analysis, as it is usually best to do at least some analysis while data are being collected. In this way it is possible to see whether interviews are asking sensible questions and observations are useful. Fine-tuning of interview schedules and observation methods are possible. Other worthwhile issues may be discovered.

Some degree of analysis while collecting data can also give a guide to when sufficient data have been gathered. If no new insights appear after a number of interviews, it may be time to stop collecting data. This principle also applies to sections of interviews on individual topics. If the answers to a set of questions on a particular issue seem to yield consistent responses after a time, it is worth considering removing this section from the interviews.

Analysis exercise

To introduce qualitative analysis, we suggest you consider how you would go about a very simple analysis task: analysing the data from 10 students' responses to one open-ended question on a questionnaire. This is a simple task that most people would do almost intuitively. But, as a way of introducing analysis, try to think about the steps you are performing.

The question was:

How could this course be improved?

Responses were:

Student 1

In general the course was good but I would have preferred more learning activities.

Student 2

Start the class later as I find it hard to get from work in time.
Provide better biscuits — we get the same ones all the time.

Student 3

A lot of information was presented which was hard to understand.
The textbook was not very helpful.

Student 4

I did not understand the lesson on differential equations.
The plastic seats are uncomfortable.

Student 5

Provide more practice sessions in class for doing typical problems.

Student 6

The material was explained well but there was not enough opportunity to practise what was taught.

Student 7

Provide more handouts as the textbook was not much help.

Student 8

The workload was too high.

Student 9

Suggest a better textbook.

Student 10

The course was demanding but by working hard at home I managed to get a grasp of the material. Perhaps there could be more chance to practise the work in class.

Analysis

A normal starting point for the analysis would be to read through to *explore* how to tackle the data. While doing this you would be looking for common themes, because *classification* of key ideas is a key step in reducing the data to manageable proportions. In this case, main classifications or categories might be:

- learning activities;
- promote understanding;
- classroom environment; and
- textbook.

The next step might be going through the comments one by one to *code* them into the appropriate category of the classification scheme. Some might treat this as a semi-quantitative exercise, noting how many codings there are for each category. You would then want to *draw conclusions* and put them in some form of *report*.

Elements of analysis

Exploring, classifying, coding, drawing conclusions and reporting are steps or stages that the researcher normally passes through within qualitative analysis. In more complex cases than that above they may not be very distinct from one another. Each step is likely to be revisited several times. There is much to-ing and fro-ing as the researcher develops, refines and reconsiders ideas.

The remainder of this chapter examines the elements of analysis in more detail. The steps are presented in roughly the order in which they would normally be performed. Bear in mind, though, that progress through the stages will be recursive rather than linear.

You will note that there are more than the five main steps derived from the exercise above. The additional ones are substeps or additional elements that are often needed once the volume of data grows to a more substantial volume and it becomes impossible to hold everything in the mind at the same time. The steps assume that interviews or observations have been conducted and transcripts produced. The explanations tend to relate more to interview data than observations.

Figure 7.1 is a representation of steps in analysis. It is a simplification, though, in that it does not fully represent the to-ing and fro-ing that normally takes place. Many more recursive arrows could be added to the diagram.

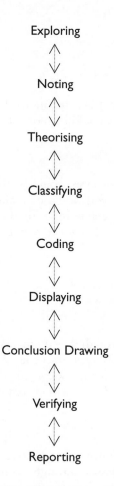

Exploring

Noting

Theorising

Classifying

Coding

Displaying

Conclusion Drawing

Verifying

Reporting

Figure 7.1 A schematic representation of qualitative data analysis

Examples

The elements of analysis are illustrated with many examples. This approach has been found to be helpful in teaching qualitative analysis. It seems to give help in envisioning the types of outcome that are possible.

In an attempt to bring some coherence to the explanation of the stages in analysis, many of the examples relate to research into conceptions of teaching. There are also examples which relate to students' approaches to learning (SAL; cf. Biggs & Tang, 2007; Entwistle, 2009; Prosser & Trigwell, 1999; Ramsden, 2003), as many readers are likely to be familiar with this field. References to the original papers are given, so that the example can be examined in context if desired.

Exploring

The initial step is to examine the data by reading it through. The greater the volume of data and the more complex it is, the more often it will be necessary to go through the material. While reading through you should be asking questions like:

- What are interviewees saying?
- What are the important ideas?
- Is there any commonality between interviewees?
- What are the important variables?
- Do any classification systems seem to be there?

The next two steps – noting and theorising – are substeps of exploring, which are needed when the amount of data becomes more substantial than that in the exercise at the start of the chapter.

Identification of variables will also be something which is considered during the initial exploration. In a substantial study, with a large body of complex data, it may be more of a separate, but overlapping, step.

Noting

When the volume of data is more substantial than the rather artificial exercise at the start of the chapter, it becomes necessary to make some form of record during the exploration. As the researcher goes through the transcripts, notes are made in the form of marginal comments, observations, self-memos, sketches, etc.

Notes tend to be at two levels, or possibly three. Initially, most notes tend to be about individual points or paragraphs within transcripts. These might pinpoint ideas or points that seem to be particularly significant. It is a form of preliminary coding. The noting is usually through making marginal comments or highlighting phrases.

At the overall level some preliminary ideas about answers to the questions posed in the section above on exploring might start to emerge. These are usually noted down separately. The form can be quite varied. Self-memos are probably the most common, while some researchers prefer graphic representations.

The third level is that of the individual interview or case. This usually happens at a later stage as individuals are allocated to defined elements of a classification system. A preliminary exploration may, though, do some sorting of cases.

The traditional approach to exploring and noting has been the use of pencil and paper. Erasers are useful as ideas change and develop as the exploration proceeds. Some favour highlighter pens, often with multiple colours.

There are computer programs such as NVivo, which you can use to record your notes. I (DK) find computers hard to use for this part of the task as only a tiny part of the data can be viewed on screen at any point in time, which makes it difficult to see the relevance of the comments in the context of the whole interview or dataset. This may be a personal preference; others raised in this IT era may find the opposite holds.

This observation about the use of computer programs in qualitative data analysis does not apply to other elements of analysis. My research team and I have found NVivo very useful for coding and sorting large bodies of complex data.

Theorising

Theorising consists of initial attempts to answer the questions posed in the above section. Important variables will be identified. There might be some early ideas on a classification system. At this stage you may have some initial ideas as to what is the main message from the data.

Identifying variables

One outcome of the initial exploration and theorising will be the identification of ideas, themes or variables which seem to be important. For convenience we will call all of these *variables*.

Identified variables may be only loosely related to the actual questions asked in an interview. These are often just initial probes to define the topic area, but leave it open to interviewees to raise issues which concern them.

Defining variables

Some variables may be quite straightforward in nature. Others will need careful definition or characterisation if readers are to understand the nature of the variable. Still others may need extensive investigation to uncover the characteristics of the variable. The main point of the early research into SAL was to identify the nature of an approach to learning (Marton & Säljö, 1976).

The ways of identifying and defining variables are similar to those for characterising categories of a variable. Some of the more common ways are given below.

Label

A label is needed so that you have a way of referring to the variable. Obviously, a good label conveys the nature of the variable. With straightforward variables a label may be all that is needed.

Definition

Some researchers tend to use labels for constructs such as reflection or conceptions with the assumption that everyone understands the nature of the variables. These, though, are quite complex constructs and the terms have been used in different ways by various writers. It is good practice, therefore, to ensure that variables are properly defined where necessary.

Even with more straightforward variables it may be necessary to set some limits on the variable. For example, it may be quite straightforward for readers to understand the variable *university student*. It would, though, be helpful to say whether it includes part-time and full-time, undergraduate and post-graduate, sub-degree and degree, etc. Other studies might concentrate exclusively on particular types of student, such as mature students or those from disadvantaged socio-economic backgrounds.

Written description

A major outcome from a project can be a detailed or 'thick' description of a variable. The researcher aims to convey to the reader an understanding of the nature of the variable through its description. The characterisation of an approach to learning is a good example again (Marton & Säljö, 1976).

Classifying

The next step is devising ways to classify the types of variable into a category scheme. Classification is a process of dividing variables into identified subsets. Variables or phenomena are rarely uniform, so most disciplines have developed schemes for classifying concepts into subgroups. An example with which everyone should be familiar is the way biologists classify plants and animals into species and subspecies.

There are several different ways of classifying phenomena. All of these have logical ways of representing both the scheme and the individual classifications. Part of the analysis is determining which (if any) of the classification systems best fit the data or apply to each variable. This is clearly a matter of informed judgement, as more than one possibility will exist in most cases.

Age, for example, can be shown by any of the following category schemes, and several more besides:

- Broad developmental categories, such as toddler, child, adolescent, etc.
- Student levels, such as primary school student, secondary school student, undergraduate, mature student.
- Small age groups, such as 6–10, 11–15, 16–20, etc.
- Larger age groups, such as 0–30, 31–60, 61–90, etc.
- A specific age on the continuum from 0 to death.

It is poor technique to apply the same type of classification scheme to all variables and sets of data, though many researchers seem to do this. The next sections examine types of classification schemes.

Discrete categories

A scheme of discrete categories implies dividing a variable into two or more separate categories. Deep and surface approaches to learning are a good example, though later research has shown that approaches to learning may not be best described as two discrete categories. Discrete categories are probably the most commonly used type of category scheme, with two to five categories being common. This is probably because it is hard to keep more than five categories in mind, rather than any reflection on the nature of knowledge.

Hierarchical structure of categories and subcategories

Hierarchical structures result from splitting individual categories into subcategories. If subcategories are then split into sub-subcategories and so on, the structure can become quite complex. Biological classification systems for species use this type of structure.

The computer program NVivo and its predecessor started out using hierarchical classification schemes. Figure 7.2 is an example showing a coding scheme for generic capabilities or graduate attributes. The top part of the diagram shows the hierarchical structure graphically. The lower part shows the nodes of the coding structure.

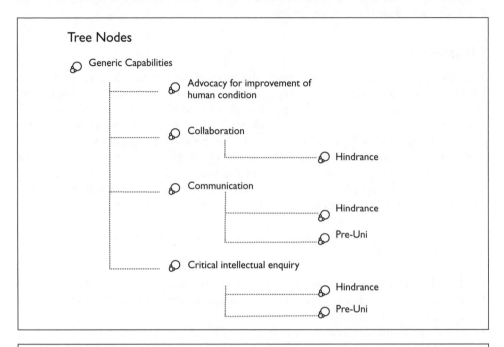

Tree Nodes

Generic Capabilities

  Advocacy for improvement of human condition

  Collaboration
    Hindrance

  Communication
    Hindrance
    Pre-Uni

  Critical intellectual enquiry
    Hindrance
    Pre-Uni

All Nodes

Name	In Folder
Generic Capabilities	Tree Nodes
Generic Capabilities\Advocacy for improvement of human condition	Tree Nodes
Generic Capabilities\Collaboration	Tree Nodes
Generic Capabilities\Collaboration\Hindrance	Tree Nodes
Generic Capabilities\Communication	Tree Nodes
Generic Capabilities\Communication\Hindrance	Tree Nodes
Generic Capabilities\Communication\Pre-Uni	Tree Nodes
Generic Capabilities\Critical intellectual enquiry	Tree Nodes
Generic Capabilities\Critical intellectual enquiry\Hindrance	Tree Nodes
Generic Capabilities\Critical intellectual enquiry\Pre-Uni	Tree Nodes
Generic Capabilities\Critical self reflection	Tree Nodes
Generic Capabilities\Critical self reflection\Hindrance	Tree Nodes
Generic Capabilities\Critical self reflection\Pre-Uni	Tree Nodes

Figure 7.2 An NVivo hierarchical tree classification system

Related or multidimensional categories

If two variables are related and both have two or more categories, it can be useful to look at the categories of each as a combined system. A 2×2 structure is the simplest design, and an example of this is displayed in the quadrant diagram shown in Figure 7.3. The variable students' conception of learning was divided into passive and active categories. Their perceptions of teaching were divided into transmissive and non-traditional categories (Kember, 2007).

Where one or both of the variables are divided into more than two categories, a table or matrix is a good way of portraying this. If one variable has x categories and the other y, it can be shown in an $x \times y$ table.

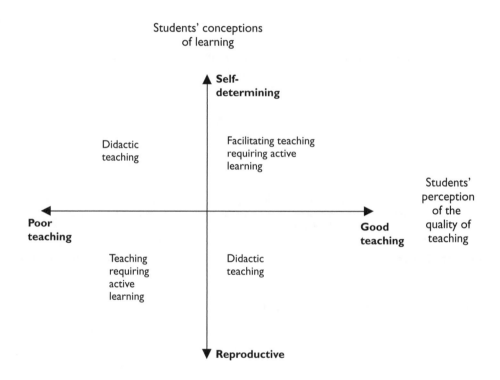

Figure 7.3 A 2×2 quadrant classification system

Overlapping categories

Most category systems are not completely separate or discrete. Complex phenomena rarely sort perfectly into a small number of totally separate categories. There may be cases that have characteristics of two or even more categories. If there seem to be a lot of in-between cases, it suggests that categories are better shown as overlapping or having indistinct boundaries.

A study of conceptions of art teaching suggested that an important dimension was whether teachers believed that they were educating students *in* art or *through* art. An appreciable number showed evidence of both beliefs. This belief was therefore judged to be a category system with a substantial overlap. Figure 7.4 represents the beliefs about education in or through art by a Venn diagram with two overlapping spheres. The spheres are shown against a continuum of conceptions of art teaching to show the relationship between the conception and the belief (Lam & Kember, 2006).

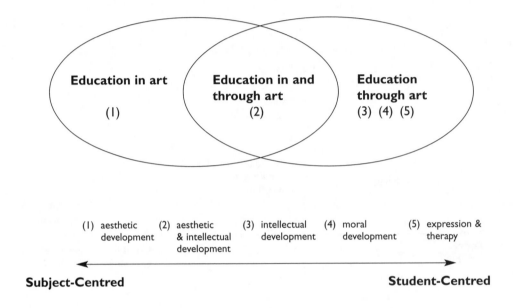

Figure 7.4 Venn diagram showing overlapping classifications

Continuum

Some variables show a range of values or have indistinct boundaries between cases. These variables can be visualised as continua or spectra. It is usual to define the ends of a continuum. Individual subjects or cases can then be allocated to any point along the continua.

Figure 7.5 shows a portrayal of approaches to teaching taken from Kember and Kwan (2000). This is partitioned into six aspects, which are subdivided into motivation and strategy categories. Each aspect was represented by a continuum as the interviews suggested a range of approaches existed. A lecturer's teaching approach was then characterised by plotting a point on each of the six continua. An overall categorisation could then be made as most lecturers had a preponderance of points at either the content-centred or learning-centred ends of the continua.

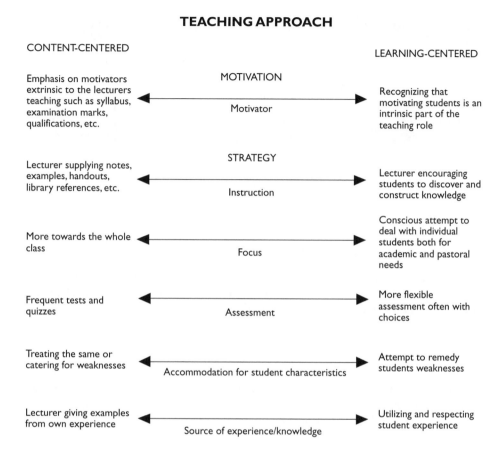

Figure 7.5 A continuum classification for approaches to teaching

More complex hybrid structures

Hybrid category schemes that are some combination of the above structures are also possible. For those with fertile minds there are probably a whole range of other possibilities too.

Figure 7.6 is one example of a hybrid structure for classifying conceptions of teaching (Kember, 1997). There is a hierarchical aspect to it, with subcategories under the teacher-centred/content-oriented and student-centred/learning-oriented main categories. Boundaries between subcategories are shown shaded to imply an indistinct boundary. A transitional student–teacher interaction subcategory is included. It is linked to the other subcategories by arrows to imply a developmental continuum.

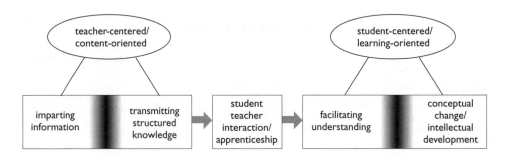

Figure 7.6 A categorisation model of conceptions of teaching

Defining categories

Whatever the classification scheme decided upon, categories within the scheme need to be defined so that others can understand how one category is distinguished from another and could place a case in an appropriate category.

Label

A label is necessary even for purposes of referring to the category. A good label will also make a head start in communicating and defining the nature of the category. For example, 'deep' and 'surface' are good labels for approaches to study. They are short and easy to use. They obviously do not fully define the categories but do seem to communicate the basic idea to most readers.

Quotations

Use of typical quotations is almost certainly the most common way of both defining and illustrating categories.

Metaphors

A less common (but potentially very effective) way of defining categories is to use a metaphor. A delightful metaphor for the nurturing conception of teaching was made by Northedge (1976, p. 68):

> ...we view the ground as already covered with vegetation (concept systems), some of which is clearly worth retaining and cultivating. ... In the garden plants will tend to grow quite readily regardless of intervention from the gardener, and it is his aim to encourage certain plants at the expense of others; finding ways of acting as a catalyst in bringing out the best he can from the available ground. The gardener does not work towards a precisely defined end, since the garden is continually changing as different plants come to their prime. He has broad plans as to

how he wants the garden to develop (probably rather flexible ones, which change as possibilities within the garden reveal themselves), but he does not attempt to specify the exact dimensions that each plant (or concept structure) is to achieve.

Elements

Variables can often be characterised by a number of dimensions or elements. The categories can then be defined in terms of the main dimensions. This approach to defining variables is strongly encouraged.

- It defines categories unambiguously.
- Clear distinction between cases, and which category they belong to, is facilitated.
- Understanding of the phenomenon is advanced as the defining characteristics of the variable, and categories of it, are clearly delineated.

Table 7.1 shows how conceptions of teaching can be defined in terms of the dimensions.

Table 7.1 Dimensions used to define categories of conceptions of teaching

	Imparting information	*Transmitting structured knowledge*	*Teacher– student interaction*	*Facilitating understanding*	*Conceptual change*
Teacher	Presenter	Presenter	Presenter and tutor	Facilitator	Change agent/ developer
Teaching	Transfer of information	Transfer of well-structured information	Interactive process	Process of helping students to learn	Development of person and conceptions
Student	Passive recipient	Recipient	Participant	Lecturer responsible for students' learning	Lecturer responsible for student development
Content	Defined by curriculum	Lecturer needs to order and structure material	Defined by teacher	Constructed by students within teacher's framework	Constructed by students but conceptions can be changed
Knowledge	Possessed by lecturer	Possessed by lecturer	Discovered by students but within lecturer's framework	Constructed by students	Socially constructed

Source: Kember (1997)

Deciding on the number of categories

There have often been disagreements in the literature about the number of categories that best represent a variable or phenomenon. Approaches to learning provide a good example. The original categorisation scheme was that of dichotomous deep and surface approaches (Marton & Säljö, 1976). Subsequent research into the Chinese learner discovered intermediate approaches. Kember (1996, 2000a) suggested that a continuum between deep and surface poles might be a better way of classifying approaches.

The review of conceptions of teaching also shows that different researchers found differing numbers of conceptions of teaching in their data. Where conceptions appear to be 'missing' it could simply be the case that a particular conception was not present within a sample. Most qualitative studies have quite small samples so this is possible.

A more fundamental issue is that there are no clear-cut rules or processes for making decisions about the number of categories. In social science research, cases will virtually never be absolutely identical, so the researcher must make judgements as to whether cases are sufficiently similar that they fit within one category. Alternatively, are they subcategories or quite different categories?

In making these judgements, it is good practice to use one, or preferably more, of the above ways to define categories so that the distinctions are clear and explicit. In the studies of conceptions of teaching, those that relied solely upon quotations to define categories ended up with the most categories and I (DK) feel that the distinction between some categories was questionable.

I have observed a similar problem with those who use a tree hierarchy, such as those in NVivo. There is a tendency to keep splitting categories into more and more subcategories or sub-subcategories. Whether these are useful divisions which represent real distinctions can become questionable, though.

Statistical analysts make use of the rule of parsimony, which says that simple is better than complex, or a smaller number of categories is better than a larger number *if* the data are adequately represented. This is a big if. A simple structure or smaller number of categories is not better if it does not adequately represent the phenomenon. As usual, informed judgement is required. The word 'informed' is important. The judgement is most likely to be informed if it is based on clear definitions of the categories.

Relationship between categories

Part of the process of definition of categories is to describe how they relate to each other. If they are categories of a single variable or phenomenon, there is normally likely to be some ordering or relationship between categories. As an example we can return to the various ways to classify age. Whichever classification scheme is chosen, it makes sense to order the categories from young to old.

The most commonly used relationship between categories is hierarchical. Conceptions of teaching, for example, are commonly seen as a hierarchy from teacher-centred conceptions to superior student-centred ones. More sophisticated ways of describing the relationship between categories make use of the dimensions inherent to the variable or phenomenon. An example for conceptions of teaching was given in Table 7.1.

Coding

Once a classification scheme has been established it is often necessary to go through at least part of the data allocating points or cases to categories within a coding scheme. This process is known as coding. Coding consists of going through a transcript paragraph-by-paragraph or case-by-case to note important points and allocate statements to categories within a classification system.

Coding often develops as the analysis proceeds. Initial coding usually takes the form of highlighting what seem to be key statements. As theorising progresses more formal classification systems can be developed with associated codes. Coding can then become more systematic. It is common for these classification and coding schemes to develop as coding takes place. New categories may be discovered or the classification system re-arranged.

Schemes

A coding scheme is a shorthand way of indicating each category within a classification scheme. It can be the label for the category, a shortened version of it or a formal hierarchical system such as the NVivo one in Figure 7.2.

When coding by hand at the paragraph level, it is common practice to write the code in the margin alongside the point. Additional notes may also be made.

Computer programs like NVivo are useful at the coding stage. Sections can be selected then coded according to pre-defined codes. Once relevant data have been coded, it is then possible to use the logic steps within the programs to examine sections of data relating to particular codes or to look for relationships between data coded under two or more categories. A common strategy is to code all instances of particular categories and then to sort the data according to the codes. It is then possible to examine together all the data referring to a particular category. This then permits more detailed analysis of that particular category.

Levels

Coding can be at a number of levels, the most common of which are the individual case level and/or the point or paragraph level within transcripts. Some projects need to systematically code all cases or even all paragraphs to examine the distribution of cases to categories within a classification system. Other projects look more for principal themes, so code only as much as is necessary to find these.

Taking the study of conceptions of teaching as an example to establish and provide illustrations of the meanings of the conceptions and approaches, it was first necessary to go through the transcripts point by point or paragraph by paragraph to code statements in terms of the categories. This was an iterative process. Initial inspection suggested some preliminary categorisation schemes. Several stages of re-examination and refinement were necessary before the final scheme was developed.

In this case it was not necessary to code every point or paragraph. Many were not relevant to the topic. Even for relevant parts of the interview, the coding did not have to be fully comprehensive. The aim was to establish what the categories were rather than to report fully everything said by each lecturer. In other types of research it may be necessary to fully code at the paragraph or point level. Studies which analyse language or communication patterns may well have to do this.

In a second level of coding, a case corresponded to a lecturer who had been interviewed. Referring to Table 7.2, as each lecturer had been allocated to a category for both conceptions of teaching and approaches to teaching, it was then possible to cross-tabulate conceptions and approaches.

Determining relationships

Qualitative research is often restricted to building descriptions or identifying categories. Establishing relationships is sometimes seen as the preserve of quantitative research, by looking for correlations between variables or increasingly commonly by looking directly at cause and effect models with techniques like structural equation modelling.

Qualitative research, though, is perfectly capable of establishing relationships. Surely important research aims are looking for explanations for observations or phenomena which means that they need to investigate causes, reasons, links, relationships between variables and/or categories within variables. Several methods for doing this are given.

Direct observation

The most obvious way of establishing is a cause–effect relationship is through observation. Classroom observation has been a common research method for school research, but has not been so popular in higher education.

Quotations mentioning relationships

Interviewees can mention relationships in interviews. Typical statements might be 'I did this because ...' or 'The course is X, so ...'. Sometimes these statements need to be treated cautiously. People tend to attribute their successes to their own actions but attribute their failures to others or factors outside their own control. In the latter case, particularly, the reasons given may not be the real ones.

For example, students who are awarded good grades in a course are likely to explain their success as resulting from hard work, being clever, having a good understanding of the material or other personal factors. However, those who fail are more likely to blame the course design, the tutor, not having enough time or anything other than themselves. This means that the researcher needs to look carefully at statements like these to see whether they should be taken at face value.

Proximity in transcript

In some projects it can be found that two variables often appear close together within transcripts, without prompting by the interviewer. This can mean that the interviewees see the two variables as in some way related. Again, the researcher needs to make an intelligent judgement about whether there is any relationship. The nature of any relationship may be less apparent with this type of evidence. A similar case for a relationship can be made if a variable or category commonly occurs in the same case or interview.

Comparing classifications for 2 variables

A powerful way of establishing a relationship is by comparing codings for two variables. The best way to explain this technique is with examples. Table 7.2, which is taken from Kember and Kwan (2000), compares codings for conceptions of teaching with those for teaching approaches. With two exceptions, those with transmission conceptions are coded as having a content-centred approach, while those with a learning facilitation conception show evidence of learning-centred approaches. It seems reasonable to conclude that a lecturer's conception of teaching strongly influences the way in which they approach teaching.

When cross-correlation is used to examine relationships in qualitative research, the most common approach seems to have relied on inviting the reader to inspect the tabulation, as in Table 7.2. In the example in Table 7.2 it is quite obvious that there is a clear relationship. Most cases in the literature appear like this. When the relationship is this clear, it seems unnecessary to calculate a correlation, particularly when the data comes from qualitative work.

Table 7.2 Establishing a relationship between conceptions of good teaching and approaches to teaching

Conceptions of good teaching	Faculty code	Teaching approaches	
		Content-centred	Learning-centred
Transmission of knowledge			
T1	ENG-1	X	
	ENG-2	X	
	ENG-3	X	
	ENG-4	X	
T2	SS-3	X	
	SS-5		X
	ENG-7	X	
	PM-1	X	
	PM-2	X	
Learning facilitation			
F3	SS-1	X	
	ENG-5		X
	ENG-6		X
	PM-4		X
F4	SS-2		X
	SS-4		X
	SS-6		X
	PM-3		X

Verification

It is always good practice to check and verify conclusions from research. In the case of qualitative research it is particularly worthwhile since there are still people who are suspicious of any qualitative research. Careful verification of results can make the conclusions from the research more believable.

Various approaches to verifying conclusions are described below. They apply at various stages of the process of analysis and to different outcome elements.

Multiple coders

A common strategy applies to coding of categories by more than one researcher. This is a way of convincing readers that the coding was not subjective.

Two or more researchers independently code the data following an agreed coding procedure. The coding outcomes are then compared to see the level of agreement. Quantitative estimates of inter-rater reliability (IRR; see LeBreton & Senter, 2008, for a review) may be calculated at this stage. A common method of reporting this is the percentage of cases in which the coding was the same. Cohen's kappa is another commonly reported metric of agreement, where values of 0.61–0.80 and 0.80–1.00 are commonly held to represent good and very good levels of IRR, respectively (Altman, 1991). Another more general form of IRR is Krippendorf's alpha (Morley, 2009). There may be a second round of comparison in which cases with differing codings are discussed to see whether the researchers can reach agreement.

Verification of transcripts by interviewees

When interviews are conducted it is often necessary to produce a transcript of the interview. In Hong Kong there can be the extra dimension of translating and transcribing an interview if it is conducted in Cantonese and the researchers need to analyse and report the data in English.

If transcripts are produced it is good practice to ask interviewees to check through them. This not only provides a check for errors but also gives interviewees an opportunity to clarify any statements which are not clear or add anything which did not occur to them at the time of the interview.

Excluded cases

After establishing a classification system and doing any necessary coding, it is good practice to check to see whether any significant cases or variables have not been included. It is possible that a category may have been missed.

It is not necessary to account for every case and comment – you have to make a judgement about what is significant. There are usually comments which are not relevant to the topic under investigation or individuals with views which are quite different to everyone else in the sample. These can be excluded quite legitimately.

Relating conclusions to other applications

Once you reach a conclusion, a good check is to see whether it can explain other observations.

Applying same constructs to other situations

A rigorous approach to verifying conclusions is to do a replication study. This means repeating the study in another quite different situation with a different sample to see whether the same conclusions result. Obviously this requires extra time and resources, so is not common.

Drawing conclusions

Analysis is about reducing a body of data to manageable proportions and presenting logical conclusions in ways in which they can be readily understood. An important step is trying to develop answers to the question about what the data has to say. This implies drawing together overall conclusions and working out the lessons that can be drawn from the data.

Writing up a project is an integral and important part of the process of analysis and conclusion drawing. The writing up will include the reporting of all the parts of the analysis covered so far. It often takes the process further. The process of writing up requires thinking through what has been learned and producing a logical ordered conclusion. Ways of conceptualising results can occur during the writing process.

Reporting and display of qualitative data

The outcome of qualitative data analysis is almost always some form of report. The aim of the report is to communicate to the reader or audience what the data has to say. For the message to be read and understood, it needs to be succinct.

The most common reporting form is the written word. Within written reports, though, it is often good practice to make use of some of the ways of describing and displaying data which have been introduced in this chapter. A summary of some of the more useful forms is given below.

The displaying step consists of finding succinct and understandable ways to communicate what the data has to say. The main section on displaying has a selection of examples of common forms of display.

Typical quotations

Typical quotations are the most common way of reporting conclusions. It is not necessary to give an example of the use of quotations as most qualitative papers use quotations. Those using qualitative research methods will surely be familiar with the use of quotations.

Case study

A case study is a detailed description of one case or interviewee. The purpose is to give the reader a vivid insight into the topic from the perspective of one case from the sample. The aim is to provide illustration and illumination. Giving a case study is particularly valuable if you are dealing with multiple variables or influences. A case can show how the variables interact and how multiple influences come into play. Such detail can often be lost if variables are dealt with separately.

Thick description

Thick description is a term used by a school of qualitative researchers to denote detailed and explicit descriptions of observed phenomena and situations. This type of writing commonly results from field studies or classroom observations.

Metaphors

An example of a metaphor for a conception of teaching by Northedge (1976) was given in an earlier section of the chapter.

Quadrants

Quadrants are useful for looking at the relationship between two variables, each of which has two subcategories. Figure 7.3 uses a quadrant to model the relationship between student's conception of learning and their perception of their instructors' conception of teaching (Kember, 2007).

Tables

Tables are commonly used for a variety of purposes. Table 7.1 presents the dimensions used to define the five conceptions of teaching (Kember, 1997). Table 7.2 is an example of using a table to look at the relationship between two variables (Kember & Kwan, 2000).

Discrete categories

A very common outcome of qualitative research is describing a phenomenon in terms of a small number of discrete categories. Deep and surface approaches to learning provides an example of a two category division. Papers normally just list these categories and illustrate each category with a quotation or two.

Tree diagrams

Other studies have split categories into subcategories. These are commonly presented in the form of a tree diagram, of which Figure 7.2 is a good example.

Spectrum

Phenomena cannot always be well described in terms of separate categories. A spectrum or continuum sometimes provides a better representation. Figure 7.5 shows a way of representing aspects of approaches to teaching as a set of continua (Kember & Kwan, 2000).

Venn diagrams

Venn diagrams have frequently been used to show overlaps between concepts or categories. Figure 7.4 shows a diagram from a study of conceptions of art teaching, showing how the conception is manifest as teaching-in-art or teaching-through-art.

More complex diagrams

For those with imagination, there must be an almost infinite number of ways of portraying information. Figure 7.4 is an example of a diagram that does not fit into any of the above categories, but has elements of several (Kember, 1997).

Relationship or causal model

The end result of reviewing the research into conceptions of teaching (Kember, 1997) was a model which shows the causal relationship between conceptions of teaching and other aspects of teaching and learning. This is shown in Figure 7.7.

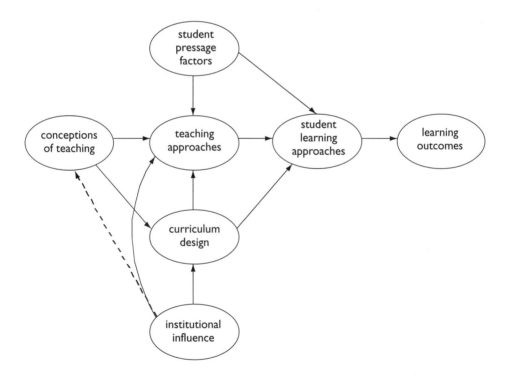

Figure 7.7 A causal model

Conclusion

Qualitative data analysis is often not described clearly. It can also be portrayed as an almost mystical art form that is the preserve of an initiated elite. Neither approach is useful to the uninitiated.

The approach taken here is an attempt to demistify. It takes the main elements of qualitative analysis and gives lots of examples of how they can be performed and what the outcomes will look like. There is a constant caution given, which is well worth reiterating here. In portraying qualitative analysis as a series of elements it can start to look like a step-by-step process. There are steps, but they are not linear. There is usually a lot of to-ing and fro-ing.

Chapter 8

Observation

Introduction

Classroom observation has been a common form of research at the school level. In higher education, though, it has been a lot less common. There are two probable reasons for this. The first is that most academics treat their classroom or lecture theatre as a sanctum. Observers or researchers are not welcome.

The other reason is what there is to observe in the classroom. School classrooms, particularly at primary school level, usually have an interesting pattern of interaction between teacher and pupils, and between the children themselves. There are also a wide variety of activities and actions to observe. The classrooms themselves can even be of interest, the walls replete with the students' work and other artefacts. By contrast, the university classroom or lecture theatre is usually a rather drab and lifeless affair. It is not easy to draw interesting and profound conclusions from a series of observations that almost all of the class time was taken up by a monologue from the lecturer.

Transforming college teaching so that classroom observation becomes a worthwhile and productive activity is clearly a task beyond the ambit of a book like this. A far more modest aim is attempted instead. Two reflective checklists for small and large classes are introduced. These enable teachers to reflect upon their own teaching. They can also be used by a mentor, observing the class, to provide feedback.

The main aim, when using these checklists, has normally been helping teachers to improve their own teaching through cycles of reflection and iterative improvement. Both protocols, though, provide a method for systematic observation of teaching, which could contribute to an evidence base.

Class observation

A stereotypical portrait of a poor university teacher is of one who keeps his (yes, the stereotype is male) head down to read a lecture from his notes. Slipping into this 'knowledge transmission' mentality results in loss of contact with the class. In the extreme, students effectively cease to exist in the vision of the lecturer, and indeed may well have voted with their feet.

Better teachers maintain eye contact with their students. This is a psychological principle of good communication. More important for the subject matter of this book, looking up enables the teacher to observe the class. This is an essential prerequisite to making use of either of the following checklists.

Reflection

Chapter 1 suggested that award-winning teachers are prone to reflect upon their teaching as part of the process of iterative improvement. This chapter gives two checklists, for large and small classes, to help make this process more systematic and insightful.

Both checklists contain a small number of criteria for a good large or small class. Each criterion has a brief description of good quality with respect to the criterion. Alongside each is a space for a comment.

Large class checklist

The large class checklist is designed for use with presentations or lectures, the predominant form of teaching in higher education. The first set of criteria in the checklist, plus the final one, examine the structure of the talk. The other three consider the presentation.

Table 8.1 Large class reflection checklist for lectures

Criteria	Rating	Comment
Introduction – clear purpose statement or roadmap		
Body – coherent logical structure		
Fundamental concepts – made explicit		
Fundamental concepts – avoided excess detail		
Relevance – gave examples to show relevance of theory		
Visual aids – helped understanding of concepts		
Delivery – spoke clearly and audibly		
Feedback – maintained eye contact for monitoring		
Conclusion – gave summary of key concepts		
Overall reflection		

Note: This checklist can be used to reflect on lectures and large classes. It is suitable for individual reflection after a class or for use with a colleague as an observer. It can also be used in conjunction with an audio- or video-recording. Scoring:

1 = needs improvement   2 = good   3 = excellent

Seminar/tutorial checklist

The other checklist is appropriate for smaller classes, such as tutorials or seminars. It assumes there will be interactions between teacher and students. The criteria also refer to activities.

Table 8.2 Seminar/tutorial checklist for small classes

Criteria	Rating	Comment
Planning – planned content and activities		
Time management – planning and execution		
Organisation – prepared teaching materials		
Introduction – purpose established at start		
Activities – clear direction and management		
Questioning – managed discussion with questions		
Questioning – used range of prompts and probes		
Flexibility – adapted plans in response to feedback		
Debriefing – summarised key concepts		

Note: This checklist can be used to reflect on seminars and tutorials. It is suitable for individual reflection after a class or for use with a colleague as an observer. It can also be used in conjunction with an audio- or video-recording. Scoring:

1 = needs improvement   2 = good   3 = excellent

Mentoring

The two checklists can be used for self-observation and self-reflection by the teacher. They can also be used by a mentor invited into the class to observe the teaching. It is normal to hold a debriefing session after the observation in which the mentor and teacher discuss the comments or recommendations.

If conducted as a collegial exercise, mentoring can be a valuable approach to staff development or teaching quality enhancement. It can be particularly helpful for new teachers to obtain advice from a more experienced mentor.

Chapter 9

Use of assessment for evaluation

Limitations

Intuitively, assessment results should be a powerful form of evaluation. Assessment fulfils the function of certifying students' achievements in a course of study. The level of performance should be a measure of the quality of learning, which should be related to the effectiveness of the teaching.

However, all too often assessment results provide little in the way of feedback to teachers. They are not often cited as evidence in articles based on the scholarship of teaching and learning. Presumably those engaged in such scholarship did not think that assessment outcomes provided diagnostic evidence relating to their study, or were unable to persuade reviewers that it was the case.

The reasons that assessment commonly fails to provide useful evaluation data are the two fundamentals of measurement, namely validity and reliability. Assessment results are only useful if the assessment gives a valid measure of the intended outcomes specified for the course or project. Also, there needs to a convincing case that the way the assignment is set and marked gives results that can reliably be compared from one case to another. If reliability in measurement cannot be established, comparison cannot be made between results from one year to the next, from one course to another, or from one form of teaching to another.

Alignment of assessment

Assessment will only satisfy validity requirements if there is alignment between the nature of the assessment and the intended outcomes of a course. This is an issue raised in textbooks on teaching in higher education. Biggs and Tang (2007) introduce the concept of constructive alignment. Kember with McNaught (2007) deals specifically with the need for valid or authentic assessment. Examples from award-winning teachers are given to show how this can be achieved through consistency with the curriculum or professional needs, or through the application of theory to personal contexts.

The textbooks need to include calls for the alignment of assessment with intended outcomes because of the evidence that there is often a lack of alignment. The most common form of misalignment is probably when the assignments require reproduction, whereas the outcomes specified are higher-order intellectual ones.

Evidence of another common form of a lack of alignment is given below in the section on *concept inventories*. Students have managed to pass university courses, but are subsequently found to have fundamental misunderstandings of key concepts in the discipline. The majority of the examples cited have been in science. Students are commonly asked examination questions about a concept which can be answered by substituting numbers into a formula and algebraically manipulating it. The process, though, requires no understanding of the concept itself.

There is therefore a strong case for assessment to be consistent with desired learning outcomes from the perspective of ensuring quality in student learning. Facilitating the use of assessment results in evaluation provides an additional reason.

Outcomes-based/criterion-based assessment

To be of use for evaluation purposes, assessment needs to give a reliable measure, as well as being of a valid form. In practical terms, for the scholarship of teaching, reliability in assessment implies that assessment results can legitimately be compared between courses or from one year to the next. This means that the assignments set have to be of a comparable standard. More significantly, the marking should be based on the same standards.

The most commonly used approach to grading in higher education has been norm-based assessment. In this approach grades are supposedly distributed according to a normal distribution, though it is often a distorted curve, with a bias towards higher grades and few failures. Norm-based marking does not give useable evaluation results as, however well or badly students perform, the same percentage are awarded a particular grade.

The alternative is criterion-, standards-, or outcomes-based assessment. Under this model, criteria or a rubric are defined for a pass or for the award of each grade. Criterion-based assessment has commonly been used to test performance of procedures or physical skills. A well-known example is the driving test. Candidates have to perform a set of designated procedures, such as a three-point turn and parallel parking, accurately and safely. Those who perform all the procedures to the required standard pass their driving test. It is important to have criterion-based testing, as only those who are competent to drive safely should be passed.

Higher education has found it more difficult to introduce standards-based assessment. The difficulty of setting reliable standards for the complex and diverse cognitive assignments set in higher education deters many from moving towards standards-based assessment. However, the drive towards an outcomes-based approach has seen recent attempts to deploy outcomes-based assessment more widely.

We do not intend to write a treatise on standards-based assessment – that would be a book in itself. What we will do, though, is give three examples of protocols which have been used to grade assignments in a reliable and reproducible manner.

1   A checklist for grading student presentations.
2   SOLO taxonomy.
3   Four-category protocol for assessing level of reflection.

Performance in presentations

Chapter 8 introduced a reflective checklist as a reflective tool for those teaching in large classes. The protocol was originally developed to assess student presentations, and works well for this purpose.

The protocol provides a good introduction to the nature of a rubric for standards-based assessment. It specifies nine criteria for a good presentation, including the structure of the talk, the nature of the content and the quality of the delivery. It is better to keep the number of criteria fairly small, otherwise the process becomes unmanageable. For each criterion there is a brief definition of what constitutes good performance. Judgement is still needed, but there is guidance in making that judgement, which leads to a high degree of consistency and comparability. Judgement is given using a three-category scale, plus space for feedback on each criterion. Normally, it was the constructive feedback that was most helpful.

The checklist was commonly used for peer assessment. Students gave presentations to their classmates and each member of the class was asked to complete a checklist for each presentation. The degree of consistency between members of the class in assessing the quality of presentations was high. The peer assessment exercise was a valuable learning experience as it taught the students what constituted a good presentation.

Table 9.1 Presentation checklist

Criteria	Rating	Comment
Introduction – clear purpose statement or roadmap		
Body – coherent logical structure		
Fundamental concepts – made explicit		
Fundamental concepts – avoided excess detail		
Relevance – gave examples to show relevance of theory		
Visual aids – helped understanding of concepts		
Delivery – spoke clearly and audibly		
Feedback – maintained eye contact for monitoring		
Conclusion – gave summary of key concepts		
Overall reflection		

Note: The checklist above can be used to provide feedback and give ratings for student presentations. Scoring:

1 = needs improvement   2 = good   3 = excellent

The format of the presentation checklist is suitable for adapting to assess other forms of assignment, particularly performance- or skill-based ones. The essential steps are selecting a small number of criteria for identifying high quality work and defining each of the criteria.

SOLO taxonomy

The structure of observed learning outcome (SOLO) taxonomy is a classification scheme that provides criteria to guide grading of extended pieces of writing, such as essays (Biggs & Collis, 1982). The category scheme distinguishes the structural quality of written work by defining five categories for the degree of logical structure in an essay.

By concentrating on the structure of the argument, the taxonomy can be applied to any discipline. This is clearly a great advantage as any essay can be categorised according to the taxonomy. It can also be seen as a limitation, though, as the quality of the content is also important in written work.

Use of SOLO for grading

The SOLO taxonomy is most commonly used as a guide to marking essays. It has five qualitative categories distinguishing the structure of the piece of writing. In the following descriptions of the categories we will use labels introduced in Kember with McNaught (2007), rather than the original ones given by Biggs and Collis (1982), which are given in parentheses. In the table below the category labels are given in the first column, with our version on top and the original beneath it.

An answer in the *missing the point* (pre-structural category) has failed to address the issue at all. This type of answer arises in examinations when students know nothing about the question. They also occur when students misinterpret an essay topic.

Single point (unistructural) answers deal with just one issue of a complex problem, though the single point may be presented in several ways. This type of answer may arise because students' schooling has conditioned them to expect problems with right or wrong answers. They therefore expect all questions to have single answers.

The structure of a *multiple unrelated points* (multistructural) essay is like a bulleted list. The material may be appropriate in answering the question, but the essay has little structuring. The points are not properly linked together. There is little in the way of introduction or conclusion to tie the ideas together. Essays like this can arise all too often when students do an internet search and add each point to the list as it is found. The result is reproduction without interpretation.

A *logically related answer* (relational) could have the same points as a multiple unrelated one, but has a coherent structure. This time each point is related to the others so that there is a logical flow to the essay. There are introductions and conclusions that tie the essay together and provide the coherence of interpretation and argument.

An *unanticipated extension* (extended abstract) would have the same logical coherent structure as a logically related answer. Something in the answer, though, goes beyond what the teacher could reasonably have expected. The student could have found some recent research or related theory to local conditions.

As with most qualitative categorisation schemes, the categories should be treated as a guide rather than as fixed or mutually exclusive. Judgements have to be made as to which category an essay is closest to. Intermediate cases are common. Particularly common are essays between multiple unrelated and logically related. These essays will have some degree of linking between points and an attempt at an introduction or conclusion, but not the good structure of a fully logically related answer. Answers between these points are so common that an intermediate category has been added to the following table. Intermediate positions between other categories also occur.

When the SOLO taxonomy is used as a framework for marking essays it should be treated flexibly. Essays with an intermediate structure deserve an intermediate grade. Subject knowledge also needs to be taken into account as well as structure. Even if an essay has a perfect structure, it does not deserve the grade associated with a logically related answer if it contains material that is incorrect, out of date or irrelevant.

The SOLO category can then be used as a guide to marking assignments and awarding grades. Using the traditional grading scale, the categories are normally equated as follows. The grades can be adjusted for intermediate categories in the normal way by using + and −.

A = unanticipated extension
B = logically related answer
C = multiple unrelated points
D = single point
F = missing the point

Allocating grades based on SOLO means that there are criteria for grading. Judgements still have to be made, but there is a basis for making the judgement, which makes for reasonably reliable grading. Reliability can be improved if markers perform exercises in which they discuss the category to be allocated to a range of scripts, to enhance consistency between markers.

The final column of the following table describes the structure of an essay for each SOLO level. Although the SOLO taxonomy is most commonly associated with essays, it can also be used for marking other types of assignment. Column four in the table shows how the categories might be applied to simple problems, complex problems, practical reports and to the outcomes of projects.

The SOLO taxonomy has been used quite widely in research studies. It is particularly suitable for those conducting scholarship on courses they teach themselves as it provides a method for utilising student performance in assessment as evidence for the attainment of desired learning outcomes.

A good example, relating to the learning of anatomy, is given in Pandey and Zimitat (2007). Students' approaches to learning were measured with the R-SPQ (see Chapter 3). The quality of learning outcomes was determined by using the SOLO taxonomy to categorise answers to written questions in the final examination. Students' answers were placed into the five SOLO categories by two independent markers. Ratings by the two markers were compared and any discrepancies discussed. Students with higher deep approach scores tended to produce answers in the higher SOLO categories, but anatomy appears to be a subject which requires memorisation in conjunction with understanding.

Table 9.2 The SOLO taxonomy as a guide to setting and marking assessment

SOLO category	Representation	Type of outcome	Solution to problem	Structure of essay
Unanticipated extension		Create Synthesise Hypothesise Validate Predict Debate Theorise	Solution to problem which goes beyond anticipated answer.	Well-structured essay with clear introduction and conclusion. Issues clearly identified; clear framework for organizing discussion; appropriate material selected. Evidence of wide reading from many sources. Clear evidence of sophisticated analysis or innovative thinking.
Extended abstract			Project or practical report dealing with real world ill-defined topic.	
Logically related answer		Apply Outline Distinguish Analyse Classify Contrast Summarise Categorise	Elegant solution to complex problem requiring identification of variables to be evaluated or hypotheses to be tested.	Essay well structured, with a clear introduction and conclusion. Framework exists which is well developed. Appropriate material. Content has logical flow, with ideas clearly expressed. Clearly identifiable structure to the argument with discussion of differing views.
Relational			Well-structured project or practical report on open task.	
Intermediate			Solution to multiple part problem with most parts correctly solved but some errors. Reasonably well structured project or practical report on open task.	Essay fairly well structured. Some issues identified. Attempt at a limited framework. Most of the material selected is appropriate. Introduction and conclusion exists. Logical presentation attempted and successful in a limited way. Some structure to the argument but only limited number of differing views and no new ideas.
Multiple unrelated points		Explain Define List Solve Describe Interpret	Correct solution to multiple part problem requiring substitution of data from one part to the next.	Essay poorly structured. A range of material has been selected and most of the material selected is appropriate. Weak introduction and conclusion. Little attempt to provide a clear logical structure. Focus on a large number of facts with little attempt at conceptual explanations. Very little linking of material between sections in the essay or report.
Multistructural			Poorly structured project report or practical report on open task.	

Table 9.2 (continued)

SOLO category	Representation	Type of outcome	Solution to problem	Structure of essay
Single point	▬	State	Correct answer to simple algorithmic problem requiring substitution of data into formula.	Poor essay structure. One issue identified and this becomes the sole focus; no framework for organizing discussion. Dogmatic presentation of a single solution to the set task. This idea may be restated in different ways. Little support from the literature.
Unistructural		Recognise Recall		
		Quote Note Name	Correct solution of one part of more complex problem.	
Misses the point			Completely incorrect solution.	Inappropriate or few issues identified. No framework for discussion and little relevant material selected. Poor structure to the essay. Irrelevant detail and some misinterpretation of the question. Little logical relationship to the topic and poor use of examples.
Pre-structural				

Protocol for assessing level of reflection

Where courses have as an aim the promotion of reflective practice, it will enhance the achievement of the goal if the level of reflective thinking is assessed. To do this in a satisfactory way requires a reliable protocol for assessing the level of reflection in written work. We present here a protocol that can be used to guide the allocation of work to four categories, namely: habitual action/non-reflection; understanding; reflection; and critical reflection. Intermediate categories can also be used.

Below are brief descriptors of each category to guide the process. More detailed descriptions of each category were provided in Kember, Leung Jones, Loke, McKay, Sinclair, Tse, Webb, Wong, F.K.Y., Wong, M.W.L., and Yeung (2000). As usual with qualitative protocols, intermediate categories are permitted.

The protocol was tested by four assessors independently using it to grade a set of written work, and very good agreement was obtained. Note that the four reflection categories correspond with the four scales in the reflection questionnaire, given in Chapter 3.

Non-reflection

- The answer shows no evidence of the student attempting to reach an understanding of the concept or theory that underpins the topic.
- Material has been placed into an essay without the student thinking seriously about it, trying to interpret the material, or forming a view.
- Largely reproduction, with or without adaptation, of the work of others.

Understanding

- Evidence of understanding of a concept or topic.
- Material is confined to theory.
- Reliance upon what was in the textbook or the lecture notes.
- Theory is not related to personal experiences, real-life applications or to practical situations.

Reflection

- Theory is applied to practical situations.
- Situations encountered in practice will be considered and successfully discussed in relationship to what has been taught. There will be personal insights that go beyond book theory.

Critical reflection

- Evidence of a change in perspective over a fundamental belief of the understanding of a key concept or phenomenon.
- Critical reflection is unlikely to occur frequently.

Concept inventories

Concept inventories are a form of assessment task that have been used in higher education to both assess student learning and to evaluate curricula. Concept inventories assess students' understandings of foundational concepts in a particular discipline.

Often, the conceptions of a topic that students bring to university-level study are inaccurate and, moreover, surprisingly resistant to change over the course of extended periods of study. Disturbingly, students may also often perform well on standard examinations involving calculations, but will not understand key ideas at the conceptual level. For example, Philip Sadler, a Harvard astrophysicist, interviewed recent science graduates from Ivy League universities about their understanding of core scientific ideas, such as the model of the solar system underpinning seasonal change on Earth. He found many students had failed to grasp key ideas that would reflect 'scientific literacy', despite having successfully passed multiple exams during their degrees (Private Universe Project in Science, 1995). Such a disconnect between assessment performance and underlying understanding strongly suggests a lack of alignment between the instructor's learning objectives and the standard assessment tools used in higher education (Wright & Hamilton, 2008).

At around the same time as the Private Universe Project was being conducted, David Hestenes and colleagues at Arizona State University were developing the Mechanics Diagnostic Test (MDT), followed by the Force Concept Inventory (FCI) (Hestenes, Wells, & Swackhamer, 1992). J. Richardson (2005) provides a personal communication in which Hestenes described the catalyst for the MDT's subsequent development:

> One of my graduate students approached me with a set of questions related to Newtonian mechanics and asked me to give these questions to my Physics I students. I looked at the questions and told him, 'These questions are trivial. This is a waste of time.' He finally succeeded in convincing me to give the questions to my students. When I looked at the student responses, I was astonished. Large numbers of my students had failed to answer the questions correctly.

These examples of the often large distance between the expectations of educators who are experts in a field and the actual conceptual functioning of relative novices reflect the need for assessment tasks that span the full range of understanding of key ideas in the field.

Using concept inventories for curriculum evaluation

While concept inventories may be useful assessments of learning in their own right, they have also fostered substantial reflection on and redesign of curricula. The effectiveness of curriculum redesigns might be evaluated in several ways, including changes in students' performances on standard assessment tasks, CTEQ instruments, and/or through approaches to learning inventories (e.g. Gordon & Debus, 2002). The focus of concept inventories on assessing core concepts in a field supports their use for curriculum evaluation, when at least one of the goals of a curriculum is developing fundamental understanding of a field (as is usually the case).

The Force Concept Inventory, described above, is particularly noteworthy in this respect. Using the FCI, a Harvard physicist, Eric Mazur, found his own students were failing to develop advanced conceptions of force, prompting him to reconsider his entire approach to teaching introductory physics (Mazur, 1992, 1997). Rather than traditional lecturing, this approach emphasises student engagement during lectures through the following cycle. The lecturer gives a series of short presentations, each of which is focused on a key point. After each presentation, the lecturer then poses a conceptual problem to gauge student understanding of the key point just taught. Students are given a few minutes to formulate an individual answer, which is then reported back to the lecturer using one of several possible methods (e.g. an audience response system, or numbered cards). Students then debate their answers to this conceptual problem with each other for two to four minutes, with the goal of convincing others of the correctness of their answer; the lecturer moves around the room at this point, listening to answers. The lecturer then polls students again for their answers, and possibly for confidence in their answers, explains the answer to the problem, and then moves on to the next conceptual problem.

Marks are not assigned for students' answers to questions posed in class, but a small class participation mark may be assigned if tracking of individuals is possible through the audience response system. Alignment with other assessment tasks is achieved through the inclusion of questions like those posed in class on mid-term and final exams (Crouch & Mazur, 2001).

Mazur's leadership in the physics education community led to the dissemination of both interactive engagement methods, as well as the use of the MBT and FCI for assessing learning. Hake (1998) compared the results on the MBT and FCI of students across 62 introductory physics courses taught using 'interactive engagement' methods such as those advocated by Mazur, and more traditional lecturing methods. Hake used the average normalised gain, g, as a measure of students' conceptual change over a semester. Here g is the ratio of the actual average gain (percentage correct on post-test minus percentage correct on pre-test) to the maximum possible average gain (100 minus percentage correct on pre-test). Hake found an average gain of 0.23 for 14 traditional courses, but 0.48 for 48 interactive engagement courses.

Hake interpreted these results as providing substantial support for interactive engagement methods in supporting conceptual change. Savinainen and Scott (2002) used the FCI to evaluate a high school physics curriculum building on peer instruction, which added an emphasis on research-based materials and the use of texts to promote understanding (e.g. textbook annotation, summarising, concept mapping). The authors report a pre-post gain of 0.57, which they argued benchmarks well against the average gain of 0.48 for interactive engagement high school and university classes reported by Hake (1998). Outside the discipline of physics, Carlson, Oehrtman, and Engelke (2010) note the use of their Precalculus Concept Assessment inventory to assess pre-post gains across a traditionally taught curriculum ($g = 0.80$) with a curriculum strongly promoting covariational reasoning ability ($g = 3.60$). Taken together, these investigations suggest that concept inventories are sufficiently sensitive measures for evaluating the effects of curriculum change on learning.

Concept inventories as a focus for scholarship of teaching and learning

Concept inventories may play a role in both assessment and evaluation, but, more generally, their development may provide a focus for scholarship of teaching and learning (SoTL). Developing such inventories requires careful, extended consideration of what constitutes deep understanding within a particular discipline, a process that is best established within a community of scholars so that ideas can be tested and debated. Having developed such an inventory, members of such a community will possess an instrument which provides a 'common language' for assessing and benchmarking student learning across multiple sites.

At present, published concept inventories have largely come from STEM (science, technology, engineering and mathematics) disciplines, perhaps reflecting the epistemological maturity of these disciplines. Developing such instruments in the humanities and social sciences may be difficult at present because 'core understandings' in these fields are in many cases still matters for debate.

J. Richardson (2005) describes 5 steps in the development of a concept inventory:

1   *Determine the concepts to be included in the inventory.* As limitations on class time mean most instruments should be administered in under 30 minutes, a relatively small number of core concepts in the field should be identified. The Delphi method has been used by some concept inventory developers (e.g. Streveler, Olds, Miller, & Nelson, 2003) to manage the process of distilling expert opinion about core concepts, as the basis for ensuring the instrument's content validity.

2   *Study and articulate the student learning process regarding those concepts.* This step is required because an important part of novice–expert differences in a field is the nature of the mental constructs experts have in an area. Experts may take these constructs for granted, but the lack of these constructs may explain many learning problems novices have. Concept inventory developers may use a variety of methods to understand student learning processes at this stage, including interviews, focus groups, and responses to open-ended questions.

3   *Construct several multiple-choice questions for each concept.* For each core concept, designers develop several questions focusing on that concept only. (Items addressing multiple core concepts are problematic because they are essentially 'double-barrelled' – if a student answers such a question incorrectly, it will be difficult to understand where exactly the misconception lies.) Incorrect answers to questions from student responses, gathered in the previous stage reflecting misconceptions, are an important source of 'distractor' responses to questions.

4   *Administer the beta (trial) version of the inventory to as many students as possible. Perform statistical analyses on the results to establish reliability, validity, and fairness.* Trials of the draft version of the instrument are best undertaken with large numbers of students; this might be achieved working with colleagues across institutions. Reliability refers to the consistency of measurement of a construct, and could be assessed by the internal consistency of student responses using the Kuder-Richardson 20 analysis for dichotomous (correct/incorrect) responses, or test–retest reliability. Validity is assessed in a number of ways, including through expert review (content validity), factor analysis and/or Rasch analysis (construct validity), and examining correlations of student scores with other forms of assessment (criterion-related validity). Fairness could be assessed by assessing performance of equity groups; J. Richardson (2005) notes that the often small number of enrolments from such groups in a single institution's programme supports the involvement of programmes from multiple institutions at this stage.

5   *Revise the inventory to improve readability, validity, reliability, and fairness.* Several iterations of the process may often be required to refine the instrument until its operating characteristics are suitable for widespread use.

A non-exhaustive list of concept inventories described in peer-reviewed journal articles or scholarly texts, reflecting the breadth of disciplines in which such instruments have been developed, includes the Force Concept Inventory and Mechanics Baseline Test (Mazur, 1997), the Precalculus Concept Assessment (Carlson, Oehrtman, & Engelke, 2010), the Genetics Concept Assessment (Smith, Wood, & Knight, 2008), the Signals and Systems Concept Inventory (Wage, Buck, Wright, & Welch, 2005), the Biology Concept Inventory (Garvin-Doxas & Klymkowsky, 2008), the Molecular Life Sciences Concept Inventory (Howitt, Anderson, Costa, Hamilton, & Wright, 2008) and the Geoscience Concept Inventory (Libarkin & Anderson, 2005).

An extensive list of additional concept inventories is given at www.foundationcoalition.org/home/keycomponents/concept/index.html.

Chapter 10

Using evaluation data for the scholarship of teaching

Strengths and limitations of experimental designs

Those engaged in the scholarship of teaching come from just about any discipline. For most, research into teaching and learning is therefore venturing into a different discipline. This can present problems at times as newcomers to SoTL are uncertain whether research skills and methods learned in another field will be suitable for educational research.

From experience, those who hail from scientific or technological disciplines tend to be the least certain about the transition to a new field. They tend to be uncertain as to whether the experimental designs of the scientific method can be transported into educational research.

They are often surprised to find that a lot of educational research does not use experimental designs. While working on Kember (2003), I examined the three most recent issues of four of the better-quality higher education journals. As somewhat different approaches to research have tended to develop in the US and elsewhere, two journals were from the US and two were European. Of the 65 articles, just one had any sort of experimental design, and that was a comparison between two different instructional treatments.

The same process was followed with four of the highest-rated educational psychology journals, again split evenly between US and European journals. This time the three most recent issues had a mean, across the four journals, of 20.3 per cent of articles with some sort of experimental design. Educational psychology is the educational discipline most closely associated with experimental designs, and yet the large majority of work published in its journals did not use an experimental design.

While experimental designs may not be a common methodology in research in higher education, this should not be seen as precluding their use for SoTL. If experimental methods are typically used within your discipline (e.g. psychology, medicine, agriculture, science, engineering), you may consider experimentation to be the most desirable methodology for conducting SoTL research. Expertise in such methods may support the creative use of experimentation to test meaningful questions about teaching and learning in higher education (e.g. End, Worthman, Mathews, & Wetterau, 2010; Huck, 2007). Experimentation is a methodology which has enjoyed widespread application in the social sciences, including education, with a recent renaissance following the implementation of the *No Child Left Behind* bill in the USA (Schneider, Carnoy, Kilpatrick, Schmidt, & Shavelson, 2007).

Pitfalls in experimental designs

Those who choose to employ experimental designs should, though, be aware that there are a number of potential threats. The following issues may need to be addressed for an experiment to be successful. For a more detailed discussion, see Kember (2003).

- In biological field trials, the control would typically be a plot that received no treatment, while in medical trials the control group receive a placebo. An educational equivalent is problematic, as offering a group of students no instruction is impracticable. It is certainly not obvious what the educational equivalent of a placebo is. Experimental trials normally introduce some form of innovative teaching, so it has become the convention that the other group receive teaching that is more normal, which is usually the type of teaching used prior to the introduction of the innovation. In the case of higher education this usually means a lecture format.
- Cohorts of students are commonly taught within one class, so splitting them into two or more groups requires special arrangements and extra resources. Where it has been feasible to introduce experimental designs in higher education, it has often occurred when intakes are divided into parallel tutorial groups.
- There are ethical issues as one or more groups accorded different treatments may be disadvantaged.
- Even if it is possible to set up trial groups, students can readily undermine the experimental design by contamination across the supposedly discrete groups (Craven et al., 2001). A good example is that of a project for teaching mathematics to engineering students. Students in the experimental group were allowed to make use of software that enabled them to visualise and manipulate mathematical relationships, which the students found to be very helpful to their understanding of the underlying concepts. The message soon spread to the control group, and before too long just about everyone in the class was using the software.
- Innovations to university teaching normally operate over the duration of the course in which they are situated. The majority, therefore, last for a period of one semester, with some extending for the whole academic year. Designing different teaching programmes, arranging for the separation of groups and holding extraneous variables constant becomes more difficult as the length of the trial increases.
- Experiment/control designs reduce the degree of adaptation that can be made to innovations. Comparison of treatments implies making advance plans and keeping conditions constant between the treatment groups. If the innovation is adapted it can often be hard to make a comparable adaptation to the control without invalidating the design. However, with curriculum innovations it is extremely difficult to foresee all eventualities, so successful implementations almost invariably require some modifications to initial plans in the light of experience.
- Experimental designs originated from scientific disciplines which normally deal with a very limited number of variables for any given conceptual area. Educational constructs, like those in other social sciences, are more complex, consisting of an array of contextual factors that can interact with each other and the variables under study. If it is possible to identify and define relevant factors, and it can often be hard to do so, their number causes problems for experimental designs.

- Generalisability can be harder in education than in some other disciplines as treatments are not normally reproducible. The types of claim that tend to be made, for example, are that problem-based learning enhances students' problem-solving skills, or that web-based teaching is effective. The problem with claims like these is that implementations of a type of innovation can differ radically. Just because one case of implementing a particular innovation proved effective does not imply that generalisations can be made to all cases, because the other cases can differ quite markedly in the way they are designed and implemented.

The list of potential pitfalls in experimental designs may have put some readers off using an experimental design. Fortunately, there are alternatives that most find straightforward to adopt.

Survey study

The latter part of this chapter contains two case studies. The second of these is a study of the student experience in an education course offered in first semester. This study could be characterised as a survey study, because data were collected through a set of questionnaires. Conclusions were then drawn by analysing the data to look for relationships between variables in the study.

This has been a common research method, which can deal with a wide variety of topics – essentially, anything for which there is a questionnaire to obtain measures of the relevant variables. Triangulation with qualitative data is not precluded. This could be as a preliminary study to check that relevant variables are included. Alternatively, interview data could be used to amplify and illuminate results.

Action research

Action research is a logical method for SoTL in that it is a research method that aims to bring about change, which is consistent with most SoTL projects. A typical venture in classroom research involves teachers who try out some method of innovative teaching in one of their courses. In the higher education sector this can be interpreted as being almost anything that ventures away from the traditional lecture format.

Action research proceeds through a cyclical process of:

- reflection;
- planning;
- action;
- observation; and
- back to reflection.

Usually there are at least two such cycles, as the aim is iterative improvement. Lessons learned during the first cycle are drawn upon to improve the initiative in the second cycle.

Evaluation data are collected as part of the observation step. In higher education, action research projects commonly use questionnaires and/or interviews. Observations and reflections on observations are also legitimate forms of evaluation data.

There is an extensive literature on action research. For a general background to educational action research see Carr and Kemmis (1986), Elliott (1991), McKernan (1991) or McNiff (1992). For the application of action research to teaching and learning in the higher education sector, the following references are useful: Kember and Gow (1992), Kember and Kelly (1993), Kember and McKay (1996), Kember (2000), Schratz (1992), and Zuber-Skerrit (1992).

Triangulation

One principle that has been widely followed in better SoTL studies, and which is accepted as good practice, is that of triangulation across multiple evaluation methods and sources of evidence. This implies the use of a range of evaluation techniques appropriate to the nature and intended outcomes of the particular project.

It is also desirable to obtain input from as many relevant sources as possible. Students are the most obvious and the most common source, and the input of the teachers is valuable. Other voices will be relevant for particular projects, including demonstrators, clinical practice supervisors, clients in practice situations and eventual employers.

In general, the aim of the evaluation will be that of establishing a claim beyond reasonable doubt rather than absolute proof or causality. If a number of types of evaluation seeking data from multiple sources indicate that there was a measure of improvement in the targeted outcome, it seems reasonable to conclude that the innovation was effective. If the participants themselves attribute any outcomes to the innovation, it would seem that it would be the most likely cause. It is clearly not absolute proof, but the arguments above suggest that the supposed proof of experimental designs can be illusory.

Generalisation by triangulation across projects

As the projects adopting such evaluation styles tend to aim for evidence at the 'beyond reasonable doubt' level, rather than absolute proof, it makes sense to triangulate across projects introducing similar innovations to enhance the level of credibility. If several innovations of the same type and with similar curriculum characteristics have been effective in influencing related outcomes, there should be more confidence in others modelling their own teaching on the results than if the study was an isolated one.

Combination of evidence is often not as straightforward as that in many conventional meta-analyses, which aggregate effect sizes from very similar experiments using the same outcome measures. Evaluation designs and evidence should be specific to the rationale for the innovation, so the measures used tend to be diverse, and therefore less easy to aggregate. There are also normally variations in the format of particular innovations, which can complicate comparison.

Reviews across a number of similar innovations can still be valuable, though, if approached with an appropriate orientation. A good example comes from a review of peer student assessment in higher education (Topping, 1998). The review concluded that there was sufficient variation in the way in which peer assessment had been implemented to require a 17-element typology to characterise studies. With this lack of homogeneity it was clearly inappropriate to make sweeping generalisations. Instead, the conclusions were of the form of deriving recommendations about how to organise particular parameters for a quality implementation of peer assessment.

A rather different way of triangulating across projects is that of synthesis of conclusions through a meta-project with subprojects on related themes. An example is that of five action research projects concerned with developing curricula to promote reflective practice in health science disciplines (Kember *et al.*, 2001). By joining the five subprojects together into one related venture, it proved possible to synthesise recommendations for curriculum design that could be used more widely. Regular critical discussion meetings between participants enabled comparisons to be made across subprojects, which led to insights which would not have been discovered from individual innovations.

Longitudinal measures of a deep approach

The first case study is of a series of measures aiming to improve the curriculum and teaching and learning environment in a radiography programme. The project was an exercise in staff development and curriculum reform, which encompassed a whole programme and the department which taught it.

Before describing the project itself, we will introduce a commonly used strategy to evaluate the impact of a teaching and learning innovation, which is the use of longitudinal measures of approaches to learning, or often just a deep approach. The rationale is that approaches to learning are influenced by students' perceptions of the teaching and learning environment. Changes in deep approach scores, from the beginning to the end of an innovation, should therefore show the influence of the teaching innovation on approaches to learning.

The strategy is operationalised by asking students to complete the study process questionnaire (SPQ) at the start of the course. For this completion they are asked to complete it for their normal or typical approach to study. The SPQ is then administered at the end of the course or innovation. This time the students are asked to complete the questionnaire by reporting how they had studied for the course in question. The difference between the two sets of results can reasonably be attributed as the effect of the innovation on approaches to learning.

Kember, Charlesworth, Davies, McKay, and Stott (1997) provides a rationale for this approach to evaluation for the scholarship of teaching. It uses three cases as examples, one of which is given here.

Base comparison data

Longitudinal change in deep approach scores can be an effective indicator of the effectiveness of educational innovation because it seems to be quite difficult to design curricula which promote increasing deep approach scores. Figure 10.1 shows deep approach scores by year of study gathered from a sample of 4,863 students from over half of the departments in one university in Hong Kong. The data were gathered with the original version of the SPQ. Year zero is when students enter the programme, while year three data were gathered at the completion of the final year of their programme.

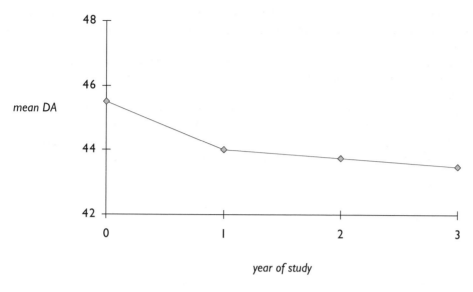

Figure 10.1 Deep approach scores by year of study

The data show that as students proceeded through their programme their interest declines and they became less inclined to try to understand material. Unfortunately this is not just the effect of one atypical university. A similar finding seems to occur whenever a large sample of SPQ data has been gathered from across a range of departments (e.g. Biggs, 1987, 1992; Gow & Kember, 1990; Watkins & Hattie, 1985). It appears to be quite normal for universities to demotivate their students and encourage them to use less desirable approaches to learning as they proceed through their programme.

An example of successful curriculum innovation

Fortunately, the outcome depicted in the above graph does not always occur. There are examples from more restricted samples, such as single programmes or degrees, for which deep approach scores rise by year of study. The action research case study is a prime example.

The radiography department wished to upgrade its offering from a professional diploma to a BSc degree. For purposes of external accreditation, the curriculum had to undergo major changes, and the staff of the department engaged in staff development activities for teaching and curriculum development. The revised course shifted away from the content-centred didactically taught diploma to more student-centred teaching. The number of hours of lectures was reduced significantly and students spent more time on self-directed learning and activities such as projects. More details about the changes to the curriculum are given in Kember and McKay (1996) and McKay and Kember (1997).

The project had a clear action research methodology from the curriculum change and involvement of staff from the department. There was triangulation of qualitative and quantitative data. The qualitative data included curriculum documents and records of meetings. There were also extensive interviews with students and teachers. Those with students aimed to find out how the old curriculum could be improved and gauge the impact of the new curriculum.

The main quantitative data were SPQ data from four successive intakes to the radiography department (Kember & McKay, 1996; McKay & Kember, 1997). Intakes RPD1 and RPD2 were the final two cohorts for a Professional Diploma in radiography. Their SPQ data show a pattern of declining scores similar to those in Figure 10.1.

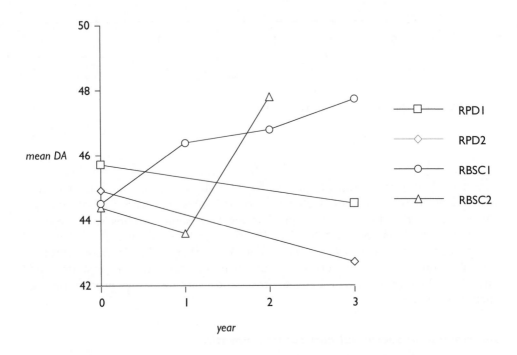

Figure 10.2 Longitudinal SPQ scores for the old diploma and new degree programmes

In addition to RPD1 and RPD2, the other two lines in Figure 10.2 are the first (RBSC1) and second (RBSC2) intakes to the revised degree curriculum. Apart from the small dip for year one of the second intake, the SPQ scores for the revised degree curriculum show increases over time. The marked contrast to the pattern of scores between the old diploma programme and the revised degree curriculum provides compelling evidence for the success of the curriculum reform.

Student experience in the first semester

The second case study is a survey study. Understanding the quality of experience for first year students is of particular importance to the second author (PG), who is responsible for a large, introductory education course in his faculty. Below, a research study is briefly outlined in which existing student experience and deep approach scales developed by the first author (DK) were tested in a novel setting, then used to determine if certain groups of first-year students differed systematically across these measures.

The 3P (presage–process–product) model (Biggs, 1993a) posits that the quality of student learning (product) is driven by the equilibrium found between student characteristics (presage), perceptions of the teaching and learning environment, and the approaches to learning students take (process). In the study described below, we focus on first-year students' perceptions of the teaching and learning environment and the extent to which they report using a deep approach to learning.

There are several ways in which the experience of students can be understood. Broadly, we can distinguish between *variable-centred* and *person-centred* approaches. The former approach uses methods such as correlation, regression, exploratory or confirmatory factor analysis, path analysis or structural modelling (see the Appendix for descriptions of these methods) to understand the relations between variables. The latter approach, using methods such as cluster analysis (see Appendix), aims to identify relatively homogeneous groups of students, where members of groups 'cluster together' as a result of similar responses on a range of variables. Student learning researchers (e.g. Crawford, Gordon, Nicholas, & Prosser; Ellis, Ginns, & Piggott, 1998; Ginns & Ellis, 2007) have often used this latter approach because such analyses aid understanding of how groups are similar or different within a particular context. Pragmatically, such analyses may also assist in identifying students whose profile of responses, and hence group membership, places them at academic risk (e.g. Bowers, 2010).

In the first, variable-centred phase of the study, the aim is to determine if a modified version of the student engagement questionnaire (see Chapter 3) previously validated in a Hong Kong context (Kember & Leung, 2009) shows suitable levels of construct validity in an Australian context; that is, do the constructs hypothesised to be measured by this instrument emerge out of students' responses to this instrument in a new context? In the second, person-centred phase, the results of the first phase are used to investigate whether distinctive groups of students can be identified within particular programmes.

The student engagement questionnaire

The survey consisted of three sections. The first section consisted of demographic questions, including age, gender, self-reported Australian Tertiary Admission Rank (ATAR) and first language. The second section, 'About your degree programme', consisted of 19 items drawn from Kember and Leung's SEQ (Kember & Leung, 2009), to measure nine dimensions of students' programmes: 'Active learning', 'Teaching for understanding', 'Assessment', 'Coherence of curriculum', 'Relationship between teachers and students', 'Feedback to assist learning', 'Relationship with other students', 'Cooperative learning', and 'Workload'. Kember and Leung hypothesised that the first four dimensions constituted a higher-order factor labelled 'Teaching'; the fifth and sixth dimensions constituted a higher order factor labelled 'Teacher–student relationship'; and the seventh and eighth dimensions constituted a higher-order factor labelled 'Student–student relationship'. Kember and Leung noted that 'workload can be modelled as being weakly influenced by most of the variables in this characterisation of a teaching and learning environment' (Kember & Leung, 2009, p. 22); hence, it was not included in Kember and Leung's model, nor in that tested below.

In the third section, an additional two items were drawn from the e-learning scale described in Ginns and Ellis (2009). Many universities are investing heavily in information and communication technology (ICT) to support learning, creating a need to evaluate how students perceive ICT in relation to this goal. A key purpose of this study was to validate a short form (2 items) of the original 5-item scale described in Ginns and Ellis (2009), following Kember and Leung's (2009) development of scales that were both short and psychometrically acceptable.

The two items were selected from the longer scale using the 'alphamax' procedure (Hayes, 2005), an SPSS macro that generates a spreadsheet containing each possible short form and its psychometric properties based on existing data (in this case, the data set used by Ginns and Ellis). Examining the earlier dataset with the alphamax procedure, two items – 'My online experiences helped me engage actively in my learning' and 'The online learning experiences of my degree course were well-integrated with my face-to-face learning' – could be used to constitute a short version with a good level of internal consistency (Cronbach's alpha = 0.78). Evidence for the construct validity of this short form would be provided by a strong loading of this facet on a higher order 'Teaching' factor similar to that tested by Kember and Leung (2009).

In addition to examining the construct validity of the modified SEQ, the present study aimed to validate the hypothesised higher order factors against students' self-reports of a deep approach to learning. Kember and Leung (2009) argued that the facets of the SEQ focusing on the teaching and learning environment demonstrated suitable levels of external validity as these constructs were associated with students' self-reports of generic capability development (e.g. critical thinking, problem-solving, communication skills). This approach to demonstrating external validity involves examining the set of relationships between constructs in a broader nomological network (Anderson, 1987). A key component of the nomological network outlined in the 3P model is students' approaches to learning. Thus, the last section of the SEQ consisted of the ten deep approach items from the R-SPQ-2F (Biggs, Kember, & Leung, 2001), to examine whether the hypothesised higher-order factors constituted by the above SEQ scales were meaningfully related to self-reports of a deep approach to learning.

The nature of the relationship between students' perceptions of the teaching and learning environment and approaches to learning needs careful consideration. Early interview-based research (e.g. Marton, 1976; Ramsden, 1979) was used to justify arguments for a functional relationship between these sets of constructs; that is, that perceptions of the learning and teaching environment influenced students' subsequent approaches to learning. Richardson (2006) reviewed arguments for several alternate relationships between perceptions and approaches, and concluded, on the basis of path analysis of two datasets, that a bidirectional relationship exists between perceptions and approaches, such that:

(a)...approaches to studying in higher education are driven in part by the students' perceptions of their academic environment, but (b) equally...students' perceptions of their academic environment are driven in part by the extent to which they are able to adopt congenial approaches to studying. Consequently, attempts to enhance the quality of student learning in higher education need to address both students' perceptions of their academic context and their study behaviour within that context.

(Richardson, 2006, p. 890)

Consistent with this argument, in the present analysis, confirmatory factor analysis is used to specify correlational relationships between the teaching and learning environment factors and a deep approach to learning, rather than causal relationships.

Participants

Participants were 270 first year education students enrolled in a metropolitan university in Australia. The majority of students (89.9%) were between 17 and 20 years old, were female (73%), and spoke English as their first language (77.8%). While all students were enrolled in a Bachelor of Education, the specific focus of the programme included Early Childhood (6.7% of respondents), Primary Education (25.6%), Humanities (33%), Maths/Science (15.2%), and Human Movement and Health Studies (19.6%).

Variable-centred analyses

Prior to analysis, the extent of missing data across the SEQ and Deep Approach items was examined. As fewer than 5 per cent of cells were missing, the missing data were imputed with the Expectation Maximisation algorithm using SPSS 17 (Graham & Hofer, 2000). Confirmatory factor analysis (CFA) was used to test a hypothesised model of the relations between the SEQ and deep approach scale items, and their expected scales; between the SEQ scales and hypothesised higher-order factors; and between the higher-order factors and a deep approach to learning.

A confirmatory factor analysis was conducted with M*plus* (Muthén & Muthén, 1998–2010), using the robust maximum likelihood estimator (MLR). Following Marsh, Hau, and Wen's (2004) guidelines, the comparative fit index (CFI), the root mean square error of approximation (RMSEA) and an inspection of parameter estimates were used to assess model fit. CFI values at or greater than 0.90 and 0.95 were considered to reflect acceptable and excellent fit to the data, respectively, while RMSEA values at or less than 0.08 and 0.05 were considered to reflect acceptable and excellent fit, respectively.

Initial inspection of item functioning revealed the 'Active learning', 'Feedback to assist learning' and 'Assessment' items did not form scales with suitable reliability levels (Cronbach's alpha equalling 0.41, 0.41 and 0.47 for the three scales, respectively). Hence, these items were excluded from the subsequent CFA. Another difference between the model tested here and that presented by Kember and Leung (2009) lies in the incorporation of the 'Relationship between teachers and students' construct into the 'Teaching' higher-order factor. This was justified on the basis that the very high latent correlation (0.93) between the 'Teaching' and 'Teacher–student relationships' higher-order factors found by Kember and Leung, suggesting a possible third-order factor. The hypothesised model and estimated parameters are given below in Figure 10.3.

Based on the above criteria for model fit, the model had acceptable fit to the data: CFI = 0.92 and RMSEA = 0.048 (90% confidence interval 0.038–0.057). Inspection of Table 10.1 reveals the scale scores were reasonably well distributed, with skewness and kurtosis estimates not greater than ±1. Reliability analyses for each of the scales indicated generally acceptable levels of internal consistency.

Table 10.1 Descriptive statistics and Cronbach's alpha for SEQ and Deep Approach scales

Scale	Mean	S.D.	Skewness	Kurtosis	Cronbach's alpha
Teaching for understanding	3.64	0.75	−0.81	0.84	0.72
E-learning	3.00	1.11	−0.13	−0.37	0.86
Coherence of curriculum	3.44	0.83	−0.61	0.28	0.79
Teacher–student relations	3.68	0.80	−0.63	0.45	0.71
Relations with other students	3.51	0.97	−0.63	0.31	0.76
Cooperative learning	3.41	1.05	−0.51	−0.54	0.81
Deep approach	2.89	0.63	0.07	−0.37	0.79

Several conclusions can be drawn from these results. First, the acceptable model fit leads us to conclude that students in a different cultural setting to that of the original study distinguished suitably between the different hypothesised dimensions (both lower- and higher-order) of the teaching and learning environment, as well as a deep approach to learning. Second, item loadings on the six hypothesised SEQ scales all had loadings greater than 0.70, indicating items were suitable indicators of their hypothesised constructs. Third, for the most part, the teaching and learning environment scales evinced good to excellent levels of reliability, despite their short length. In particular, the proposed short e-learning scale showed excellent levels of reliability (Cronbach's alpha = 0.86). However, the low levels of reliability for the 'Active learning', 'Feedback to assist learning' and 'Assessment' scales mean these scales may require revision in the Australian context. Fourth, the substantial correlations between the higher-order factor of 'Teaching' and deep approach ($r = 0.61$), and between the higher-order factor of 'Student–student relationships' and deep approach ($r = 0.40$), provide evidence of the external validity of these higher order constructs, adding to the evidence for external validity given by Kember and Leung (2009) based on relations with generic capabilities.

Person-centred analyses

Having provided evidence for the validity and reliability of the SEQ constructs described above, in this section we outline a person-centred approach to analysis, using cluster analysis. As noted above, such analyses are often used in higher education

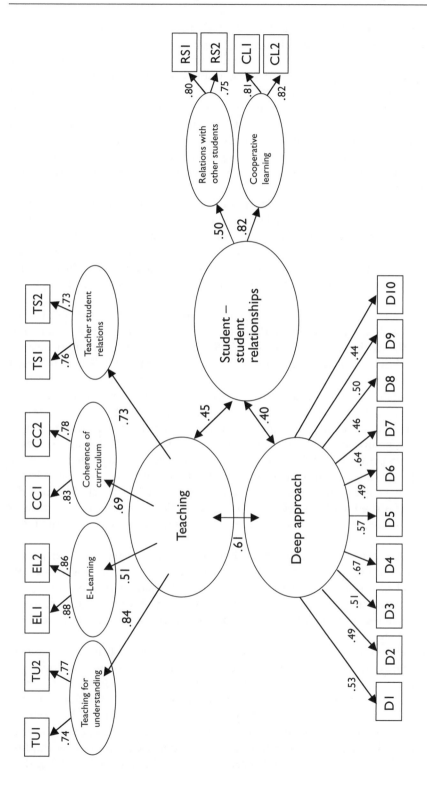

Figure 10.3 CFA model of the teaching and learning environment and relations to a deep approach

research to identify groups of students who show similar profiles across a range of variables (Huberty, Jordan, & Brandt, 2005).

From the 3P model perspective, students in distinct clusters may be expected to vary systematically according to presage factors (e.g. prior knowledge, conceptions of learning or the topic of study), process factors (e.g. perceptions of the teaching and learning environment; approaches to learning) and product factors (e.g. self-reports of skill development; assessment outcomes). The SEQ described above supports such analyses in providing a presage variable (prior academic achievement, as measured by ATAR) and process variables (described above). A product variable measuring academic achievement across the first semester of study, weighted average mark (WAM), was accessed from student records.

As noted above, the sample of students consisted of students studying in several programmes. As these constitute specific learning contexts, it is appropriate to focus analyses on particular programmes; analysing responses from all students risks 'mixing apples and oranges', particularly given the likelihood of differing teaching approaches, assessment methods and learning objectives in different programmes. We illustrate this approach using the largest cohort of respondents (Bachelor of Education/Bachelor of Arts; $n = 90$).

Following standardisation of ATAR, SEQ, deep approach and WAM scores, hierarchical cluster analysis was conducted using Ward's minimum variance method. Inspection of the agglomeration coefficient indicated a two-cluster solution was the best representation of similarities and dissimilarities between groups of students. Based on this two-group solution, t-tests were conducted to determine if group differences on the above variates were statistically reliable. Table 10.2 gives the means and standard deviations on each variable for each cluster; the results of a t-test on the differences between means; and the standardised mean difference, d, an effect size measure, calculated as the difference between the mean scores divided by the average standard deviation. The 95 per cent confidence interval for d is also given, as an indication of the plausible range of values of this effect size given the sample size. We consider the magnitude of effect sizes using benchmarks recommended by Hattie (2009): small $d = 0.20$, medium $d = 0.40$, and large $d = 0.60$ or greater. Note that the signs of most of the effect sizes are negative; this is simply a result of using the first cluster as the reference group.

We interpret the cluster analysis results as follows. The first cluster of students could be characterised as a group that, on average, entered their university studies with a relatively high level of capacity, as measured by their ATAR mark. However, this group gave relatively low ratings of teaching for understanding, e-learning, coherence of curriculum, teacher–student relations and cooperative learning, and had relatively low self-ratings of a deep approach to learning.

The second cluster, in comparison, gave relatively high ratings of teaching for understanding, e-learning, coherence of curriculum, teacher–student relation, and cooperative learning, and had relatively high self-ratings of a deep approach to learning. These statistically reliable differences between the two clusters, as indicated by the standardised mean differences, were generally quite large. The differences between the clusters on relations with other students and weighted average mark were not statistically significant. Notably, the advantage in academic attainment enjoyed by the first cluster on entry to university (as measured by the ATAR score) has diminished

Table 10.2 Comparisons across presage, process and product variables

Variable	Cluster 1 (n = 35)		Cluster 2 (n = 55)		t-test	d	95% CI of d
	Mean	SD	Mean	SD			
Presage							
ATAR	0.34	0.71	−0.22	1.10	t(88) = 2.67, p = 0.009	0.58	0.14, 1.46
Process							
Teaching for understanding	−0.74	0.83	0.45	0.79	t(88) = 6.82, p < 0.001	−1.48	−1.94, −0.99
E-learning	−0.89	0.69	0.50	0.77	t(88) = 8.75, p < 0.001	−1.88	−2.36, −1.36
Coherence of curriculum	−0.57	0.98	0.33	0.88	t(88) = 4.56, p < 0.001	−0.98	−1.42, 0.52
Teacher–student relations	−0.88	0.88	0.61	0.57	t(88) = 9.76, p < 0.001	−2.11	−2.61, −1.57
Relations with other students	0.04	0.88	0.09	1.01	t(88) = 0.21, p = .831	−0.05	−0.48, 0.37
Cooperative learning	−0.43	1.14	0.32	0.77	t(88) = 3.70, p < .001	−0.81	−1.24, −0.36
Deep approach	−0.72	0.96	0.40	0.76	t(88) = 6.19, p < 0.001	−1.33	−1.78, −0.85
Product							
Weighted average mark	0.22	0.65	−0.10	1.09	t(88) = 1.55, p = 0.125	0.34	−0.09, 0.76

substantially by the end of the first semester, as indicated by the lack of a statistically reliable difference between clusters on the weighted average mark.

On face value, the finding is somewhat paradoxical: students in this cohort entering university studies with a higher level of attainment perceive many aspects of the teaching and learning environment less favourably, as well as reporting lower levels of a deep approach to study. One possible explanation of this pattern of results relates to the previous learning context of most of these students: the final years of high school, involving the Higher School Certificate (HSC), a high-stakes assessment process. Anecdotal evidence based on conversations with students suggests the use of rote memorisation strategies (encouraged by many teachers) in the HSC context is widespread, despite evidence that the very best HSC teachers (as measured by student achievement) teach for understanding (Ayres, Sawyer, & Dinham, 2004). This leads to the conjecture that at least some students attempt to maximise their ATAR for university entry using conceptions and strategies of learning that are counter-productive to success within this programme.

Some limitations of the present study deserve consideration. The most important limitation is the use of a cross-sectional design; that is, all variables (with the exception of the weighted average mark) were collected at the same time. A more nuanced understanding of the relationships between the variables examined in this study, including questions of causal influence between perceptions and approaches, would have arisen out of multiple waves of data; for example, measurement of conceptions of and approaches to learning at the start of the programme, followed by measurement of perceptions and approaches at the end of the first and second semesters of study. Crawford *et al.* (1998) provide an example of a longitudinal investigation of these variables across a semester.

In addition, the use of the self-reported ATAR mark as the sole presage variable might be criticised as being limited. Although prior academic achievement is generally held to be a very important predictor of subsequent attainment (see Hattie, 2009, pp.41–42), other possible presage variables that would be expected to play a role in first-year university studies include self-efficacy for self-regulated learning (Usher & Pajares, 2008), self-efficacy for academic writing (Pajares, Hartley, & Valiante, 2001) and conceptions of learning (Purdie & Hattie, 2002).

As an example of the scholarship of teaching, the study described above is presented as aiming to meet several goals. First, it aimed to build clearly on previous research, testing Kember and Leung's (2009) SEQ in a new context, and against a key variable (deep approach) in student learning theory's nomological network. Second, it aimed to generate an understanding of the experience of a specific group of students that might be used to improve teaching and learning. The results of the cluster analysis reported above suggest the need to strongly emphasise the change in teaching and learning context from high school to university, and the concomitant expectations around quality learning. In effect, part of PG's responsibility towards his first year students is to make them aware of their 'conditioning' from their high school studies, and the limitations of this conditioning in the present environment; the results of studies such as this provide a starting point for both staff and students in achieving this understanding.

Conclusion

The aim of this chapter has been to help those who need to integrate evaluation into the design of an SoTL project. The first part of the chapter dealt with paradigmatic issues. For those accustomed to using experimental methods in their disciplinary research, there is a discussion of the suitability of the experimental method for SoTL research. We give a list of ways in which experimental designs might fail to work effectively for SoTL projects. However, we present these as pitfalls to avoid rather than reasons for not adopting experimental designs. Those from traditionally experimental disciplines may prefer not to venture outside their comfort zone.

As an alternative we present the action research approach, which is suited to SoTL in that it is a research approach which specifically aims to bring about change, whereas most others try to avoid perturbing the phenomenon studied. Action research employs a series of cycles of planning, action, observation and reflection to bring about change and hopefully improvement. This is similar to other developmental processes, such as the test and development phases used in product development, so most find it straightforward to adopt.

Another alternative to experimental designs is the survey method. For this approach data are collected from questionnaires. In the example given in this chapter we present two distinct ways of analysing survey data. The more common method is a variable-centred one that looks for relationships between variables in the study. The other method is person-centred because it seeks to identify relatively homogeneous groups of students who are likely to behave in a similar way in a given circumstance.

The other methodological approach dealt with is triangulation. Most commonly this implies collection of data through multiple methods. The rationale is that complementary evidence from contrasting forms of data provides a more convincing claim than that from a single method. Another form of triangulation is that of multiple sources. In the case of SoTL this normally implies collecting data from sources besides students.

Chapter 11

International perspectives on teaching evaluation

In national higher education sectors, common CTEQ instruments are increasingly used across institutions. These provide institutions with data useful to a variety of stakeholders (e.g. students, funding bodies, accreditation bodies), but can also provide a source of data for benchmarking across institutions. This chapter describes the most common programme-level or institution-level instruments used in North America (the National Survey of Student Engagement), Australia (the Course Experience Questionnaire and the Australasian Survey of Student Engagement), and the UK (the National Student Survey), as well as the theoretical frameworks underlying their design. The benefits of aligning the design of internal CTEQ instruments (e.g. at the course level) with instruments used for external benchmarking (i.e. at the programme or institution level) are discussed.

North America: The National Survey of Student Engagement

The USA does not have an institution responsible for assuring higher education quality through governmental mandate, as do the other countries discussed in this chapter. Thus, a variety of questionnaires have been developed over the past decades which have subsequently been used by multiple institutions. Currently, the most widely used such instrument is the National Survey of Student Engagement (NSSE), administered by the Center for Postsecondary Research (CPR) in the Indiana University School of Education. Since the NSSE was first administered in 2000, over 1400 Canadian and US higher education institutions have participated in the NSSE. In the most recent (2010) administration, students from 595 Canadian and US institutions participated.

The NSSE is based on the core construct of student engagement, which builds on constructs including time on task, quality of effort, student involvement, social and academic integration, and effective practices in undergraduate education. We discuss these foundation constructs briefly below.

Theoretical background

Kuh (2009) tracks the development of the student engagement construct in American education back to the 1930s, beginning with Tyler's research on the positive effects of *time on task* on learning. During the 1960s and 1970s, C. Robert Pace developed the notion of *quality of effort*, arguing that while universities and colleges can provide resources and the conditions that give students the opportunity to learn, students must still make use of these opportunities in order to learn. Resources for learning are therefore viewed as necessary but not sufficient conditions for learning; institutions are therefore responsible for providing learning opportunities, but ultimately the responsibility for learning rests with the student.

Alexander Astin's notion of *involvement* (e.g. Astin, 1984, 1985) was developed as part of a broader conceptualisation of the nature of education. He argued that thinking of education as anything like an industrial production process was misguided. Rather, education is more like a service, in particular because students are not blank slates when they arrive at university; they are subjects, not objects. The university's role, according to Astin, is to enhance or add value to the student's situation. Educational outcomes are therefore dependent not only on the environment and process, but how individuals behave in those circumstances. According to Astin:

> Students learn by becoming involved . . . Quite simply, student involvement refers to the amount of physical and psychological energy that the student devotes to the educational experience. A highly involved student is one who, for example, devotes considerable energy to studying, spends a lot of time on campus, participates actively in student organisations, and interacts frequently with faculty members and other students.
>
> (Astin, 1985, p. 134)

Vincent Tinto's model of student retention (e.g. Tinto, 1975, 1987) focuses on academic and social integration into a higher education institution. Braxton, Milem, and Sullivan (1997) summarised the key empirically supported propositions of Tinto's revised (1987) model as follows:

> . . . student entry characteristics affect the level of initial commitment to the institution. These student entry characteristics include family background characteristics (e.g. socio-economic status, parental educational level), individual attributes (e.g. academic ability, race, and gender) and pre-college schooling experiences (e.g. high school academic achievement). The initial level of commitment to the institution influences the subsequent level of commitment to the institution. This subsequent level of institutional commitment is also positively affected by the extent of a student's integration into the social communities of the college. The greater the level subsequent commitment to the institution, the greater the likelihood of student of persistence in college.
>
> (Braxton et al., 1997, p. 570)

Arthur Chickering and Zelda Gamson (1987) proposed seven principles for good practice in undergraduate education. This paper, published in the *American Association for Higher Education Bulletin*, was an effort to make findings from research on university teaching and learning accessible to a wider audience. The principles comprised encouraging student–faculty contact, encouraging cooperation among students, encouraging active learning, giving prompt feedback, emphasising time on task, communicating high expectations, and respecting diverse talents and ways of learning.

The above frameworks have informed the development of the broad student engagement construct, defined by Kuh, Kinzie, Schuh, Whitt et al. (2005) as having two key aspects. The first aspect is the amount of time and effort students direct towards their studies and other activities, which leads to productive learning experiences and outcomes. The second aspect is a function of the institution's resource allocation and curriculum design, increasing the likelihood of student engagement in productive learning experiences. The NSSE aims to measure both of these aspects of engagement.

NSSE survey administration, surveying methodology and design

The NSSE is centrally administered by the Center for Postsecondary Research (CPR) in the Indiana University School of Education. Institutions provide a full dataset of student contact details to CPR, which is used for either population sampling of freshman and senior year classes in the case of smaller institutions, or random sampling of these classes for larger institutions.

Institutions may choose one of three survey modes. The Web-only mode consists of up to 5 contacts by email only. The Web+ mode consists of up to three initial email contacts, followed by a paper survey being sent to a subgroup of non-respondents (with the student retaining the option to complete the survey online), and a final fifth email contact for non-respondents. The paper option consists of an initial paper-based contact (institutional letter and survey), with an option to complete online, followed by a second letter and survey, again with the online completion option. The third contact is either a follow-up email or postcard, and the fourth and fifth contacts are email reminders.

Core items of the NSSE survey instrument, referred to as the College Student Report, can be viewed at http://nsse.iub.edu/pdf/US_paper_10.pdf (2010 version). The first section of items asks how often a respondent has engaged in a variety of 'educationally purposeful activities' (Kuh, 2009, p. 11) either by herself or in collaboration with students or staff. The second section captures the extent to which a respondent has engaged in learning-related cognitive processes (e.g. memorizing, applying theories or concepts to practical problems). The third section captures how much reading and writing the respondent has done over the school year. The fourth section asks about homework completion in a typical week, while the fifth section asks about academic challenge in examinations.

The sixth section asks about engagement in a variety of extra-curricular activities (e.g. attendance of artistic performances, participation in physical fitness activities). The seventh section asks about planned extra-curricular activities before graduation (e.g. study abroad). The eighth section asks about quality of relationships with other students, staff, and administrative personnel in the institution. The ninth section has respondents estimate the number of hours spent in a typical 7-day week on a variety of academic and non-academic activities. Section 10 asks students about their perceptions of their institution's emphases (e.g. spending time on studying; encouraging contact among diverse students).

Section 11 asks respondents to estimate the institution's contribution to development of their knowledge, skills, and personal development. Sections 12 and 13 ask respondents to evaluate the quality of academic advising and overall educational experience, respectively, while Section 14 asks students to rate whether they would still attend the same institution if starting over. Sections 15 to 28 gather a variety of data on background characteristics, such as age, gender, race/ethnicity, grade point average and major field. Consortia of at least six institutions can add up to twenty additional items specific to the interests of that group.

NSSE institutional reporting

Following data collection, raw data files and a codebook are also returned to institutions. CPR generates the 'Institutional Report' for participating institutions, which includes an overview of the data, a number of standard reports and supporting resources. Standard reports include respondent characteristics, selected comparison groups, frequency distributions, mean comparisons, benchmark comparisons, a multi-year benchmark report, the student experience in brief, between- and within-major fields reports, and an Executive Snapshot. Examples of standard reports and institutional report resources are given at http://nsse.iub.edu/_/?cid=402.

Five core benchmark scales are a key focus of NSSE reports and subsequent institutional activity. These scales are:

1   Active and Collaborative Learning – students' efforts to actively construct knowledge.
2   Level of Academic Challenge – the extent to which expectations and assessments challenge students to learn.
3   Student–Faculty Interactions – the level and nature of students' contact and interaction with teaching staff.
4   Enriching Educational Experiences – students' participation in broadening educational activities.
5   Supportive Campus Environment – students' feelings of support within the university community.

Psychometric properties of the NSSE

CPR provides summary reports of the psychometric properties of the NSSE through its 'Psychometric Portfolio' webpage http://nsse.iub.edu/_/?cid=154.

Institutional and public use of NSSE results

At a national level, two organisations representing public baccalaureate colleges and universities (the American Association of State Colleges and Universities, and the Association of Public and Land-Grant Universities) developed the Voluntary System of Accountability Program (VSA; see www.voluntarysystem.org/index.cfm), in which NSSE results (as one option) may be used for reporting student experiences and perceptions. Another widespread use of NSSE results for public accountability is through USA Today's NSSE report site which includes results from over 400 institutions (www.usatoday.com/news/education/nsse.htm).

In common with many other surveys, NSSE results are used for a range of purposes by institutions. Institutions have made internal use of NSSE results in a large number of ways, including accreditation, departmental use, faculty and staff development, and marketing. CPR provides a searchable database of examples of NSSE, FSSE (Faculty Survey of Student Engagement) and BCSSE (Beginning College Survey of Student Engagement) data use at http://nsse.iub.edu/html/using_nsse_db. Specific examples of the use of NSSE data to understand the policies and practices of institutions achieving higher than expected outcomes are provided in Kuh, Kinzie, Schuh, Whitt, and associates (2005) and Nelson Laird, Chen, and Kuh (2008).

The provision of the raw dataset back to institutions supports many forms of institutional research. Chen, Gonyea, Sarraf, BrkaLorenz, *et al.* (2009) provide a comprehensive overview of recommended analytic strategies for NSSE data, and SPSS syntax for common recodes and analyses is provided at http://nsse.iub.edu/html/analysis_resources.cfm.

As noted above, the USA Today NSSE site is a resource available to the public. One of the stated goals of this site is to help potential students to 'evaluate whether a particular campus offers the kinds of experiences and opportunities that are known to benefit students' (USA Today, 2010). CPR also supports decision making by students, parents, and counsellors using the student engagement framework through its Pocket Guide to Choosing a College (http://nsse.iub.edu/html/pocket_guide_intro.cfm).

Australia: the Course Experience Questionnaire

Theoretical background

The constructs measured by the Course Experience Questionnaire (CEQ) exist within a larger theoretical network of constructs within student learning theory (SLT; Biggs & Tang, 2007; Entwistle, 2009; Prosser & Trigwell, 1999; Ramsden, 2003). SLT seeks to understand the elements of a student's experience of higher education associated with qualitative differences in the approaches to study (Biggs, Kember, & Leung, 2001) that student takes, as well as the subsequent quality of learning. The CEQ was derived from an earlier instrument, the Course Perceptions Questionnaire (CPQ; Ramsden, 1979; Entwistle & Ramsden, 1983; Ramsden & Entwistle, 1981). Initial item development for the CPQ drew on interviews with UK students about their perceptions of the academic context. In these interviews, students often identified functional relationships between their perceptions of the academic context and their subsequent approaches to study (Entwistle & Ramsden, 1983; Ramsden, 1979). Thus, SLT theorists argue approaches to learning should not be considered as stable individual differences, but as potentially malleable responses to the perceived demands of the teaching and learning environment (Biggs, 1993b; Eley, 1992). From the SLT perspective, higher-quality approaches to learning and subsequent performance are more likely when constructive alignment is achieved between teaching and learning outcomes, the teaching and learning activities used to achieve those outcomes, and the assessment tasks used to evaluate whether those outcomes have been reached (Biggs, 1996). Understanding how students perceive these elements is an important part of the process of achieving constructive alignment, and a key use of the CEQ.

Psychometric limitations of the CPQ motivated the subsequent development of the CEQ (Elphinstone, 1989), and a national trial of a revised, shortened 30-item version of the CEQ to test its suitability as a performance indicator in the Australian context, providing 'quantitative data which permit ordinal ranking of units in different institutions, within comparable subject areas, in terms of perceived teaching quality' (Ramsden, 1991, pp. 132–133). Historically, the most widely used Australian version of the CEQ consists of 23 items, measuring five domains: good teaching, clear goals and standards, appropriate workload, appropriate assessment, and generic skills development. A single final item is used to evaluate satisfaction with the overall quality of the degree programme. On the nationally used CEQ instrument, 'course experience' is defined as follows: 'The term "course" in the questions below refers to the major field(s) of education or program(s) of study that made up your qualification(s).' Respondents are asked to write their major field of education or programme in a text box above the Likert (strongly disagree to strongly agree) response scale. Two columns of Likert response scales allow students with double majors to respond about more than one programme or degree.

Griffin, Coates, McInnis, and James (2003, p. 260) argued that 'the original CEQ was based on a theory of learning which emphasises the primary forces in the under-graduate experience as located within the classroom setting', making the five-scale version described above potentially limited, given subsequent developments in higher education. Griffin *et al.* developed an expanded range of CEQ scales so as to expand the range of performance indicators available to institutions. The expanded scales address both programme- and institution-level concerns, focusing on student support, learning resources, course organisation, learning community, graduate qualities, and intellectual motivation. The development of these additional scales was informed by student engagement theorizing rather than SLT, with a strong focus on students' out-of-class experiences. However, J. T. E. Richardson (2005, p. 400) cautions:

> the new scales were introduced for largely pragmatic reasons and are not grounded in research on the student experience. Hence, although the extended CEQ taps a broader range of students' opinions, it may be less appropriate for measuring their perceptions of the more formal aspects of the curriculum that are usually taken to define teaching quality.

CEQ survey administration, surveying methodology and design

The CEQ is centrally managed by Graduate Careers Australia, and is delivered as part of a larger survey of Australian graduates, the Australian Graduate Survey (AGS), which also collects data on a range of employment-related processes and outcomes (referred to as the Graduate Destination Survey, or GDS). Responsibility for conducting the AGS is devolved to individual institutions, with an expectation that institutions will comply with a general code of conduct and specific guidelines provided in a provided manual (GCA, 2011). Two survey rounds are conducted per year (April and October), targeting graduates who have completed studies in either the second semester of the previous year (April round) or the first semester (October round).

Institutions are encouraged to use multiple survey modes to maximise the response rate, with a minimum of two follow-ups of non-respondents. These include paper-based surveys in a standardised format, an online version using a system (oAGS) developed by GCA, and phone surveying using a standardised script.

As the AGS is a census survey, all graduates of Australian universities (excluding those studying at offshore campuses) are invited to complete it, and response rates are calculated according to the proportion of potential respondents identified from institutional records. The AGS code of practice stipulates that an institution should not publish AGS data outside of the institution where the relevant response rate falls below 50 per cent. The 50 per cent response rate applies separately to the GDS and CEQ components of the AGS. The code of conduct also stipulates restrictions on external publication if the response rate for local or international respondents falls below 50 per cent. Response rates for the CEQ specifically are calculated on the basis that respondents must have given responses to at least four items for either the Good Teaching Scale (GTS), or the Generic Skills Scale (GSS), or a response to the Overall Satisfaction Indicator (OSI), as well as supplying a valid CEQ major field of education.

For the purposes of benchmarking in the Australian context, the GTS, GSS and OSI comprise the core scales of the CEQ. All institutions must include items from these scales as a minimum requirement. Within the constraint of fitting all desired scales onto the last page of the paper version of the AGS, institutions may also choose to include additional scales from the original form of the CEQ; additional scales from Griffin *et al.*'s (2003) extended CEQ; or a combination of original and extended CEQ scales.

CEQ institutional reporting

Following data collection by institutions, data entry may be conducted either by the institution, or by GCA, although GCA recommends certain variables such as field of study be coded by the institution to ensure accuracy based on local knowledge. Data are 'cleaned' by GCA and final data files are returned to institutions. GCA generates a range of sector-wide reports from both the GDS and CEQ data; these are provided to institutions and are also available for purchase from GCA. The key report (e.g. GCA and ACER, 2010) summarises the characteristics of CEQ respondents and responses, describes national patterns and trends for CEQ scales and items, and summarises the experience of specific groups. Specific analyses are provided for effects of institution, broad field of education, detailed field of education, qualification level, the means by which study has been financed, attendance type, mode of study, gender, age, identification as Aboriginal or Torres Strait Islander, identification as Permanent Resident, language background, self-report of disability, participating in paid work in the final year of study, and being in paid work at the AGS census date. Reports use two different metrics: descriptive statistics based on a transformation of responses to a −100 to +100 scale, and a 'percentage agreement' metric calculated by the proportion of 4 (agree) and 5 (strongly agree) responses to items across a given scale.

Psychometric properties of the CEQ

The measurement properties of the original CEQ have been investigated in a large number of studies, using both exploratory and confirmatory techniques (for a review, see J. T. E. Richardson, 2005). Generally, the original CEQ evinces reasonable levels of construct validity as measured by the clarity of the factor structure using exploratory methods. A recent analysis (Marsh, Ginns, Morin, Nagengast, & Martin, 2011) of the last national dataset (2001) to use the full original CEQ found marginal levels of model fit using confirmatory methods, but substantially better fit using exploratory structural equation modelling. The construct validity of the extended CEQ was demonstrated by McInnis, Griffin, James, and Coates (2001) using confirmatory factor analysis of response to both the original and extended CEQ scale items.

A reliability generalisation study given in the 2006 annual report (GCA & ACER, 2007) found the 10 original and extended scales had consistent measurement properties across contexts, and that the reliability of the Appropriate Assessment and Appropriate Workload Scales was consistently lower (ranging from 0.65 to 0.70) than other scale reliabilities, which generally reach levels between 0.70 to 0.80. This is attributable to a combination of factors, including fewer items than other scales, as well as the use of both negatively and positively worded items.

The suitability of the CEQ to benchmark Australian universities and programmes has been questioned by Marsh, Ginns, Morin, Nagengast, and Martin (2011). The hypothesised five factor CEQ scale model had acceptable fit to the data at the level of the individual student. Individual-level analyses, however, do not take into account the 'nestedness' in the data's structure, where students are clustered within programmes and/or fields of study, which are in turn nested within universities. Marsh *et al.* argued that '[i]n order for CEQ ratings to reliably differentiate between universities and courses within universities, the associated variance components have to be substantial' (Marsh *et al.*, 2011, p. 17).

A set of 12 three-level models (level 1 = students, level 2 = programme, level 3 = university) of the scale scores and the overall satisfaction were tested using the CEQ 2001 Australian national dataset (*n* = 44,932 students from 41 institutions). The models differed as to the number of programme classifications included as random effects (10, 43 or 186 classifications), the number of discipline classifications included as fixed effects (0, 10, 43 or 186 classifications) and inclusion or non-inclusion of 12 student characteristics as fixed effects. Interpreting the relative size of variance components at each level and visual inspection of caterpillar plots, Marsh *et al.* concluded that, across all models, 'there is little evidence that any of the five specific CEQ factors is able to differentiate reliably between either universities or courses within universities – the primary purpose for which they were designed'. Follow-up profile analyses also failed to support the benchmarking of profiles of the average of the five CEQ scores, or unique profiles of CEQ scores.

While the above results call into question the use of CEQ scores for benchmarking across universities or degree programmes at one point in time, benchmarking the same degree programme over time may be a more productive use of the CEQ, particularly for tracking the impact of curriculum change (e.g. Taylor & Canfield, 2007). Among several recommended uses of the CEQ, Wilson, Lizzio, and Ramsden (1997, Table 4, p. 49) emphasised intermittent planned use of the CEQ, especially for whole-course-programme evaluation over time.

Institutional and public use of CEQ results

Australian universities have made extensive use of CEQ results for internal quality assurance and improvement purposes (e.g. Lizzio, Wilson, & Symons, 2002; Lyon & Hendry, 2002; Patrick, 1999; Tucker, Jones, & Straker, 2008; Tyler & Canfield, 2007), as well as external benchmarking (e.g. Curtis & Keeves, 2000; McKinnon, Walker, & Davis, 2000) and quality assurance purposes evaluations by the Australian Universities Quality Assurance Agency (AUQA). CEQ results also feature in benchmarking across institutional groupings such as the Group of Eight (e.g. the 'Go8 Executive Dashboard'; www.go8.edu.au/government-_and_-business/benchmarking-_and_-stats) and the Australian Technology Network (Palermo, 2004).

The main publicly available reporting framework for the CEQ is the *Good Universities Guide* website at www.gooduniguide.com.au/ and annual publication (e.g. Good Universities Guide, 2011). CEQ results for good teaching, generic skills and overall satisfaction with degree quality, as well as GDS employment data, are converted into a 1–5 star rating system to support ratings and rankings of universities, as well as ratings for specific fields of study.

The inclusion of two open-ended questions with the CEQ, about the best aspects of the graduate's degree experience and those aspects that could be improved, supports triangulation of quantitative and qualitative feedback data. The CEQuery software (Scott, 2005) for analysing the open-ended questions is provided to all Australian institutions free of charge by GCA.

Australia and New Zealand: the Australasian Survey of Student Engagement

Theoretical background

The Australasian Survey of Student Engagement (AUSSE) is another widely used programme-level instrument in Australasia (Australia and New Zealand). Like the NSSE, its development was informed by student engagement theory (see above).

AUSSE survey administration, surveying methodology and design

The AUSSE is administered by the Australian Council for Educational Research (ACER). The AUSSE was first administered in 2007 in 25 Australasian universities, and as of 2010 the AUSSE is used by 55 Australasian higher education and vocational education institutions. Institutions taking part in the AUSSE provide a de-identified list of undergraduate students and/or postgraduate coursework students meeting the sampling frame (e.g. for the undergraduate frame, first- and third-year, onshore students. (A staff version of the AUSSE is also available). A stratified sample of students is then selected; ACER identifies which students have been sampled in the population list; then the updated list is returned to the institution. Student contact details are merged into this master list, which is then used to distribute the online and paper survey forms to sampled students. Completed online or paper versions of the survey are returned directly to ACER, which is responsible for data entry, preparation of analysis files and response weighting.

In addition to demographic information, the AUSSE measures six different facets of student engagement, comprising academic challenge, active learning, student and staff interactions, enriching educational experiences, supportive learning environment, and work integrated learning. Seven outcome scales measure higher order thinking, general learning outcomes, general development outcomes, average overall grade, departure intention, overall satisfaction, and career readiness.

AUSSE institutional reporting

The AUSSE Institutional Report provides national (Australia/New Zealand) and Australasian aggregate results by different subgroups. An institution's results on the engagement and outcome scales are given, as well as item-level results using proportions across the response scale. Subgroup analyses are given to support goal-setting and benchmarking. Example reports for a fictitious 'Australasian University' are provided at www.acer.edu.au/research/ausse/australasian-university.

Psychometric properties of the AUSSE

ACER provides a Research Briefing of the psychometric properties of the AUSSE at www.acer.edu.au/documents/aussereports/AUSSE_Research_Briefing_Vol7.pdf.

Institutional and public use of AUSSE results

The provision of SPSS and Excel datasets is intended to support within-institution research, such as group comparisons. Institutions are encouraged to use the AUSSE for external quality assurance reporting, setting targets for specific aspects of student engagement, and benchmarking against appropriate institutions (e.g. those with similar institutions, or those with similar engagement profiles). The capacity of institutions to link responses on the AUSSE to student records supports research on links between student engagement and institutional performance indicators such as retention or attrition.

A series of student engagement enhancement guides targeted at a range of university staff is provided at www.acer.edu.au/research/ausse/enhancement, and a series of research briefings at www.acer.edu.au/research/ausse/reports also focus on a variety of engagement issues.

Publicly available overall annual reports for the Australasian higher education sector are provided at www.acer.edu.au/research/ausse/reports.

United Kingdom: The National Student Survey

Theoretical background

Richardson, Slater, and Wilson (2007) describe the development process of the National Student Survey (NSS) as being informed by the theoretical underpinnings of student feedback instruments including the CEQ, but recognising the limitations of the CEQ specifically for certain groups (e.g. students using distance learning), and on certain aspects of the student experience (e.g. pastoral support). In the first NSS pilot study, 45 five-point Likert items were developed around broad constructs of teaching, assessment, knowledge and skills, course organisation and management, support and advice, learning resources, and overall satisfaction. Graduates from 23 UK institutions ($n = 17,173$) completed the survey. Exploratory factor analysis yielded an interpretable factor structure consisting of 7 scales (teaching, feedback, assessment, generic skills, workload, support, and resources) based on 19 items. In the second pilot study, currently enrolled students from 10 institutions ($n = 9723$) completed a questionnaire consisting of 35 items, to measure 9 aspects of the student experience: teaching, organisation and management, feedback, assessment, personal development, workload, support and advice, learning resources, and other (e.g. careers advice).

The version of the NSS currently used consists of 22 core five-point Likert items to measure teaching, assessment and feedback, academic support, organisation and management, learning resources, personal development, and overall satisfaction with course quality. In recognition that some items may not be applicable in some settings, a response option of 'not applicable' is included.

NSS survey administration, surveying methodology and design

The NSS is commissioned by the Higher Education Funding Council for England (HEFCE) on behalf of the Higher Education Funding Council for Wales (HEFCW), the Department for Employment and Learning, Northern Ireland (DEL), and the Training and Development Agency and Skills for Health, and administered by an independent research company, Ipsos MORI. The NSS is conducted in collaboration with all publicly funded higher education institutions (HEIs) in England, Wales, Northern Ireland, and some Scottish HEIs. Further education colleges (FECs) with directly funded higher education students in England have also been eligible to participate since 2008. All students whose course of study results in undergraduate credits or qualifications (such as Bachelor Degrees, Foundation Degrees, Higher Education Certificates and Diplomas) are surveyed in their final year of study, as well as students who have withdrawn from their final year of study. Institutions taking part in the NSS provide a list of eligible students to Ipsos MORI, who first contact students about completing the NSS by email, followed by postal questionnaires or telephone contact. Data for a particular institution are only published if a 50 per cent response rate is achieved.

NSS institutional reporting

Institutions and student unions receive detailed NSS reports and the anonymised qualitative comments through the Ipsos MORI NSS results website.

Psychometric properties of the NSS

Marsh and Cheng (2008) presented results of exploratory and confirmatory factor analyses of the 2005 and 2006 NSS datasets, concluding that an eight-factor solution provides the best-fitting model. In this model, assessment and feedback items form separate factors. However, Marsh and Cheng also presented multilevel analyses similar to those discussed above for the CEQ, which indicated that, once discipline and student characteristics were controlled, differences between universities explained only about 2.5 per cent of the variance in students' overall satisfaction. On the basis of these results, Marsh and Cheng called into question the appropriateness of the NSS for benchmarking universities, different disciplines within universities, or the same discipline across universities.

Institutional and public use of NSS results

The NSS is a core component of the Quality Assurance Framework developed by HEFCE. HEFCE summarises the key roles of the NSS as gathering feedback on the student experience to support institutional accountability, and informing the choices of future applicants to higher education. Sector-wide reports are published on the HEFCE website (e.g. www.hefce.ac.uk/pubs/hefce/2011/11_11/ provides results from the sixth annual NSS completed in 2010 and a five-year time series).

Investigations of the strengths and limitations of the NSS for such purposes are beginning to appear in peer-reviewed journals (e.g. Ashby, Richardson, & Woodley, 2011; Cheng & Marsh, 2010; Flint, Oxley, Helm, & Bradley, 2009; Richardson *et al.*,

2007), and an annotated bibliography on the NSS and related research on teaching evaluation is available at http://evidencenet.pbworks.com/w/page/28700535/NSS-Resources.

Decision-making by potential applicants to higher education is supported by the NSS Unistats website (http://unistats.direct.gov.uk), which provides breakdowns of NSS results by university and/or field of study, as well as other data (e.g. university admission mark for a particular field of study, percentage of graduates employed subsequent to study).

Numerous third parties use NSS results to construct institutional league tables, including *The Guardian*, *The Times*, and *The Independent* in collaboration with *The Complete University Guide*.

Aligning teaching evaluation instruments within the institution

The student experience and engagement instruments described above play important roles in a large number of institutions of higher and continuing education worldwide. However, these instruments are usually one of several in use in any given institution. Other CTEQ instruments are generally used for feedback to individual teachers, or about individual courses. This raises the question of the degree of alignment between different levels of evaluation. As noted in Chapter 1, many CTEQ instruments are developed in a piecemeal fashion, with little or no reference to guiding theoretical frameworks or other levels of evaluation. This raises challenges for institutions seeking a 'shared language' of teaching evaluation to support quality assessment and improvement.

Barrie, Ginns, and Prosser (2005) describe an institutionally aligned approach to teaching quality assurance based on student learning theory. Implementing this model was the responsibility of the University of Sydney's academic development unit, the Institute for Teaching and Learning. A key part of this model was the development of a three-tier system of teaching evaluation, which took the CEQ as its external reference point. A repeated criticism of the CEQ is its use as a 'lag indicator'. Because graduates are surveyed, this data is time-lagged. Thus, for example, a major curriculum problem at the start of the second year of a three-year programme would not surface in the survey data returned to universities until three years after the event. Additionally, the above surveys gather data on whole-programme experiences. As a result, a graduate's report of a problem with 'clarity of goals and standards' on the CEQ does not inform the university about which courses might be problematic, or in which year of a programme the problem was encountered. Notwithstanding these problems, the CEQ formed a mandated part of teaching evaluation by the University of Sydney; thus, a system was needed that was productively aligned with the CEQ and its institutional and national usage.

The three-tier teaching evaluation system sought to build on the theoretical strengths of the CEQ by designing two additional instruments. The first, the Student Course Experience Questionnaire (SCEQ; Ginns, Prosser, & Barrie, 2007), was a version of the CEQ used to survey a random stratified sample of currently enrolled undergraduate and postgraduate students annually and more recently biannually. The second, the Unit of Study Evaluation (USE; Ginns & Barrie, 2004), operated at the course level, with single items designed to capture the core CEQ and SCEQ constructs (e.g. good teaching, appropriate assessment). This level requires more explanatory and in-depth information on students' experiences to guide curriculum and teaching improvement, but still relates to data on overall programme-level experience gathered by the SCEQ for quality assurance purposes. The design of the USE is distinct in that it combines the quantitative response for each item on a Likert scale with space for comment, allowing teaching staff to triangulate between these two sources of information. University policy is that either the USE or another faculty-wide instrument must be used to evaluate the quality of individual units of study at least once every three years. Barrie *et al.* (2005) argue that this system 'encourages individual academics to focus teaching improvement and curriculum development efforts on important (from the student learning research) aspects of the student learning experience, and on the same aspects that are embodied in the faculties' and university's strategic teaching and learning plans' (pp. 645–646).

Barrie and Ginns (2007) provided evidence for the validity of this system of aligned teaching evaluation by examining the correlations between faculty-level SCEQ and USE aggregate scores. The USE data set consisted of average student ratings on the core CEQ-derived items (clear goals and standards, good teaching, appropriate workload, appropriate assessment and overall satisfaction with unit of study quality, as well as a graduate attributes item based on the equivalent SCEQ scale) of 1820 units of study, collected over a one-year period (2005) taught across 14 faculties ($n= 69,466$ individual responses; response rate = 63.3%). The SCEQ data set consisted of the equivalent faculty-average SCEQ scale ratings for the same 14 faculties, using the 2005 survey ($n = 6501$ individual undergraduate and postgraduate coursework students; response rate = 48.9%).

Initial analyses indicated there were suitable levels of inter-rater agreement (Chan, 1998; Lindell, 2001) at the Faculty level for all SCEQ and USE indices to warrant creating Faculty-level scores from the lower (programme and unit of study) levels of evaluation. Four statistically significant correlations using two-tailed significance tests were found between USE and SCEQ faculty averages for good teaching ($r = 0.77$, $p = 0.001$), clear goals and standards ($r = 0.68$, $p = 0.008$), appropriate workload ($r = 0.77$, $p = 0.001$) and appropriate assessment ($r = 0.91$, $p < 0.001$). The correlation between the scores on the Graduate Attribute Development USE item and scores on the SCEQ Graduate Attributes scale was significant, with a more liberal ($p < 0.10$) Type 1 error rate ($r = 0.45$, $p = 0.042$), as was the correlation between overall satisfaction with unit of study quality and overall satisfaction with programme quality ($r = 0.52$, $p = 0.029$). Thus, 'the aggregated data on students' experiences of a particular aspect of teaching and learning in the subjects they are studying is echoed in their overall experience of that aspect of teaching and learning for the degree those subjects contribute to' (Barrie & Ginns, 2007, p. 282). Such relationships support the expectation that targeted improvements at the subject level should eventually be reflected in improvements in students' experiences at the programme and faculty levels.

Smallwood and Ouimet (2009; see also Ouimet and Smallwood, 2005) describe a similar approach to theoretically and institutionally aligned CTEQ development. Drawing on student engagement theory, the items of the CLASSE (Classroom Survey of Student Engagement) mirror the benchmark scales of the NSSE. Smallwood (2011) argues that measuring variation in student engagement at the course level should support identifying where that variation exists within the department, college and institution. In turn, academic leaders could then use such knowledge to develop initiatives to improve engagement levels, as well as supporting and rewarding those individual faculty, department or college efforts responsible for improvements.

Summary

In this chapter, overviews of four large teaching evaluation surveys – the NSS, the CEQ, the AUSSE, and the NSS – were given. Programmes of evaluation using these surveys are underpinned, but to a greater or lesser extent, by substantial theories of higher education: student engagement theory and student learning theory.

While each theory draws on substantial research in support of key arguments, the primary use of these surveys is not primary but institutional research (i.e. informing ongoing quality improvement and quality assurance functions within institutions and across institutions). Aligning the multiple levels of evaluation can be achieved by careful 'mirroring' of key teaching and learning constructs across multiple instruments, supporting developing the quality of the overall programme experience by understanding how that quality varies across individual courses.

Chapter 12

Institutional use of teaching evaluation data

Systemic use of evaluation data

This chapter deals with procedures institutions might set up to ensure that effective use is made of evaluation data. Results from Marsh (1987, 2007) suggest that CTEQ data for individuals or groups of teachers are normally fairly stable over time. There is, though, evidence of improvement when there is counselling about the results (Marsh & Roche, 1993; Penny & Coe, 2004). These results suggest that administering questionnaires on a regular basis and simply handing over results to the respective teacher may not in itself be sufficient to improve the quality of learning.

Many universities have developed schemes that make routine use of CTEQ data, but in most cases this does not seem to have much, if anything, to do with the research cited above. The schemes referred to are the routine staff appraisal exercises that many colleges have introduced. Policy documents, at least, usually require teaching to be taken into account. CTEQ results are usually the principal, and often the only, data relating to teaching used in the exercise.

We will make little further reference to staff appraisal schemes here because we are not sure whether they have much to do with improving teaching quality through the use of evaluation. The jury is still out on whether staff appraisal impacts on teaching and learning. Clear conclusions are unlikely as there must be wide variation both within and between institutions.

Instead, this chapter deals largely with the use of programme-level evaluation data and of schemes that try to ensure that these are made use of at departmental and/or institutional level. This clearly does fall within the evaluation ambit of this book, and there is a literature to draw upon.

Importance of diagnostic power in questionnaire

This chapter gives an example from a university at which one of us previously worked. It shows how the university made use of programme-level evaluation data for quality enhancement purposes. Principles are drawn that can be applied in other contexts.

The evaluation system must be based on regular use of a suitable programme-level instrument. This example made use of the student engagement questionnaire (SEQ), given in Chapter 3. The design of this was guided by four principles (or criteria):

1   The instrument needed to be cognisant of research into teaching and learning envi-
     ronments. This led to recognition of the breadth of constructs encompassed within
     an environment that was capable of nurturing graduate attributes.
2   That body of research into teaching and learning guided the design of a section
     seeking feedback on perceptions of the quality of elements of the teaching and
     learning environment.
3   The questionnaire also needed a section seeking feedback on students' perceptions
     of the development, during their programme, of a set of generic graduate attrib-
     utes.
4   It needed to be sufficiently diagnostic to identify strengths and weaknesses, making
     it possible for feedback to lead to an action plan for improvement.

Criterion 2 implies the inclusion of a range of scales representing the breadth of
constructs implicit in a learning environment and able to provide diagnostic feedback
on teaching and curriculum design. Criterion 3 requires a scale for each targeted graduate attribute. Many universities have now drawn up a list of attributes they expect
students to have acquired on graduation.

A design restraint is that students are reluctant to complete questionnaires which
they consider overly long. The resultant questionnaire, therefore, needed to include
vital constructs without appearing daunting to complete. This implies having a wide
range of scales, as a teaching and learning environment is best envisaged as a complex
multifaceted phenomenon. In addition, graduates need to have acquired a diverse set
of attributes. As many scales are needed, it is necessary to restrict each scale to a small
number of items to prevent the questionnaire becoming too long.

The attribute scales included were:

- critical thinking;
- creative thinking;
- self-managed learning;
- adaptability;
- problem-solving;
- communication skills;
- interpersonal skills and groupwork; and
- computer literacy.

The teaching and learning environment scales included were:

- active learning;
- teaching for understanding;
- feedback to assist learning;
- assessment;
- relationship between teachers and students;
- workload;
- relationship with other students;
- cooperative learning; and
- coherence of curriculum.

Model of development of graduate attributes

The questionnaire design was based on a model of the development of graduate attributes by a teaching and learning environment providing practice in the use of the attribute. Such a model is very appropriate for use within a quality enhancement system. Specifying a set of desired graduate attributes effectively means that a university sets a target that all of its graduates should have acquired the attributes by the time they complete their programmes. The model shows that the university will come closer to the target if the teaching and learning environment is improved.

To provide evidence that the model was applicable, it was tested with data from the questionnaire using structural equation modelling (SEM). SEM models are tested by examining the goodness of fit of the model against a collection of data measuring the variables included in the model. Assessment of model fit was based on multiple criteria including both absolute misfit and relative fit indexes. The absolute misfit indexes included the root mean square error of approximation (RMSEA; Browne & Cudeck, 1993) and the standardised root mean squared residual (SRMR; Bentler, 1995). The relative goodness-of-fit index used in the study was the comparative fit index (CFI; Bentler, 1990). A model with RMSEA<0.08, SRMR<0.08 and CFI>0.95 would be considered an excellent fit to the data.

The goodness-of-fit indexes for this model were RMSEA = 0.057 (90% CI = 0.052, 0.062), SRMR = 0.042 and CFI = 0.943, which indicates a very good fit to the observed data. The standardised parameter estimates of the model are shown in Figure 12.1. All of the paths between the latent variables were statistically significant, except the one from teaching to working together. Moreover, the directions of the all the paths were positive as anticipated.

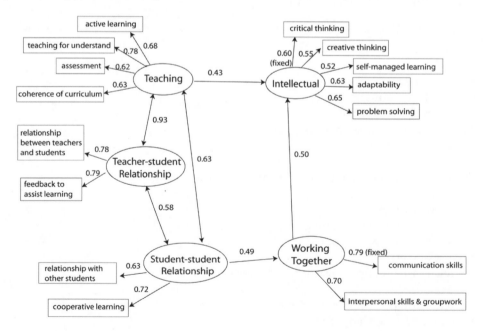

Figure 12.1 SEM model of the teaching and learning environment influencing the development of a set of attributes

Diagnostic power for quality assurance

The fit of the data to the model is of considerable value when advising departments on results from the questionnaire. Potential improvements in aspects of teaching and learning can be linked to better attainment of graduate attributes.

The existence of a coherent model also improves the diagnostic power of the instrument. Scales are related together in ways which can be understood from the model. Patterns of data can be explained.

An example is the pattern of results for the common problem of overly didactic teaching. This commonly results in low scores on scales for *active learning*, *teaching for understanding* and *critical thinking*. *Assessment* often rates low too as didactic teaching is often coupled with the type of assessment which tests recall.

Use of the questionnaire in a quality enhancement initiative

Regular administration of the SEQ was the lynchpin of a quality enhancement initiative. Each undergraduate programme was surveyed in alternate years with data collected from all first and third year students in the programme. In most cases the third year corresponded with the final year.

Degree programmes were reasonably discrete, so this was a convenient unit for collecting data and providing feedback. For most degrees, the substantial majority of courses were taught by the host department, so a programme of study was well defined and it was clear where responsibility lay for teaching quality.

When programme structures are more flexible, with a wide choice of course combinations, it can be more difficult to assign responsibility for programme-level results, particularly in the early stages of a degree. In such situations it is useful to ask students to indicate their major on the questionnaire forms. As long as returns are sufficient, feedback can then be provided to disciplines.

A typical example might be a general BA degree, in which students can pick from a wide range of courses from the arts faculty, or even other faculties. Giving feedback at the degree or faculty level often masks diagnostic information which is apparent at discipline level. This is particularly so in faculties like arts, with very diverse disciplines and styles of teaching. Relying on course evaluation from CTEQ instruments is also unsatisfactory because they do not normally give information about the development of graduate attributes or curriculum issues.

Presenting feedback

Feedback was supplied to departments by using a profile of the form shown in Figure 12.2. The departments received a profile in this form for year 1 and year 3 responses. They were also provided with a complete set of responses to the two open-ended questions.

The feedback profile included frequencies and means for each scale. Scales are shown, rather than items, so as to reduce the amount of information presented to a manageable amount. Presenting scales is also consistent with the psychometric design of the instrument, featuring a scale for each relevant construct.

Frequencies are shown graphically. The questionnaire uses a five-point scale, but for

Feedback on Programme X (Year 3, 2003) from Student Engagement Project

Development of capabilities

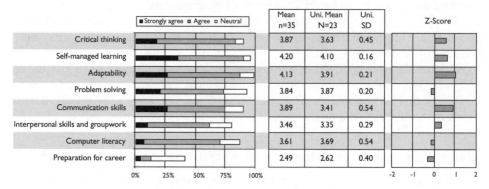

	Mean n=35	Uni. Mean N=23	Uni. SD
Critical thinking	3.87	3.63	0.45
Self-managed learning	4.20	4.10	0.16
Adaptability	4.13	3.91	0.21
Problem solving	3.84	3.87	0.20
Communication skills	3.89	3.41	0.54
Interpersonal skills and groupwork	3.46	3.35	0.29
Computer literacy	3.61	3.69	0.54
Preparation for career	2.49	2.62	0.40

Teaching and learning environment

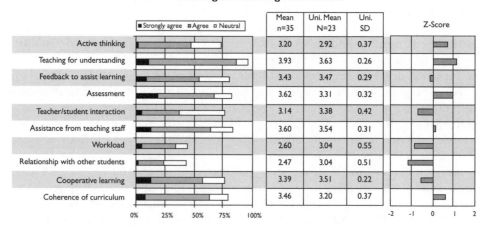

	Mean n=35	Uni. Mean N=23	Uni. SD
Active thinking	3.20	2.92	0.37
Teaching for understanding	3.93	3.63	0.26
Feedback to assist learning	3.43	3.47	0.29
Assessment	3.62	3.31	0.32
Teacher/student interaction	3.14	3.38	0.42
Assistance from teaching staff	3.60	3.54	0.31
Workload	2.60	3.04	0.55
Relationship with other students	2.47	3.04	0.51
Cooperative learning	3.39	3.51	0.22
Coherence of curriculum	3.46	3.20	0.37

Figure 12.2 Feedback profile for the case-study programme

graphic simplicity, only frequencies for strongly agree, agree and neutral are shown. An alternative approach is to collapse strongly agree and agree, and likewise disagree and strongly disagree, as in Figure 12.3. See also the discussion of the percentage agreement metric in the Appendix.

Each scale score for the programme is compared with the overall university mean for all surveyed programmes. The comparison is shown graphically in the column at the right of the feedback sheet. This gives z-scores, which are the number of standard deviations from the mean.

It will be noted that university means vary quite widely. This is mainly a feature of the nature of the variable. For example, ratings for workload are invariably on the low side. The wording of an item also has some influence on overall scores. Comparison with the university mean, therefore, gives a useful relative measure of the significance or meaning of a score. The comparison also benchmarks a programme against the rest of the university.

The feedback profile shown in Figure 12.2 is illustrative of the diagnostic power of the instrument. The z-scores indicate that the department has a generally good record in teaching. All capability development scales are ahead of or close to the university mean. Scales in the teaching and learning environment part of the questionnaire show marked variations in the z-scores, meaning that it is possible to identify relative strengths and weaknesses. Note also that the results display a logical pattern of combinations, which is expanded upon in the case study below.

The results profile is from the first year that the questionnaire was administered. There is therefore only one year of data that can be displayed. In subsequent years the profile displayed results for the current and previous administrations of the instrument. It was therefore possible to identify improvements.

More sophisticated data presentation

As a digression from the case, Figure 12.3 shows a way of presenting results from a single scale that gives more information than that shown in Figure 12.2. In practice, there would be a bar like this for each scale in the questionnaire. The method of presentation allows this year's results to be compared with last year's, and the results for the programme in question to be compared with those for the rest of the university.

Figure 12.3 A way of presenting data giving more information

Moving from left to right, the first column gives the name of the scale. Then come the bar charts showing the frequency distributions. As explained above, strongly agree and agree are combined, as are disagree and strongly disagree. The upper bar gives the frequencies for this year, and the lower bar those for the previous administration of the questionnaire.

The next column gives the mean scores for the programme, again with the current administration results above those for the previous administration. The next column gives the mean scores for the university. The next compares the mean scores for the programme to those for the university by means of effect sizes. +S means a small effect size above the university mean and N implies a negligible effect size difference. The penultimate column compares the results for the programme for this year and last. +M shows that there has been an increase of a medium effect size. The final column is a reminder of which results are compared in the upper and lower bars.

Effect sizes were calculated using the standardised mean difference, or Cohen's d. Effect sizes were designated according to the following ranges: negligible, $d = 0$ to 0.09; small, $d = 0.10$ to 0.29; medium, $d = 0.30$ to 0.49; large, $d \geq 0.50$. These cut-off values are a little lower than those commonly used in research, reflecting the difficulty of achieving meaningful improvement in teaching and learning over time.

Meeting for diagnosis and action

Returning to the case, shortly after the feedback profiles were released to departments, an appointment was made for one of the two professors in the educational development centre to meet with the department chair and other members of the department with responsibilities for teaching coordination. At this meeting there was a discussion of feedback profiles, the listings of qualitative comments and other available feedback.

Data were treated as indicative, rather than absolute, and needing intelligent inter-pretation in the particular context of the programme. The meetings therefore took the form of interactive dialogues. The aim was to identify strengths, which could be built upon, and which could inform other sections of the university, by being models of good practice. There was also an attempt to identify potential areas for improvement. If there was agreement on these, an action plan would be formulated.

Consultancy strategies

Anyone who has been involved in discussing evaluation data with senior staff will realise that the process is often not as straightforward as the preceding paragraph might imply. As with any educational development initiative, initial reactions vary considerably. Departments with better results usually find them more convincing. If feedback is less positive, the credibility of the process is usually challenged. Those most in need of help tend to be the least willing to take notice.

There is a literature on counseling individual teachers on the feedback from CTEQs. Penny and Coe (2004) performed a meta-analysis of results from experiments on the effectiveness of consultation accompanying feedback from questionnaires. Their conclusion included eight consultation strategies they found to be effective (Penny & Coe, 2004, p. 245):

1   active involvement of teachers in the learning process;
2   use of multiple sources of information;
3   interaction with peers;
4   sufficient time for dialogue and interaction;
5   use of teacher self-ratings;
6   use of high-quality feedback information;
7   examination of conception of teaching; and
8   setting of improvement goals.

There is considerably less literature on consultation strategies at institutional or programme level. This section contains ideas built up from many such meetings in three universities. It should be noted that they are generally consistent with the eight strategies above.

First: who do you meet with? Insist on meeting with senior staff, such as the head of department and/or dean, plus staff responsible for teaching coordination. It can be positive to also include interested teachers, but not these alone. There is no point meeting with those without the responsibility or power to implement change.

Teaching often follows similar patterns within broad discipline areas, so similar issues often arise. It can therefore be effective to arrange meetings by faculty or school. If, however, programmes are large, fairly discrete and show distinct differences, it is probably worth meeting by programme. For example, in my current university, meetings by faculty work well for arts, science and engineering; however, the medical faculty contains medicine, nursing and Chinese medicine, which are quite different, so separate meetings work better.

Start by asking the department for their interpretation of the data. It is better if diagnoses come from them, so that you do not have to create the impression of coming along to present a report card. Have your own diagnosis ready, though, as many find it easier to rely on those who are used to interpreting such data.

Take into account all available data. This will include other available evaluation data, such as qualitative data from sources such as staff–student consultative committees or web forums. It also includes perceptions of staff in the department about their programme. This is legitimate and useful information.

Ask if there are contextual influences that could affect results. It is important that results are treated as indicators to be interpreted in context, rather than absolute data.

Start with praising positive aspects – there is usually something to be found. Try to build on strengths, rather than asking for weaknesses to be remedied. If in a faculty meeting with several departments, look for models of good practice in constituent departments.

Try to tack improvements onto changes that will have to take place anyway. Academics are reluctant to make change for the sake of it – they have better things to do. Examples of potential prompts are starting a new programme, the need to obtain accreditation or the need to change the curriculum because of major changes in the field. Hong Kong is about to undergo a change from three- to four-year undergraduate degrees. This has made it possible to pursue major renovation and quality enhancement initiatives.

There should be some record of what was discussed and agreed in the meeting. This should note positive aspects from the evaluation. Ideally it should address aspects conducive to improvement through an action plan for dealing with them.

When consultation over programme-level evaluation is introduced it is inevitable that reactions to the initiative will vary in the initial stages. Our own experiences suggest that attitudes can change, but it does take time and is by no means easy. Working in conjunction with, and having support from, university senior management is essential.

Case study

A case study is now presented which shows how the collection of diagnostic feedback through evaluation informs and facilitates the enhancement of teaching and learning quality. The case is of the programme with the third year feedback profile shown in

Figure 12.2. The following is an extract from the meeting notes from the 2003 round of the survey, showing how some of the recommendations resulted in an improved teaching and learning environment.

Extract from meeting summary, 2003

Areas that may need further attention:

- Inconsistency appears in students' perceived low interpersonal and groupwork skills despite them having been involved in a great number of group projects.
- A low perception on problem solving and career preparation.
- Heavy workload.

Suggestions for ways forward were made during the meeting:

1   The compulsory first year courses, such as X and Y, could be examined to see if practical applications could be stressed more in order for them to become a means of developing critical thinking and problem solving ability.
2   The new module, which introduces 'Z', with guest speakers sharing their experience in their profession, seems likely to improve problem-solving and career preparation.
3   Examine the nature of group projects to see why they appear to be having negative effects on student relationships and cooperative learning. Possibly the introduction of peer assessment of contributions to the group might help.

Comparison of mean scores between 2003 and 2005 enables the department to monitor changes. In this case it can be seen that issues highlighted in the 2003 meeting notes have been acted upon in the way suggested and that significant improvements have resulted. This has been noted in the extract from the 2005 meeting notes.

Extract from meeting summary 2005

Compared to the 2003 data there were significant increases in the ratings for problem solving for both first and third years. This was attributed to teachers stressing applications to solve typical problems. This improvement is worth communicating to the Department for wider application.

There were also very major advances in student–student relationships and cooperative learning. This was attributed to better handling of group projects and the wider adoption of the assessment of individual contributions to group projects. It could be worthwhile to suggest that the purpose and anticipated outcomes of projects are clearly explained to students each time as they are a time-consuming, but very worthwhile, form of learning.

The improvements in the identified aspects of teaching and learning are shown graphically in Figure 12.4, which compares z-scores for 2003 and 2005 for the scales corresponding to the issues identified in the 2003 summary. It can be seen that there have been significant improvements.

Year 3 students:

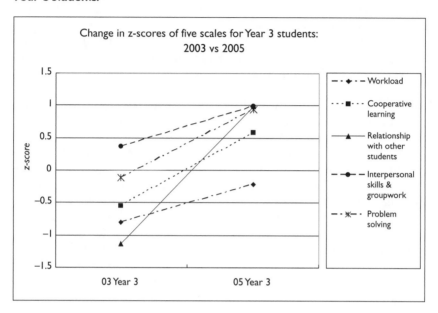

Year 1 students:

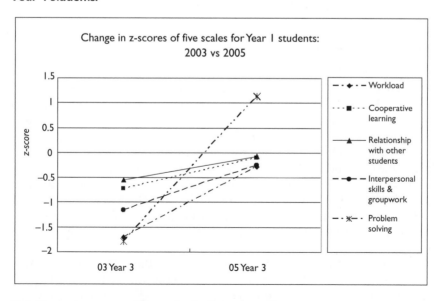

Figure 12.4 Change in z-scores of five scales for Programme X

Evaluation as part of a teaching quality enhancement initiative

Evaluation can be an integral part of a university's initiatives to promote teaching qual-ity. The main roles of the evaluation are to diagnose potential areas for improvement and hopefully to provide evidence that there has been improvement.

Educational development units are often responsible for conducting the evaluations. Whether they are or not, there should be good coordination between their efforts to enhance the quality of teaching and learning, such as academic staff development activ-ities, and the use of institutional evaluation data.

An example of a coordinated campaign is given in Kember (2009). The initiative aimed to promote student-centred forms of learning. There were five main facets to the venture, working in conjunction with each other:

1   Interviews were conducted with 18 award-winning teachers. There was evidence that they utilised active approaches to teaching and learning, which provided compelling evidence to back the campaign.
2   A compulsory course for new junior teachers was started. Material for the course was derived from the award-winning teachers. The course included a group project in which the participants were required to model a form of innovative teaching.
3   Teaching development grants were available to support projects, a fair proportion of which involved the introduction of student-centred forms of learning.
4   There was programme-level evaluation utilising the SEQ, underpinned by a supporting infrastructure along the lines described in this chapter.
5   Programme reviews were introduced. Each undergraduate degree had to be reviewed once every six years. The self-reflection document, which was the start-ing point for the review, had to include data from the programme evaluation.

Evidence for the effectiveness of the overall initiative came from increases in university-level mean scores for relevant scales of the SEQ.

Benchmarking models

There are a variety of ways CTEQs, programme-level evaluations and university-level evaluations might be used for benchmarking. In the case of Australia, the development of the Course Experience Questionnaire (CEQ) had the goal of providing 'quantitative data which permit ordinal ranking of units in different institutions, within comparable subject areas, in terms of perceived teaching quality' (Ramsden, 1991, pp. 132–133). The higher education benchmarking exercise by McKinnon, Walker, and Davis (2000) resulted in the CEQ being chosen to benchmark Australian departments and universi-ties on student experience of teaching, goals and standards, assessment practices, workload, generic skills and overall satisfaction (Benchmark 6.10). According to McKinnon *et al.*, 'Inter-university comparisons are most sensibly made across like fields of study and disciplines, or with universities that have broadly comparable profiles' (p.86).

On this basis, the Australian government mandated that all graduates of Australian universities receive the CEQ within a few months of graduation. However, as mentioned in Chapter 11, the suitability of the CEQ for this purpose has been questioned by Marsh, Ginns, Morin, Nagengast, and Martin (2011). Their analyses of the 2001 CEQ national dataset found few universities or schools/departments differed significantly or substantially from the grand mean rating. These results align with other investigations of programme-level instruments, such as the National Student Survey (Marsh & Cheng, 2008), the Postgraduate Research Experience Questionnaire (Marsh, Rowe, & Martin, 2002) and the Student Research Experience Questionnaire (Ginns, Marsh, Behnia, Cheng, & Scalas, 2009). Taken together, these results indicate that more research is needed to develop teaching performance indicators that distinguish reliably at the level of the programme, school/department and/or university.

An alternative approach to benchmarking using evaluation data is to investigate changes over time using an action research cycle, introduced in Chapter 10. Thus, staff in a degree programme, school/department or university would gather data on the student experience and/or approaches to learning (as well as other indicators), consider the data, generate and implement changes in teaching and learning, and then gather data again to examine whether those changes had the desired effect. This is the approach resulting in the changes shown in Figure 12.4.

Similar longitudinal evaluations at the school, department or faculty levels using student learning theory-derived instruments are described in Barrie, Ginns, and Prosser (2005), Gordon and Debus (2002), Gordon, Debus, Dillon, and Arthur-Kelly (2006), Govendir, Ginns, Symons, and Tammen (2009), Taylor and Canfield (2007) and Tucker, Jones, and Straker (2008). In contrast, Cope and Staehr (2008) describe a longitudinal evaluation of changes in student approaches to learning in response to curriculum changes in the context of a single course.

It should be noted that, in each of these cases of learning and teaching action research, changes when observed tended to be small and relatively slow to emerge, rather than large and immediate. Authors such as Prentice and Miller (1992) and Breaugh (2003) have called for nuanced considerations of effect sizes, especially in applied fields such as education and health. In situations where the dependent variable is complex (e.g. overall programme evaluations, driven by a wide variety of different variables), the independent variable is diffuse (e.g. a number of co-occurring interventions), even quite small effect sizes (e.g. standardised mean differences of 0.10 to 0.20) might be considered practically or educationally significant.

One of the benefits of this approach is the potential for clear goal-setting about desired changes in the quality of teaching and learning. There is a strong evidence base for the use of specific, difficult but achievable goals by individuals as well as organisations (Locke & Latham, 2002, 2006; O'Neill & Conzemius, 2006; Rodgers & Hunter, 1991). Goals for improvement could be based on the current levels of student perceptions, engagement, and/or approaches. For example, in the most recent survey of a programme, imagine that only 40 per cent of respondents respond to the active learning scale items using the 'agree' or 'strongly agree' options. This provides a current 'percentage agreement metric' benchmark (see the Appendix for more on calculating this metric) of 40 per cent. A time-based, realistic but achievable goal may be to improve to a percentage agreement result of 70 per cent by the time of the next survey in two years.

Closing the feedback loop: Communicating with students

Results of CTEQs are returned to academic staff as a matter of course, but an extra step in the process – feedback to students who gave the feedback in the first place – is often missing. Watson (2003) notes that this step in the evaluation cycle performs several functions. These include encouraging participation in further research (because the value of individuals' responses and the importance of their participation are publicly recognised), increasing confidence in the results and worth of the research when tangible actions for improvement are described, and fulfilling the ethical responsibility to debrief respondents.

Closing the feedback loop can operate at multiple levels. Individual course coordinators are responsible for communicating with students about strengths and areas for improvement following evaluations. While students are still enrolled, learning management system (e.g. Blackboard) announcements may be used, while class enrolment email lists might be used to contact the majority of students (with the exception of those who have discontinued or graduated) after the end of a semester. Several examples of such communications with students are given at www.itl.usyd.edu.au/use/feedback_response.htm.

For programme-level evaluations (e.g. the CEQ, NSSE, AUSSE or NSS), responsibilities for interpreting and acting upon student feedback may rest with more senior staff members, such as associate deans (learning and teaching). Watson (2003) reviews the variety of methods institutions use to discuss results with students, including discussions with student representatives, leaflets, newsletters, posters around campus, student handbooks, announcements on learning management systems, and emails from senior staff (e.g. deans, provosts).

Feedback loops at multiple levels can and should operate simultaneously. Tucker, Jones, and Straker (2008) present a case study of a school of physiotherapy's improvement of Course Experience Questionnaire (CEQ) results over four years, based on the development and use of a version of the CEQ for currently enrolled students and an associated CTEQ. Academics responsible for different units first reflected on and discussed results with peers, then created a summary report describing key themes from the student feedback. Students also received an outline of proposed changes for the following year and how these were linked to student feedback (Tucker, Jones, Straker, & Cole, 2003).

Conclusion

This chapter has concentrated on the evaluation of undergraduate programmes or degrees. The same principles apply to other levels of offering and other levels of award.

The first important consideration lies in the design of the questionnaire and in its administration, processing and reporting. This has been the subject of the first part of the book.

The chapter then argued that there needs to be consultancy and advice over the results. It is suggested that this is part of a regular and systematic process. Meetings should be arranged with relevant senior staff shortly after results become available. Ideally, these meetings will lead to specific plans for action. Support for implementing these plans can come from the staff and activities of the educational development unit.

Chapter 13

Conclusion

Introduction

This book has taken a wide-ranging perspective in approaching evaluation of teaching and learning in higher education. It has advocated diverse approaches including both quantitative and qualitative methods. It has catered to institutional evaluators as well as those engaged in the scholarship of teaching.

Taking this wide perspective has meant that there have been several strands through the book. The first chapter showed logical paths through the book for the two main types of reader: the institutional evaluator and those conducting SoTL.

As a result of the diverse perspective, the audiences with differing needs and the resulting strands of development, the book has not followed the classical format of progressively building an argument chapter by chapter. When this classical format is followed, the conclusion has the logical function of bringing together the step-by-step argument and drawing it together into the finale. Drawing our inter-twining strands together into a coherent whole is more difficult.

Instead we will deal with some common themes that have run through the book. We have chosen in particular ones that have sometimes been implicit and would benefit from being made more explicit. We will also provide a summary of each chapter to help the reader review the threads that have come through the book. This is mainly in the form of a series of questions, which each chapter attempts to answer.

Purpose of evaluation

Evaluation was originally defined as the collection and analysis of data for the purpose of decision-making. Colleges are continually seeking to adapt to a changing environment and new demands. Evaluation can therefore be seen as a mechanism that informs the constant stream of decisions that have to be made. As, arguably, the prime function of universities, teaching and learning is surely a vital part of the evaluation and decision-making process.

The book has been written with two audiences in mind: the institutional evaluator, and those engaged in the scholarship of teaching and learning. The role of the institutional evaluator is to provide evidence to support decision-making about teaching and learning. This implies collecting feedback at course, programme and institutional levels from relevant stakeholders with well-designed instruments. We have also argued that qualitative data should be more widely used in institutional evaluation. It is important that information from institutional evaluation is presented clearly and succinctly, in a way that facilitates decision-making.

Scholarship in teaching and learning has become increasingly popular. The most common format is when a teacher tries out a new form of teaching in a course he or she teaches. Such efforts are to be applauded and encouraged, especially since teaching in higher education has tended to be very conservative, relying over-heavily on didactic forms of teaching, which are usually less effective than student-centred forms of learning.

Focus on quality enhancement

Throughout the book, we have seen evaluation as having a justification through having a role in improving the quality of teaching and learning. At the institutional level, teaching evaluation is commonly seen as the main plank of quality assurance. We have argued that many colleges would benefit from a wider perspective in the use of evaluation for quality enhancement.

Improving the quality of teaching and learning is most commonly the aim of SoTL projects. Teachers normally introduce new forms of teaching and learning because they believe it is more likely to result in the achievement of particular desired learning outcomes.

Focus on aims

Evaluation for SoTL projects needs to be specifically designed to focus on the aims of a project. This normally means asking questions about the type of learning introduced and the intended learning outcomes. Unless this is the case, it will not be possible to determine whether the project has met its aims.

Aims at the institutional level may be more diffuse, although many universities have taken an outcomes-based approach, and it has also become common for colleges to have a statement of the graduate attributes students are expected to have acquired by graduation. If these types of outcomes have been stated, it is logical to evaluate their attainment.

Multiple methods

Triangulation is most commonly thought of as gathering data through multiple methods. The rationale for its use is that concurrent evidence from several sources is more convincing than evidence from one source.

Multiple methods are often used in SoTL projects. Collecting quantitative data through a questionnaire and qualitative data through interviews is probably the most common combination. We hope that use of this book will strengthen the use of such combinations of methods, as few researchers are trained in both quantitative and qualitative methods.

At the institutional level, many colleges use just questionnaires. Experience has shown that qualitative data can help frame the investigation of newly emerging topics by revealing key issues. Qualitative data can also provide more nuanced in-depth information to provide greater insights to questionnaire results.

Multiple perspectives

Good practice in research and evaluation also suggests that obtaining evidence from several sources will be more convincing than that obtained from one source only – again, as long as the evidence is consistent. This is another form of triangulation.

Students are the ones commonly asked for their perspectives on teaching and learning. In many cases they are the only ones. The case for moving beyond the student voice is possibly not as strong as that for adopting multiple methods in the other form of triangulation. Teachers have their say through giving their interpretation and commenting upon student feedback. Graduates or alumni have a perspective somewhat different from current students if asked relevant questions. Employers are the other obvious stakeholders, but gathering data from employers can be difficult.

Summary

Table 13.1 Summary of themes in the book

1. Evaluation principles	What is evaluation? Why is teaching and learning evaluated? What use is made of teaching and learning evaluation data?
2. Questionnaire design	Principles of writing questionnaire items. How do you ensure a questionnaire is reliable, valid and has diagnostic power?
3. Questionnaires	Lists, discusses the design of, and explains how to use results from the following standard questionnaires: exemplary teacher course questionnaire, knowledge questionnaire, skills questionnaire, experiential learning questionnaire, revised study process questionnaire, reflection questionnaire, student engagement questionnaire, taught postgraduate experience questionnaire, graduate capabilities survey, tailored outcomes-based surveys and the blended learning environment questionnaire.
4. Item bank	An extensive item bank for constructing questionnaires.
5. Collecting and processing questionnaire data	What are the advantages and disadvantages of administering questionnaires in-class, online and by post? Can sampling help reduce questionnaire fatigue?
6. Collection of qualitative data	What methods are available for gathering qualitative data? How can you conduct interviews which yield informative data? How do you plan a qualitative project?
7. Analysis of qualitative data	How do you analyse qualitative data? This chapter attempts to take the mystique out of this question by explaining and illustrating the following steps in analysis: exploring, noting, theorizing, classifying, coding, conclusion drawing, verifying and reporting.
8. Observation	How can classroom observation provide useable evidence for SoTL projects? We provide reflection protocols for small and large classes, which can be used by the teacher or a mentor.
9. Use of assessment for evaluation	Why does assessment need to be standards-based rather than norm-based, if it is to provide viable evidence? We provide three examples of assessment rubrics: the SOLO taxonomy for determining the structural quality of an essay, a four-category protocol for determining the level of reflection, and a protocol for assessing the quality of a presentation. Finally, we look at how concept inventories can be used.

10. Using evaluation data for the scholarship of teaching	How can all of the information in the previous chapters be put together into a SoTL project? Is it better for you to use an experimental design, action research or the survey method? We present two case studies: the first an action research approach to curriculum reform using longitudinal SPQ results as evidence, and the second using survey methods collecting data with several instruments presented in Chapter 3.
11. International perspectives on teaching evaluation	What are national practices for evaluation in Australasia, the UK and the USA? What are the origins and theoretical bases of the instruments and how can the results be used in practice?
12. Institutional use of teaching evaluation data	How can institutions ensure that evaluation data is effectively made use of so that there is enhancement of quality in teaching and learning? How can results be presented clearly and concisely, so that they can be interpreted diagnostically? What are effective strategies for counseling at the programme level?

Advanced statistical methods for teaching evaluation data

This appendix provides a conceptual overview of statistical methods that might be applied to teaching evaluation data. The goal of the chapter is to orient readers to the use of such analyses, particularly for SoTL purposes. Inferential statistics are discussed with reference to an exemplar study, and appropriate research methodology and statistics texts for further study are provided.

Types of variables

At the heart of statistical analysis is the idea of a *variable*. Broadly speaking, a variable is something that can be assigned a value, but the inherent meaning of a given value will depend on the type of variable. Depending on the type of variable, different kinds of statistical analyses will be appropriate for testing ideas about teaching quality or SoTL.

Hair, Anderson, Tatham, and Black (1998) make a fundamental distinction between two types of data: *non-metric* (qualitative) and *metric* (quantitative). Non-metric data describe different categories or properties of members of a dataset. Thus, in a dataset of 100 students, the *nominal* variable 'degree' may identify 60 students doing a Bachelor of Arts with the value '1'; 30 students doing a Bachelor of Science with the value '2'; and 10 students doing a Bachelor of Engineering with the value '3'. The values 1, 2 and 3 of this variable do not have any intrinsic numerical value. An *ordinal* variable is one in which values have a clear ordering (e.g. category 3 is greater than category 2, which is greater than category 1). However, in an ordinal variable, there is no clear 'zero' point, and the space between different categories is not necessarily equal. For example, different degree categories may be generally recognised as constituting a higher or lower level of knowledge of a field. Hence, having a Masters coursework degree should reflect more understanding of a field than an undergraduate degree, which in turn should reflect more understanding than a diploma. However, the exact differences between these presumed levels of understanding may not be obvious.

Metric data, on the other hand, describe differences between members of a dataset in amount or degree. An *interval* scale and a *ratio* scale both produce metric data; for both types of scale, differences between adjacent points on the scale (e.g. 3–4 vs. 5–6) will be equal, unlike differences on an ordinal scale. The major difference between the two types of metric scale is that a ratio scale (e.g. height) has a true zero point, while an interval scale (e.g. the Celsius scale) does not.

A common concern for many researchers is whether to treat data from one or more

Likert items – commonly used in educational research – as ordinal or interval variables. This is a decision that will affect decision-making about subsequent statistical analysis (see Hair *et al.*, 1998, pp. 20–21, for an example of a decision tree). However, this confuses the notion of a Likert item with a Likert scale. A Likert scale score is created from participants' responses to several items using Likert-type response categories, most often using a simple average. Often, such a scale score will approximate an interval scale, justifying parametric rather than non-parametric statistical analyses. For a review of key issues in this debate, see Carifio and Perla (2008).

Descriptive statistics

When we use *descriptive statistics*, our goal is to briefly summarise the most important characteristics of a dataset. Some key descriptive statistics are discussed in this section.

Frequency tables

A frequency table is a method for seeing 'at a glance' the characteristics of a variable, such as a response to a teaching evaluation question. Imagine you've administered a single teaching evaluation question with 5 response options – 'strongly disagree' (1), 'disagree' (2), 'neutral' (3), 'agree' (4), and 'strongly agree' (5). Fifty students respond to your short survey, and you input the data into a statistics programme such as SPSS. A frequency table (available through 'Descriptive Statistics') might look like this:

Table A.1 A frequency table

		The teacher explained things in ways I could understand.			
		Frequency	*Per cent*	*Valid per cent*	*Cumulative per cent*
Valid	1.00	9	18.0	18.4	18.4
	2.00	20	40.0	40.8	59.2
	3.00	7	14.0	14.3	73.5
	4.00	8	16.0	16.3	89.8
	5.00	4	8.0	8.2	98.0
	6.00	1	2.0	2.0	100.0
	Total	49	98.0	100.0	
Missing	System	1	2.0		
Total		50	100.0		

A frequency table will give you the frequency of different responses (in this case, 1 to 5 responses) to the question, and the percentage of the whole made up by different responses. If there are missing responses, these will also be displayed. But perhaps the best reason for examining your data using frequency tables is that they should alert you to *out-of-range responses*. In the table above, note that there is one '6' response – this was not a valid response on our 1–5 scale, and should be considered a mistake to be tracked down and corrected in the dataset. Initial inspection of the data and 'data cleaning' are extremely important if we want reliable and valid final results.

The mean (or average) score

This is calculated by adding all the responses, then dividing this figure by the number of responses. Imagine we had the following set of 'strongly disagree' (1), 'neutral' (2), or 'strongly agree' responses to the question, 'Overall, I was satisfied with the quality of this degree programme':

1, 1, 1, 2, 2, 2, 2, 2, 3, 3, 3, 3, 3, 3, 3

The mean would be calculated as follows:

$$\text{Mean score} = (1+1+1+2+2+2+2+2+3+3+3+3+3+3+3)/15$$
$$= 34/15$$
$$= 2.27$$

Standard deviation

The standard deviation gives us a sense of the variability in a set of scores. It is defined as the square root of the variance of a sum of scores. We often use the standard deviation to describe the variability of a set of scores, rather than the variance, because the standard deviation is in the same metric (e.g. a 1–5 scale) as the mean score.

Considering the size of the standard deviation of student responses to different teaching evaluation numerical questions gives us a sense of whether students tend to share the same opinion about a particular issue (small standard deviation), as opposed to having divergent opinions (larger standard deviation). For example, consider these three different patterns of 'strongly disagree' (1), 'neutral' (2), or 'strongly agree (3)' responses:

Table A.2 Standard deviation examples

Dataset	Standard deviation
1, 1, 1, 1, 1, 1, 1, 1, 1, 1, 1, 1, 1	0
1, 1, 1, 1, 1, 1, 1, 2, 2, 2, 2, 2	0.51
1, 1, 1, 1, 2, 2, 2, 2, 3, 3, 3, 3	0.85

In the first dataset, all the students gave the same rating (1, 'strongly disagree'); therefore, by definition, there was no variability in the ratings, and the standard deviation is zero. In effect, all students are in total agreement about this particular facet of teaching and learning.

In the second dataset, the majority (7/12) of students responded using 'strongly disagree', but 5 of the 7 students used the 'neutral' option; thus, there was more variability in these scores (standard deviation = 0.51) than in the first dataset. Thus, there is some disagreement about this aspect of teaching and learning.

In the third dataset, four respondents chose 'strongly disagree', four chose 'neutral', and four chose 'strongly agree'. This greater degree of variability is reflected in the larger standard deviation of this dataset (0.85) compared to datasets 1 or 2. This relatively high level of disagreement could be due to a variety of reasons, including substantial differences in students' backgrounds, and/or differences in their perceptions of course requirements. Triangulating the numerical feedback with other sources of feedback (e.g. written comments, follow-up focus groups with students) will be important in order to understand the reasons for such variation.

Skewness and kurtosis

These characteristics of a set of scores refer to the degree to which the distribution approximates a 'bell-shaped' or normal curve. Normal or approximately normal distributions have a range of desirable properties when it comes to calculating inferential statistics. However, when it comes to teaching evaluation data, it is often the case that responses are not distributed normally. In fact, in thinking about teaching evaluations, we would usually hope that students would give substantially more positive than negative responses!

Skewness occurs when a set of scores, rather than resembling a 'bell', is skewed, either to the right or the left. Kurtosis occurs when the actual 'peak' of the observed distribution differs substantially from the 'expected' peak (either above or below). We can get a good sense of skewness and kurtosis – or more generally, the degree to which data is not normally distributed – by examining a histogram of the dataset. SPSS allows a normal curve to be superimposed over the actual data. In Figure A.1 we see an artificial dataset that approximates a normal curve well:

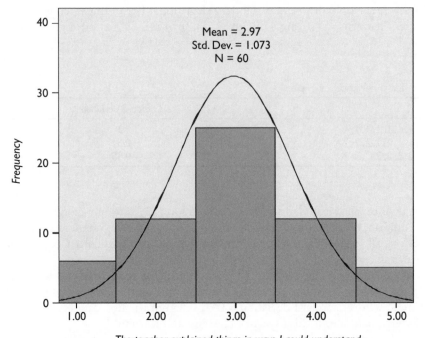

The teacher explained things in ways I could understand.

Figure A.1 A dataset with an approximately normal distribution

However, if things are going reasonably well in our teaching, a more realistic dataset might look like this:

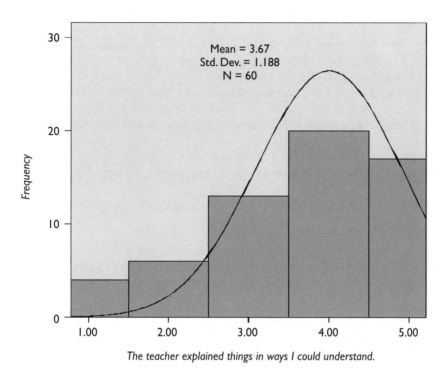

The teacher explained things in ways I could understand.

Figure A.2 A dataset with a more typical distribution for questionnaire responses

Percentage agreement/disagreement

These descriptive statistics are commonly used in reporting results from teaching evaluation surveys using the 'strongly disagree' (1), 'disagree' (2), 'neutral' (3), 'agree' (4), and 'strongly agree' (5) Likert format. Percentage agreement reports the percentage of valid responses which were either agree or strongly agree. Conversely, percentage disagreement reports the percentage of valid responses that were either strongly disagree or disagree. For example, if 34 students out of a total of 50 respondents agreed or strongly agreed with the statement, 'The teacher explained things in ways I could understand', the percentage agreement statistic would be 68 per cent.

Percentage agreement and disagreement provide a useful overview of the range of student responses. Many readers of teaching evaluation reports may be unsure whether a mean score of 3.67 out of 5 is good, bad, or neutral. Knowing that 50 per cent of respondents were positively disposed towards a particular aspect of teaching, 10 per cent were neutral, but 40 per cent were negatively disposed towards that aspect may make the numbers easier to understand.

Percentage agreement or disagreement can be derived easily from frequency tables such as the one presented above. However, the situation is more complex if we want to calculate these statistics for responses to a scale, rather than an item. SPSS syntax to create percentage agreement scores for each respondent for a three-item 1–5 scale is as follows:

```
recode teach1 (1 thru 3=0) (4,5=1) into teach1agpc
/teach2 (1 thru 3=0) (4,5=1) into teach2agpc
/teach3 (1 thru 3=0) (4,5=1) into teach3agpc.
execute.
compute teach_pc_agreement = 100*mean(teach1agpc, teach2agpc, teach3agpc).
execute.
```

To create percentage disagreement scores for each respondent, we would use:

```
recode teach1 (1 thru 2=1) (4,5=0) into teach1disagpc
/teach2 (1 thru 2=1) (4,5=0) into teach2disagpc
/teach3 (1 thru 2=1) (4,5=0)into teach3disagpc.
execute.
compute teach_pc_agreement = 100*mean(teach1disagpc, teach2disagpc, teach3disagpc).
execute.
```

We could then use SPSS descriptives to calculate the average percentage agreement or disagreement across all respondents.

Inferential statistics

While descriptive statistics are useful for describing the properties of a particular dataset, we often wish to 'move beyond' the conclusions of that dataset and infer something more general about the world (e.g. the correlates of effective learning). For example, imagine you notice there seems to be a substantial difference between the final grades of the two genders in a course you teach. This *mean difference* between the genders is a descriptive statistic. At the same time, there will probably be substantial overlap in the grade distributions of women and men; there are almost certainly other reasons than just gender for the observed differences between students (e.g. prior knowledge, motivation, study habits, etc.). Is this observed difference large enough to be unlikely to have arisen just by chance?

We use inferential statistics in order to *test models of reality* under conditions of variability. In the above example, we want to test a model which says that, over and above all the possible reasons students' grades may vary, gender is important. Field (2005; p. 27) notes that a wide variety of inferential test statistics test the same fundamental ratio:

Test statistic = variance explained by the model ÷ variance not explained by the model

If the variance explained by the model is large enough compared to variance not explained by the model, we conclude that the results are unlikely to have happened by chance.

When researchers conduct inferential statistical tests, they have historically often focused on the result of a null hypothesis significance test (NHST) – a probability (p) value indicating the likelihood of obtaining the same or more extreme pattern of results if the study was replicated, if the null hypothesis is in fact true. There are increasing calls to supplement NHST with alternative statistical reporting forms, or even eliminate NHST entirely (e.g. Kline, 2004), because NHSTs are (a) not sufficiently informative about the magnitude of an effect, (b) do not clearly communicate the impact of sampling error on population estimates, (c) encourage dichotomous thinking ('significant' vs. 'not significant') rather than a more nuanced understanding of results, and (d) are often misunderstood. Of particular concern is the fact that statistical significance is to a large extent a function of the sample size. With a large enough sample, a NHST may be 'highly significant', but this is no guarantee that a result is educationally or practically meaningful.

It is now recommended practice in the behavioural sciences (APA, 2010) to report *effect sizes* and, wherever possible, *confidence intervals* around the effect size. Cumming and Fidler (2010) define an effect size as 'simply an amount of something of interest' (p.79). There are several families of effect sizes, such as standardised estimates (e.g. Cohen's d, the standardised mean difference), as distinct from 'variance accounted for' measures (e.g. R^2, η^2, ε^2) – for an extensive review, see Grissom and Kim (2005). Cumming and Fidler (2010) argue that a focus on effect sizes is supported by language such as 'We estimate the importance of . . . ' or 'Our aim is to investigate how large an effect [X] has on [Y]'.

In considering a range of effect sizes, Cohen (1988) provided various rules of thumb for interpreting the magnitude of an effect, but also cautioned that it would be preferable to judge new results in a given field in relation to field-specific guidelines. For example, in education, a major review by Hattie (2009) of over 800 educational meta-analyses suggests an obtained standardised mean difference of 0.20 in a new study should be considered a small effect, 0.40 should be considered a medium effect and 0.60 should be considered a large effect. Equivalent correlation coefficients at each of the above levels would be 0.10, 0.20 and 0.29, respectively.

A confidence interval – typically, a 95 per cent confidence interval – around an effect size provides a range of plausible values for the population effect size, as well as communicating the degree of precision in the estimate. A larger sample size will produce a smaller (i.e. more precise) confidence interval than a smaller sample size. Cumming and Fidler (2010, p. 89) provide guidance in interpreting a 95 per cent confidence interval for an effect size, rather than focusing only on the point estimate of the effect.

Because of the relative novelty of a focus on effect sizes and confidence intervals, many commercial statistics programmes have been slow in 'hard-wiring' the above recommendations into available analyses. Fortunately, methodologists have developed a range of free stand-alone programmes, or scripts for programmes such as SPSS or SAS, to support such analyses. Grissom and Kim (2005) review a range of such resources. More recent resources have been developed by Bonett (2008) and Lorenzo-Seva, Ferrando, and Chico (2010).

Correlation/regression

Correlation occurs when at least two variables are associated in some way. An important initial consideration is the nature of the variables. For example, a correlation between two non-metric variables is calculated in a different way to a correlation between two metric variables, so it is important to have a clear understanding of the kinds of variables you are investigating. For an overview of measures of association between nominal and/or ordinal variables, see Table 14.17 in de Vaus (2002).

It can be tempting to calculate correlations between a large number of variables in a dataset, review the correlation matrix, and interpret those correlations that are statistically significant. Such 'fishing expeditions' may be useful for generating hypotheses in the initial stages of a research programme, but this practice risks over-interpretation of random variation in the data. Osborne (2010) provides a recent review of practice, arguing that high-quality correlational research starts with a strong theoretical rationale, uses high-quality measures, ensures the underlying assumptions of correlational analysis are met, and uses best practice in analysis and interpretation.

Correlational analysis is widely used in SoTL research. However, it is rarely the case that researchers examine the relationship between only two variables. More often, they will investigate the relations between a number of predictor variables, and an outcome variable. *Regression analysis* provides a highly flexible framework for such analyses. The specific goal of a regression analysis might be *prediction* (how much variance in the outcome variable is explained by this set of predictor variables), *explanation* (making a causal inference about the effect of one variable on another), or both. Kelley and Maxwell (2010) provide a thorough overview of best practice for regression analysis, noting the important caveat that causal statements about regression coefficients (as for correlation coefficients) are justified under only limited circumstances. For example, Richardson (2006) used a type of regression analysis called path analysis (see Pedhazur, 1997, ch. 18) to examine potential causal pathways between demographic variables, students' perceptions of the academic environment in a distance learning setting, their self-reports of approaches to study, and outcome measures including final marks and course satisfaction.

When a researcher has access to longitudinal data measuring the same pair of variables over time, an advanced form of regression analysis called cross-lagged panel analysis (Huck, Cormier, & Bounds, 1974) can be used to investigate causal relations. When one event (e.g. measuring academic motivation and achievement variables at Time 1) precedes another event (measuring the same variables at Time 2), such analyses allow the researcher to examine the both the plausibility and strength of competing causal interpretations. Martin and Liem (2010) used such analysis to investigate longitudinal relations between high school students' personal best (PB) orientation and measures of engagement (e.g. class participation, homework completion) and achievement. They found evidence for the relative salience of prior PBs over educational aspiration, literacy achievement and effort, and numeracy performance and effort, as well as evidence of reciprocal relationships between some pairs of variables.

Experiments

Experimentation is a research methodology with a strong focus on testing causal claims (Ginns, 2011). Typically, this is achieved through the use of random assignment of experimental units (e.g. students, classes) to alternative conditions. An alternative experimental design emphasises testing hypotheses by gathering repeated measurements from the same participant (e.g. Brünken, Plass, & Leutner, 2004; Brünken, Steinbacher, Plass, & Leutner, 2002; Huck, 2007). At least one *independent variable* (e.g. form of instruction) is manipulated, and the effects on at least one *dependent variable* (e.g. quality of learning) are observed. Random assignment to conditions provides a powerful method for 'equalising' groups with respect to the many different reasons why those groups might differ on the dependent variable/s. Thus, if a statistically significant difference is found, the researcher can be confident that this difference is due to the independent variable.

There are numerous research designs falling under the broad category of experiments. The full range of designs, and the extent to which they are subject to various *threats to validity*, are discussed by Shadish, Cook, and Campbell (2002). While a 'true' experiment may provide a strong basis for causal claims, it may often be difficult to conduct such studies in realistic higher education settings, especially when the focus is at the level of the whole curriculum or substantial parts thereof (see Kember, 2003, for a discussion of these issues). Nonetheless, there will often be questions of a more limited scope about teaching and learning design that are amenable to experimental investigation. For example, Marsh and Roche (1993) investigated the effectiveness of individualised teaching evaluation feedback by randomly assigning 92 higher education teachers into one of three conditions: targeted feedback following student evaluations in the middle of the semester (MT group), targeted feedback following student evaluations at the end of the semester (ET group), or a no-feedback control condition. In both the MT and ET conditions, using quantitative and qualitative feedback data, a consultant worked with teachers to determine two or three areas for improvement based on teaching strategy booklets (see Marsh & Roche, 1994, for copies). Marsh and Roche found that teachers in the ET condition showed greater improvements on subsequent teaching evaluations than those in the ET or control conditions, with these improvements being more substantial in targeted than non-targeted dimensions of teaching quality.

The increasing use of information and communication technologies for learning likewise provides many opportunities for experimental validations of instructional design decisions. For example, Mayer's (2009) cognitive theory of multimedia learning is based on extensive use of experiments, demonstrating that learning from multimedia can be substantially improved through a focus on strengths and limits of the human cognitive architecture (see also van Merriënboer & Sweller, 2010). Although such experiments are often conducted using relatively short learning interventions, the strengths of this body of research lie in the simplicity of the instructional redesign, the use of multiple experiments to replicate initial findings and the often large effects on learning. For meta-analytic reviews of instructional redesigns generated by these theories, see Crissman (2006) and Ginns (2005, 2006).

Cluster analysis and latent cluster analysis

Cluster analysis is used to classify objects (e.g. students, teachers, courses) into groups on the basis of scores on a set of variables. As a 'person-oriented' method of analysis, it can complement other 'variable-oriented' analyses (e.g. correlation) by helping the researcher understand the nature of subgroups in a sample. For example, Crawford,

Gordon, Nicholas, and Prosser (1998) surveyed university students studying first-year mathematics regarding their conceptions of mathematics (fragmented and cohesive) and their approaches to learning mathematics (deep and surface) at the beginning of their degree and at the start of the second semester, and their experiences of studying mathematics using a subject-specific version of the Course Experience Questionnaire. Prior academic achievement results from high school using the Higher School Certificate, and the final grade in first year mathematics, were also collected. Cluster analysis of the above variables suggested two distinct groups. The more highly achieving group had more cohesive conceptions of mathematics, more deep and less surface approaches to learning, and more positive experiences of teaching than the less highly achieving group.

As a family of related methods, cluster analysis requires a number of methodological decisions, such as choice of variables for inclusion, choice of clustering method, and method for choosing the final cluster solution (see Pastor, 2010, for a review).

Researchers in higher education are increasingly using methods for identifying unobserved groups using structural equation models (see Samuelsen & Dayton, 2010, for recommended practice). For example, Heikkilä, Niemivirta, Nieminen, and Lonka (2011) investigated associations between approaches to learning, regulation of learning, cognitive and attributional strategies, stress, exhaustion and academic achievement among 437 Finnish university students across three faculties. Participants completed a questionnaire measuring self-reported study behaviour, cognitive strategies and well-being. Latent class clustering suggested three distinct groups of students: non-academic, self-directed and helpless students. Responses from helpless students indicated higher levels of stress and exhaustion than for students in the other groups. In contrast, self-directed students performed at higher average levels of academic achievement.

Multilevel modelling

One of the most salient features of education settings (e.g. schools, universities) is the presence of nestedness: that is, people learn in social settings, and sometimes this creates similarities between group members (e.g. children in classrooms; adults in higher education programmes) that may be of substantive importance. Inferential statistics such as those described above do not take this *intra-class correlation* into account, and may therefore be biased, meaning that standard analyses are more likely to detect spurious effects or relationships. Multilevel models are also known as hierarchical linear models, mixed models or random effects models (see McCoach, 2010, for an extensive review).

In higher education teaching evaluation, it has long been recognised that nestedness of teaching evaluation data required specific analytic methods. Over and above estimates of reliability of ratings based on internal consistency estimates (e.g. Cronbach, 1951), estimates of inter-rater reliability (IRR) are often considered. The IRR is a function related to the number of student ratings, with reliabilities ranging from 0.70 to 0.90 when ratings of at least 20 to 25 students are averaged (Feldman, 1977). One-way analyses of variance, using the lecturer as the level of the independent variable, can be used to calculate an item or scale's IRR, by dividing the mean square between minus mean square within by mean square between, or $(F-1)/F$ (Gillmore, 2000; Winer, Brown, & Michels, 1991; see also LeBreton & Senter, 2008).

More recent considerations of nestedness in teaching evaluation data have been made possible by developments in multilevel modelling (e.g. Goldstein, 2003; Hox, 2010; Snijders & Bosker, 1999). In particular, variance components models are important 'base' analyses for estimating the proportion of variance in participant responses at each level of analysis. For example:

$$\text{student} \rightarrow \text{programme} \rightarrow \text{school/department} \rightarrow \text{university} \rightarrow \text{country.}$$

More complex models may then be estimated by adding predictor variables (e.g. student demographics), and observing the effects and influences on the variance components (e.g. Ginns, Marsh, Behnia, Cheng, & Scalas, 2009; Marsh, Ginns, Morin, Nagengast, & Martin, 2011; Marsh, Rowe, & Martin, 2002).

Exploratory and confirmatory factor analysis

Exploratory factor analysis (EFA) is a method for determining whether a smaller number of latent constructs can be used to explain variability among a larger set of observed variables, such as items on a teaching evaluation instrument. Confirmatory factor analysis (CFA) differs from EFA in that a researcher will use the latter method to test an explicit hypothetical model of the relations between items and latent factors (Bandalos & Finney, 2010). Typically, EFA tends to be used at the beginning of a programme of research into a construct or set of constructs, while CFA tends to be used when a mature programme of research has resulted in instruments with good psychometric properties; but this is not a hard and fast rule. As for cluster analysis, EFA and CFA require many careful decisions given the nature of the substantive question and the data itself. In particular, in the case of EFA, many of the 'default settings' for EFA in statistics programmes do not represent current recommendations for best practice (for recent reviews of recommended practice, see Bandalos & Finney, 2010; Henson & Roberts, 2006; Preacher & MacCallum, 2003).

As noted in Chapter 2, a core goal of both EFA and CFA is assessing evidence for construct validity. When CFA is used for this purpose, the researcher specifies a model in which variance among items is explained by one or more latent factors, then tests the fit of the model to the data. An example of this use of CFA is given in Chapter 10. Raykov (2009) provides a method for using CFA to test construct validity and reliability of a single scale simultaneously. A useful feature of this approach is the production of a confidence interval for the reliability estimate, reflecting the fact that reliability coefficients, like other estimates of population parameters, are subject to sampling error (Thompson & Vacha-Haase, 2000).

Structural equation modelling

Structural equation modelling (SEM), like CFA, involves specifying a theoretical model, testing the fit of data to that model, and evaluating the model's fit (Kline, 2005). On the basis of initial results, under some circumstances, the model may be modified and re-tested. The primary difference between these analytic methods is the inclusion of both *measurement* and *structural* components in the structural equation model; thus, many structural models can be thought of as using a combination of factor analysis and multiple regression. These structural components are typically included to test hypotheses about associations between latent factors, rather than observed variables.

Structural models have several advantages for testing theoretical models. First, by including both measurement and structural components in the same model, the structural components are 'purged' of measurement error associated with unreliability in the measurement component. This means that more accurate estimates of the structural components of a model are estimated. Second, theory-testing is supported by the provision of fit indices. Third, model modification is supported by modification indices for parameters in the model, although such modifications should be conceptually or methodologically defensible rather than simply expedient. Fourth, as a multivariate method of analysis, SEM supports the potential investigation of relations between multiple predictors and multiple outcomes. Kember and Leung's (2009) validation of the Student Experience Questionnaire, reviewed in Chapter 12, provides a recent example of the use of structural modeling with a programme-level instrument.

Mueller and Hancock (2010) describe a range of best practice considerations when testing structural models. It is vital to realise that, despite the power of such methods, structural models support causal hypothesis testing only under relatively limited circumstances. Valid causal statements are a function of study design and strong theory, not simply statistical analysis. For considerations of the circumstances under which SEM might be used to test causal hypotheses and make prescriptive statements, see Martin, Green, Colmar, Liem, and Marsh (2011) and Martin (2011).

Meta-analysis

Meta-analysis (Hattie, 2009; Lipsey & Wilson, 2001) involves the statistical synthesis of results of disparate studies in a common area, resulting in more accurate estimates of population parameters (e.g. correlations, standardised mean differences, odds ratios) than is possible in any single study. Meta-analysis typically generates an estimate of the average effect size across included studies, but also provides a confidence interval around this average effect. When there is significant heterogeneity among individual effects, follow-up analyses can be used to determine what variables (either categorical or continuous) moderate the overall effect.

One common research methodology for assessing the association between a teaching quality construct (e.g. teacher enthusiasm; clarity of explanations) and learning outcomes (e.g. final grade on a course) is the multisection validity study. Such studies involve teachers in different 'sections' teaching a standardised course being evaluated by their students on a common teaching evaluation instrument. Across sections, the teacher-average evaluations are then correlated with the average student learning outcomes. Meta-analyses of the multisection validity study research literature (e.g. Cohen, 1981; Feldman, 1989) have consistently found moderate to strong correlations between overall course or teacher ratings and student achievement. Feldman (1989) also meta-analysed the associations between specific dimensions of teaching quality and student achievement; for example, the average correlation between ratings of teacher's preparation and student achievement was 0.57, and the correlation between teacher clarity and learning was 0.56. Meta-analyses such as these provide important summaries of teaching evaluation and SoTL research, as well as benchmarks for judging the relative importance of novel constructs or interventions (cf. Hattie, 2009).

References

Altman, D.G. (1991). *Practical statistics for medical research*. London: Chapman and Hall.

American Psychological Association (2010). *Publication manual of the American Psychological Association* (6th Ed.). Washington, DC: Author.

Anderson, J.C. (1987). An approach for confirmatory measurement and structural equation modeling of organizational properties. *Management Science, 33*, 525–541. DOI:10.1287/mnsc.33.4.525.

Ashby, A., Richardson, J.T.E., & Woodley, A. (2011). National student feedback surveys in distance education: An investigation at the UK Open University. *Open Learning, 26*, 5–25. DOI: 10.1080/02680513.2011.538560

Astin, A.W. (1984). Student involvement: A developmental theory for higher education. *Journal of College Student Development, 25*, 297–308.

Astin, A.W. (1985). *Achieving educational excellence: A critical assessment of priorities and practices in higher education*. San Francisco, CA: Jossey–Bass.

Ayres, P., Sawyer, W., & Dinham, S. (2004). Effective teaching in the context of a Grade 12 high–stakes external examination in New South Wales, Australia. *British Educational Research Journal, 30*, 141–165. http://www.jstor.org/stable/1502207

Bandalos, D.L. & Finney, S.J. (2010). Factor analysis: Exploratory and confirmatory. In G.R. Hancock and R.O. Mueller (eds), *The reviewer's guide to quantitative methods in the social sciences* (pp. 93–114). New York: Routledge.

Barrie, S. & Ginns, P. (2007). The linking of institutional performance indicators to improvements in teaching and learning in classrooms. *Quality in Higher Education, 13*, 275–286. DOI: 10.1080/13538320701800175

Barrie, S.C., Ginns, P., & Prosser, M. (2005). Early impact and outcomes of an institutionally aligned, student focused learning perspective on teaching quality assurance. *Assessment and Evaluation in Higher Education, 30*, 641–656. DOI: 10.1080/02602930500260761

Bennett, L., Nair, C.S., & Wayland, C. (2006). Love it or hate it: Participation a key ingredient in closing the loop. Paper presented at the Australian Universities Quality Forum, Perth, 5–7 July. Retrieved from http://www.auqa.edu.au/auqf/pastfora/2006/program/paper/paper_d2.pdf

Bentler, P.M. (1990). Comparative fit indices in structural models. *Psychological Bulletin, 107*, 238–246.

Bentler, P.M. (1995). *EQS Structural equations program manual*. Encino, CA: Multivariate Software.

Beran, T., Violato, C., Kline, D., & Frideres, J. (2009). What do students consider useful about student ratings? *Assessment & Evaluation in Higher Education, 34*, 519–527. DOI: 10.1080/02602930802082228

Biggs, J. (1987). *Student approaches to learning and studying*. Melbourne: Australian Council for Educational Research.

Biggs, J. (1992). *Why and how do Hong Kong students learn? Using the Learning and Study Process Questionnaires.* Hong Kong: Hong Kong University.

Biggs, J.B. (1993a). From theory to practice: A cognitive systems approach. *Higher Education Research and Development, 12,* 73–85. DOI: 10.1080/0729436930120107

Biggs, J. (1993b). What do inventories of students' learning processes really measure? A theoretical review and clarification. *British Journal of Educational Psychology, 63,* 3–19. DOI: 10.1111/j.2044-8279.1993.tb01038.x

Biggs, J. (1996). Enhancing teaching through constructive alignment. *Higher Education, 32,* 347–364. DOI: 10.1007/BF00138871

Biggs, J.B. & Collis, K.F. (1982). *Evaluating the quality of learning: the SOLO taxonomy (structure of the observed learning outcome).* New York: Academic Press.

Biggs, J.B. & Tang, C. (2007). *Teaching for quality learning at university: What the student does.* Maidenhead, UK: McGraw–Hill/Society for Research into Higher Education & Open University Press.

Biggs, J.B., Kember, D., & Leung, D.Y.P. (2001). The revised two–factor study process questionnaire: R–SPQ2F. *British Journal of Educational Psychology, 71,* 133–149. DOI: 10.1348/000709901158433

Bonett, D.G. (2008). Confidence intervals for standardized linear contrasts of means. *Psychological Methods, 13,* 99–109. DOI:10.1037/1082–989X.13.2.99

Bowers, Alex J. (2010). Analyzing the longitudinal K–12 grading histories of entire cohorts of students: Grades, data driven decision making, dropping out and hierarchical cluster analysis. *Practical Assessment, Research & Evaluation, 15.* Available online: http://pareonline.net/getvn.asp?v=15&n=7

Boyer, E.L. (1990). *Scholarship reconsidered: Priorities of the professoriate.* San Francisco, CA: The Carnegie Foundation for the Advancement of Teaching.

Braxton, J.M., Milem, J.F., & Sullivan, A.S. (1997). The influence of active learning on the college student departure process. *The Journal of Higher Education, 71,* 569–590. http://www.jstor.org/stable/2649260

Breaugh, J.A. (2003). Effect size estimation: Factors to consider and mistakes to avoid. *Journal of Management, 29,* 79–97. DOI: 10.1177/014920630302900106

Browne, M.W. & Cudeck, R. (1993). Alternative ways of assessing model fit. In K.A. Bollen & J.S. Long (eds), *Testing structural equation models* (pp. 136–162). Newbury Park, CA: Sage.

Brünken, R., Plass, J.L., & Leutner, D. (2004). Assessment of cognitive load in multimedia learning with dual-task methodology: Auditory load and modality effects. *Instructional Science, 32,* 115–132. DOI: 10.1023/B:TRUC.0000021812.96911.c5

Brünken, R., Steinbacher, S., Plass, J.L., & Leutner, D. (2002). Assessment of cognitive load in multimedia learning using dual-task methodology. *Experimental Psychology, 49,* 109–119. DOI: 10.1027//1618-3169.49.2.109

Carifio, J. & Perla, R. (2008). Resolving the 50–year debate around using and misusing Likert scales. *Medical Education, 42,* 1150–1152. DOI: 10.1111/j.1365–2923.2008.03172.x

Carlson, M., Oehrtman, M., & Engelke, N. (2010). The Precalculus Concept Assessment: A tool for assessing students' reasoning abilities and understandings. *Cognition and Instruction, 28,* 113–145. DOI: 10.1080/07370001003676587

Carr, W. & Kemmis, S. (1986). *Becoming critical: Education, knowledge and action research.* Brighton, UK: Falmer Press.

Caulfield, J. (2007). What motivates students to provide feedback to teachers about teaching and learning? An expectancy theory perspective. *International Journal for the Scholarship of Teaching and Learning, 1.* Retrieved 22 July 2009 from http://academics.georgiasouthern.edu/ijsotl/v1n1/caulfield/IJ_Caulfield.pdf

Centra, J. (1993). *Reflective faculty evaluation.* San Francisco, CA: Jossey Bass.

Chan, D. (1998). Functional relations among constructs in the same content domain at different levels of analysis: A typology of composition models. *Journal of Applied Psychology, 83,* 234–246. DOI: 10.1037/0021-9010.83.2.234

Chen, P.D., Gonyea, R.M., Sarraf, S.A., BrkaLorenz, A., Korkmaz, A., Lambert, A.D., Shoup, R., & Williams, J.A. (2009). Analyzing and interpreting NSSE data. *New Directions for Institutional Research, 141,* 35–54. DOI: 10.1002/ir.285

Cheng, J.H.S. & Marsh, H.W. (2010). National Student Survey: Are differences between universities and courses reliable and meaningful? *Oxford Review of Education, 36,* 693–712. DOI: 10.1080/03054985.2010.491179

Chickering, A.W. & Gamson, Z. (1987). Seven principles for good practice in undergraduate education. *American Association for Higher Education Bulletin, 39,* 3–7.

Church, A. (1993). Estimating the effect of incentives on mail survey response rates: A meta-analysis. *Public Opinion Quarterly, 57,* 62–79. DOI: 10.1086/269355

Cohen, J. (1988). *Statistical power analysis for the behavioural sciences.* (2nd Ed.). Hillsdale, NJ: Erlbaum.

Cohen, P.A. (1981). Student ratings of instruction and student achievement: A meta-analysis of multisection validity studies. *Review of Educational Research, 51,* 281–309. DOI: 10.3102/00346543051003281

Cope, L. & Staehr, L. (2008). Improving students' learning approaches through intervention in an information systems learning environment. *Studies in Higher Education, 30,* 181–197. DOI: 10.1080/03075070500043275

Craven, R.G., Marsh, H.W., Debus, R.L., & Jayasinghe, U. (2001). Diffusion effects: Control group contamination threats to the validity of teacher–administered interventions. *Journal of Educational Psychology, 93,* 639–645. DOI: 10.1037/0022-0663.93.3.639

Crawford, K., Gordon, S., Nicholas, J., & Prosser, M. (1998). Qualitatively different experiences of learning mathematics at university. *Learning and Instruction, 8,* 455?468. DOI:10.1016/S0959-4752(98)00005-X

Crissman, J. (2006). *The design and utilization of effective worked examples: A meta-analysis.* Unpublished Ph.D., University of Nebraska – Lincoln. (UMI No. 3208114).

Cronbach, L. J. (1951). Coefficient alpha and the internal structure of tests. *Psychometrika, 35,* 297–334. DOI: 10.1007/BF02310555

Crouch, C.H. & Mazur, E. (2001). Peer Instruction: Ten years of experience and results. *American Journal of Physics, 69,* 970–977. DOI: 10.1119/1.1374249

Cumming, G. & Fidler, F. (2010). Effect sizes and confidence intervals. In G.R. Hancock and R.O. Mueller (eds), *The reviewer's guide to quantitative methods in the social sciences* (pp. 79–92). New York: Routledge.

Curtis, D. & Keeves, J. (2000). The Course Experience Questionnaire as an institutional performance indicator. *International Education Journal, 1,* 73–82.

d'Appollonia, S. & Abrami, P.C. (1997). Navigating student ratings of instruction. *American Psychologist, 52,* 1198–1208.

de Vaus, D.A. (2002). *Surveys in social research* (5th ed). Crows Nest, Australia: Allen & Unwin.

Dillman, D. (2000). *Internet, mail, and mixed-mode surveys: The tailored design method* (2nd Ed.). New York, NY: John Wiley & Sons.

Dillman, D. (2009). *Internet, mail, and mixed-mode surveys: The tailored design method* (3rd Ed.). Hoboken, NJ: John Wiley & Sons.

Dommeyer, C.J., Elganayan, D., & Umans, C. (1991). Increasing mail survey response with an envelope teaser. *Journal of the Marketing Research Society, 33,* 137–40.

Edwards, P., Roberts, I., Clarke, M., DiGuiseppi, C., Pratap, S., Wentz, R., & Kwan, I. (2002). Increasing response rates to postal questionnaires: systematic review. *British Medical Journal, 324,* 1183. DOI: 10.1136/bmj.324.7347.1183

Eisner, E.W. (1991). *The enlightened eye: Qualitative inquiry and the enhancement of educational practice*. New York: Macmillan Publishing.

Eley, M.G. (1992). Differential adoption of study approaches within individual students. *Higher Education, 23*, 231–254. http://www.jstor.org/stable/3447375

Elliott, J. (1991). *Action research for educational change*. Milton Keynes: Open University Press.

Ellis, R.A., Ginns, P., & Piggott, L. (2009). eLearning in higher education: Some key aspects and their relationship to approaches to study. *Higher Education Research and Development, 28*, 303–318. DOI: 10.1080/07294360902839909

Elphinstone, L. J. (1989). *Development of the course experience questionnaire*. Unpublished Masters thesis. Melbourne University: Melbourne, Australia.

End, C.M., Worthman, S., Mathews, M.B., & Wetterau, K. (2010). Costly cell phones: The impact of cell phone rings on academic performance. *Teaching of Psychology, 37*, 55–57. DOI: 10.1080/00986280903425912

Entwistle, N. & Ramsden, P. (1983). *Understanding student learning*. London: Croom Helm.

Entwistle, N.J. (2009). *Teaching for understanding at university: Deep approaches and distinctive ways of thinking*. New York: Palgrave Macmillan.

Feldman, K. (1977). Consistency and variability among college students in rating their teachers and courses: A review and analysis. *Research in Higher Education, 6*, 223–274.

Feldman, K.A. (1989). The association between student ratings of specific instructional dimensions and student achievement: Refining and extending the synthesis of data from multisection validity studies. *Research in Higher Education, 30*, 583–645.

Field, A. (2005). *Discovering statistics using SPSS*. London: Sage.

Flint, A., Oxley, A., Helm, P., & Bradley, S. (2009). Preparing for success: One institution's aspirational and student focused response to the National Student Survey. *Teaching in Higher Education, 14*, 607–618. DOI: 10.1080/13562510903315035

Franklin, J. (2001). Interpreting the numbers: Using a narrative to help others read student evaluations of your teaching accurately. *New Directions for Teaching and Learning, 87*, 85–100. DOI: 10.1002/tl.10001

Garvin–Doxas, K., & Klymkowsky, M.W. (2008). Understanding randomness and its impact on student learning: Lessons learned from building the Biology Concept Inventory (BCI). *CBE Life Sciences Education, 7*, 227–233. DOI: 10.1187/cbe.07-08-0063

GCA (2011). Survey Training and Resource Tool for university survey managers: Key documents and files. Retrieved from http://start.graduatecareers.com.au/Resourcelibrary/KeyDocuments/index.htm

GCA & ACER (2007). *Graduate Course Experience, 2006: The report of the Course Experience Questionnaire*. Parkville: Graduate Careers Australia.

GCA & ACER (2010). *Graduate Course Experience, 2009: The report of the Course Experience Questionnaire*. Parkville: Graduate Careers Australia.

Gerbing, D.W. & Anderson, J.C. (1988). An updated paradigm for scale development incorporating unidimensionality and its assessment. *Journal of Marketing Research, 25*, 186–192. http://www.jstor.org/stable/3172650

Gillmore, G.M. (2000). Drawing inferences about instructors: the inter–class reliability of student ratings of instruction. University of Washington Office of Educational Assessment. Retrieved from http://www.washington.edu/oea/pdfs/reports/OEAReport0002.pdf

Ginns, P. (2005). Meta–analysis of the modality effect. *Learning and Instruction, 15*, 313–331. DOI:10.1016/j.learninstruc.2005.07.001

Ginns, P. (2006). Integrating information: Meta–analyses of the spatial contiguity and temporal contiguity effects. *Learning and Instruction, 16*, 511–525. DOI:10.1016/j.learninstruc.2006.10.001

Ginns, P. (2011). Quantitative modeling of experimental data in educational research: Current practice, future possibilities. In L. Markauskaite, P. Freebody, and J. Irwin (eds),

Methodological choice and design: Scholarship, policy and practice in social and educational research (pp. 225-234). Dordrecht, The Netherlands: Springer.

Ginns, P. & Barrie, S.C. (2004). Reliability of single–item ratings of quality in higher education: A replication. *Psychological Reports, 95*, 1023–1030.

Ginns, P. & Ellis, R. (2007). Quality in blended learning: Exploring the relations between on-line and face-to-face teaching and learning. *Internet and Higher Education, 10*, 53–64. DOI:10.1016/j.iheduc.2006.10.003

Ginns, P. & Ellis, R. (2009). Evaluating the quality of e–Learning at the degree level in a campus–based university. *British Journal of Educational Technology, 40*, 652–663. DOI:10.1111/j.1467–8535.2008.00861.x

Ginns, P., Marsh, H.W., Behnia, M., Cheng, J.H., & Scalas, F. (2009). Using postgraduate students' evaluations of research experience to benchmark departments and faculties: Issues and challenges. *British Journal of Educational Psychology, 79*, 577–598. DOI:10.1348/978185408X394347

Ginns, P., Prosser, M., & Barrie, S. (2007). Students' perceptions of teaching quality in higher education: The perspective of currently enrolled students. *Studies in Higher Education, 32*, 603–615. DOI: 10.1080/03075070701573773

Glaser, B.G. & Strauss, A.L. (1967). *The discovery of grounded theory.* Chicago, IL: Aldine.

Goldstein, H. (2003). *Multilevel statistical models* (3rd Ed.). London: Arnold.

Good Universities Guide (2011). *Good Universities Guide, 2011.* Melbourne: Hobsons Australia.

Gordon, C. & Debus, R. (2002). Developing deep learning approaches and personal teaching efficacy within a preservice teacher education context. *British Journal of Educational Psychology, 72*, 483–511. DOI: 10.1348/00070990260377488

Gordon, C., Debus, R., Dillon, J., & Arthur–Kelly, M. (2006). Using action research to develop deep learning outcomes within a preservice teacher education context. *Educational Research and Review, 1*, 337–346.

Govendir, M., Ginns, P., Symons, R., & Tammen, I. (2009). Improving the research higher degree experience at the Faculty of Veterinary Science, The University of Sydney. Proceedings of international conference of HERDSA, Darwin, Australia, 6–9 July. Retrieved from http://www.herdsa.org.au/wp–content/uploads/conference/2009/papers/HERDSA2009_Govendir_M.pdf

Gow, L. & Kember, D. (1990). Does higher education promote independent learning? *Higher Education, 19*, 307–322. http://www.jstor.org/stable/3447274

Graham, J.W., & Hofer, S.M. (2000). Multiple imputation in multivariate research. In T. D. Little, K. U. Schnabel, & J. Baumert (eds), *Modeling longitudinal and multiple–group data: Practical issues, applied approaches, and specific examples* (pp. 201–218). Hillsdale, NJ: Erlbaum.

Green, D. (1994). *What is quality in higher education?* Buckingham: SRHE and Open University Press.

Green, J.M. (1996). Warning that reminders will be sent increased response rate. *Quality and Quantity, 30*, 449–450. DOI: 10.1007/BF00170147

Green, K.E. & Hutchinson, S.R. (1996). Reviewing the research on mail survey response rates: Meta–analysis. Paper presented at the annual meeting of the American Educational Research Association, New York, April 1996.

Green, S.B., Lissitz, R.W., & Mulaik, S.A. (1977). Limitations of coefficient alpha as an index of test unidimensionality. *Educational and Psychological Measurement, 37*, 827–838. DOI: 10.1177/001316447703700403

Griffin, G., Coates, H., McInnis, C., & James, J. (2003). The development of an extended course experience questionnaire. *Quality in Higher Education, 9*, 259–266. DOI: 10.1080/13538320320015111

Grissom, R.J. and Kim, J.J. (2005). *Effect sizes for research: A broad practical approach.* Mahwah, NJ: Erlbaum.

Hair, J.F., Anderson, R.E., Tatham, R.L., & Black, W.C. (1998). *Multivariate data analysis* (5th Ed.). Upper Saddle River, NJ: Prentice Hall.

Hake, R.R. (1998). Interactive–engagement vs. traditional methods: A six–thousand–student survey of mechanics test data for introductory physics courses. *American Journal of Physics, 66*, 64–74.

Hattie, J. (1985). Methodology review: Assessing unidimensionality of tests and items. *Applied Psychological Measurement, 9*, 139–164. DOI: 10.1177/014662168500900204

Hattie, J.A.C. (2009). *Visible learning: A synthesis of over 800 meta–analyses relating to achievement.* Abingdon, UK: Routledge.

Hayes, A.F. (2005). A computational tool for survey shortening applicable to composite attitude, opinion, and personality measurement scales. Paper presented at the meeting of the Midwestern Association for Public Opinion Research, Chicago, IL: November 2005. Retrieved from http://www.afhayes.com/public/alphamax.pdf

Heberlein, T.A. & Baumgartner, R. (1978). Factors affecting response rates to mailed surveys: A quantitative analysis of the published literature. *American Sociological Review, 43*, 447–462.

Heerwegh, D. (2005). Effects of personal salutations in e-mail invitations to participate in a web survey. *Public Opinion Quarterly, 69*, 588–598. DOI: 10.1093/poq/nfi053

Heikkilä, A., Niemivirta, M., Nieminen, J., & Lonka, K. (2011). Interrelations among university students' approaches to learning, regulation of learning, and cognitive and attributional strategies: A person oriented approach. *Higher Education, 61*, 513–529. DOI: 10.1007/s10734–010–9346–2

Henson, R.K. & Roberts, J.K. (2006). Use of exploratory factor analysis in published research: Common errors and some comment on improved practice. *Educational and Psychological Measurement, 66*, 393–416. DOI: 10.1177/0013164405282485

Hestenes, D., Wells, M., & Swackhamer, G. (1992). Force concept inventory. *The Physics Teacher, 30*, 141–158.

Hinkin, T.R. & Tracey, J.B. (1999). An analysis of variance approach to content validation. *Organizational Research Methods, 2*, 175–186. DOI: 10.1177/109442819922004

Howitt, S., Anderson, T., Costa, M., Hamilton, S., & Wright, T. (2008). A concept inventory for molecular life sciences: How will it help your teaching practice? *Australian Biochemist, 39*, 14–17.

Hox, J.J. (2010). *Multilevel analysis: Techniques and applications* (2nd Ed.). New York: Routledge.

Huberty, C.J., Jordan, E.M., & Brandt, W.C. (2005). Cluster analysis in higher education research. In J. C. Smart (ed.), *Higher Education: Handbook of theory and research* (Vol. 20, pp. 437–457). Great Britain: Springer.

Huck, S.W. (2007). Using e-mail messages to help students prepare for a statistics exam. In S. Sawilowsky (ed.), *Real data analysis* (pp. 107–113). Charlotte, NC: Information Age Publishing.

Huck, S.W., Cormier, W.H., & Bounds, W.G. (1974). *Reading statistics and research.* New York: Harper and Row.

Jochems, W., van Merriënboer, J., & Koper, R. (2004). An introduction to integrated e–learning. In W. Jochems, J. vanMerriënboer & R. Koper (eds), *Integrated e-learning: Implications for pedagogy, technology and organization* (pp. 1–12). London: RoutledgeFalmer.

Kelley, K. & Maxwell, S.E. (2010). Multiple regression. In G.R. Hancock and R.O. Mueller (eds), *The reviewer's guide to quantitative methods in the social sciences* (pp. 281–298). New York: Routledge.

Kember, D. (1996). The intention to both memorise and understand: Another approach to learning? *Higher Education, 31*, 341–351. http://www.jstor.org/stable/3447651

Kember, D. (1997). A reconceptualisation of the research into university academics' conceptions of teaching. *Learning and Instruction, 7*, 255–275. DOI: 10.1016/S0959-4752(96)00028-X

Kember, D. (2000a). Misconceptions about the learning approaches, motivation and study practices of Asian students. *Higher Education, 40,* 99–121.

Kember, D. (2000b). *Action learning and action research: Improving the quality of teaching and learning.* London: Kogan Page.

Kember, D. (2003). To control or not to control: The question whether experimental designs are appropriate for evaluating teaching innovations in higher education. *Assessment & Evaluation in Higher Education, 28,* 89–101. DOI: 10.1080/02602930301684

Kember, D. (2007). *Reconsidering open and distance learning in the developing world: Meeting students' learning needs.* Abingdon, UK: Routledge.

Kember, D. (2009). Promoting student–centred forms of learning across an entire university. *Higher Education, 58,* 1–13. DOI: 10.1007/s10734–008–9177–6

Kember, D. & Gow, L. (1992). Action research as a form of staff development in higher education. *Higher Education, 23,* 297–310. http://www.jstor.org/stable/3447378

Kember, D. & Kelly, M. (1993). *Improving teaching through action research.* N.S.W.: HERDSA Green Guide No. 14.

Kember, D. & Kwan, K.P. (2000). Lecturers' approaches to teaching and their relationship to conceptions of good teaching. *Instructional Science, 28,* 469–490. DOI: 10.1023/A:1026569608656

Kember, D. & Leung, D.Y.P. (2008). Establishing the validity and reliability of course evaluation questionnaires. *Assessment and Evaluation in Higher Education, 33,* 341–353. DOI: 10.1080/02602930701563070

Kember, D. & Leung, D.Y.P. (2009). Development of a questionnaire for assessing students' perceptions of the teaching and learning environment and its use in quality assurance. *Learning Environments Research, 12,* 15–29. DOI: 10.1007/s10984–008–9050–7

Kember, D. & McKay, J. (1996). Action research into the quality of student learning: A paradigm for faculty development. *Journal of Higher Education, 67,* 528–554. http://www.jstor.org/stable/2943867

Kember, D. *et al.* (2001). *Reflective teaching and learning in the health professions.* Oxford: Blackwell Science.

Kember, D. with McNaught, C. (2007). *Enhancing university teaching: Lessons from research into award winning teachers.* Abingdon, Oxfordshire: Routledge.

Kember, D., Biggs, J., & Leung, D.Y.P. (2004). Examining the multidimensionality of approaches to learning through the development of a revised version of the Learning Process Questionnaire. *British Journal of Educational Psychology, 74,* 261–280. DOI: 10.1348/000709904773839879

Kember, D., Charlesworth, M., Davies, H., McKay, J., and Stott, V. (1997). Evaluating the effectiveness of educational innovations: Using the Study Process Questionnaire to show that meaningful learning occurs. *Studies in Educational Evaluation, 23,* 141–157. DOI:10.1016/S0191-491X(97)00009-6

Kember, D., Leung, D.Y.P., Jones, A., Loke, A.Y., McKay, J., Sinclair, K., Tse, H., Webb, C., Wong, F.K.Y., Wong, M.W.L., & Yeung, E. (2000). Development of a questionnaire to measure the level of reflective thinking. *Assessment and Evaluation in Higher Education, 25,* 381–395. DOI: 10.1080/713611442

Kember, D., Leung, D.Y.P., & Kwan, K.P. (2002). Does the use of student feedback questionnaires improve the overall quality of teaching? *Assessment and Evaluation in Higher Education, 27,* 411–425. DOI: 10.1080/0260293022000009294

Kember, D., Leung, D.Y.P., & Ma, R.S.F. (2007). Characterizing learning environments capable of nurturing generic capabilities in higher education. *Research in Higher Education, 48,* 609–632. DOI: 10.1007/s11162-006-9037-0

King, P.M. & Kitchener, K.S. (1994). *Developing reflective judgement: Understanding and promoting intellectual growth and critical thinking in adolescents and adults.* San Francisco, CA: Jossey-Bass.

Kline, R.B. (2004). *Beyond significance testing: Reforming data analysis methods in behavioral research.* Washington, DC: American Psychological Association.

Kline, R.B. (2005). *Principles and practice of structural equation modeling* (2nd Ed.). New York: Guilford Press.

Kolitch, E. & Dean, A.V. (1999). Student ratings of instruction in the USA: Hidden assumptions and missing conceptions about 'good' teaching. *Studies in Higher Education, 24,* 27–42. DOI: 10.1080/03075079912331380128

Kreiter, C.D. & Lakshman, V. (2005). Investigation of the use of sampling for maximising the efficiency of student–generated faculty teaching evaluations. *Medical Education, 39,* 171–175. DOI: 10.1111/j.1365-2929.2004.02066.x

Kuh, G.D. (2009). The National Survey of Student Engagement: Conceptual and empirical foundations. *New Directions for Institutional Research, 141,* 5–20.

Kuh, G.D., Kinzie, J., Schuh, J.H., Whitt, E.J., and associates (2005). *Student success in college: Creating conditions that matter.* San Francisco: Jossey Bass.

Lam, B.-H., & Kember, D. (2006). The relationship between conceptions of teaching and approaches to teaching. *Teachers and Teaching, 12,* 693–713. DOI: 10.1080/13540600601029744

LeBreton, J.M. & Senter, J.L. (2008). Answers to 20 questions about interrater reliability and interrater agreement. *Organizational Research Methods, 11,* 815–852. DOI: 10.1177/1094428106296642

Lei, P. & Wu, Q. (2007). CTTITEM: SAS macro and SPSS syntax for classical item analysis. *Behavior Research Methods, 39,* 527–530. DOI: 10.3758/BF03193021

Leung, D.Y.P. & Kember, D. (2003). The relationship between approaches to learning and reflection upon practice. *Educational Psychology, 23,* 61–71. DOI: 10.1080/01443410303221

Leung, D.Y.P. & Kember, D. (2006). The influence of teaching approach and teacher–student interaction on the development of graduate capabilities. *Structural Equation Modeling, 13,* 264–286. DOI: 10.1207/s15328007sem1302_6

Levy, P.S. & Lemeshow, S. (2008). *Sampling of populations: Methods and applications.* Hoboken, NJ: Wiley.

Libarkin, J.C. & Anderson, S.W. (2005). Assessment of learning in entry–level Geoscience courses: Results from the Geoscience Concept Inventory. *Journal of Geoscience Education, 53,* 394–401.

Lincoln, Y. & Guber, E. (1985). *Naturalistic inquiry.* Newbury Park, CA: Sage.

Lindell, M.K. (2001). Assessing and testing interrater agreement on a single target using multi–item rating scales. *Applied Psychological Measurement, 25,* 89–99. DOI: 10.1177/01466216010251007

Lipsey, M. W. & Wilson, D. B. (2001). *Practical meta–analysis.* Thousand Oaks, CA: Sage.

Lizzio, A., Wilson, K., & Simons, R. (2002). University students' perceptions of the learning environment and academic outcomes: Implications for theory and practice. *Studies in Higher Education, 27,* 27–51. DOI: 10.1080/03075070120099359

Locke, E.A. & Latham, G.P. (2002). Building a practically useful theory of goal setting and task motivation: A 35–year odyssey. *American Psychologist, 57,* 705–717.

Locke, E.A. & Latham, G.P. (2006). New directions in goal–setting theory. *Current Directions in Psychological Science, 15,* 265–268. DOI: 10.1111/j.1467–8721.2006.00449.x

Lorenzo–Seva, U., Ferrando, P.J., & Chico, E. (2010) Two SPSS programs for interpreting multiple regression results. *Behavior Research Methods, 42,* 29–35. DOI: 10.3758/BRM.42.1.29

Lyon, P.M. & Hendry, G.D. (2002). The Use of the Course Experience Questionnaire as a monitoring evaluation tool in a problem–based medical programme. *Assessment & Evaluation in Higher Education, 27,* 339–352. DOI: 10.1080/0260293022000001355

Marsh, H.W. (1987). Students' evaluations of university teaching: Research findings, methodological issues, and directions for future research. *International Journal of Educational Research, 11,* 253–388.

Marsh, H.W. (2007). Students' evaluations of university teaching: Dimensionality, reliability, validity, potential biases and usefulness. In R.P. Perry & J.C. Smart (eds). *The scholarship of teaching and learning in higher education: An evidence–based perspective* (pp. 319–383). New York: Springer.

Marsh, H.W. & Cheng, J.H.S. (2008). *Dimensionality, multilevel structure, and differentiation at the level of university and discipline: Preliminary results.* http://www.heacademy.ac.uk/resources/detail/ourwork/research/NSS_herb_marsh

Marsh, H.W. & Roche, L. (1993). The use of students' evaluations and an individually structured intervention to enhance university teaching effectiveness. *American Educational Research Journal, 30,* 217–251. DOI: 10.3102/00028312030001217

Marsh, H.W. & Roche, L. (1994). *The use of students' evaluations of university teaching to improve teaching effectiveness.* Canberra, Australia: Australian Government Publishing Service.

Marsh, H.W., Ginns, P., Morin, A.J.S., Nagengast, B., & Martin, A.J. (2011). Use of student ratings to benchmark universities: Multilevel modeling of responses to the Australian Course Experience Questionnaire (CEQ). *Journal of Educational Psychology, 103,* 733-748. DOI: 10.1037/a0024221

Marsh, H.W., Hau, K.–T., & Wen, Z. (2004). In search of golden rules: Comment on hypothesis testing approaches to setting cut–off values for fit indexes and dangers in overgeneralising Hu & Bentler's (1999) findings. *Structural Equation Modeling, 11,* 320–341. DOI: 10.1207/s15328007sem1103_2

Marsh, H.W., Rowe, K.J., & Martin, A. (2002). PhD students' evaluation of research supervision: Issues, complexities, and challenges in a nationwide Australian experiment in benchmarking universities. *Journal of Higher Education, 73,* 313–348. http://www.jstor.org/stable/1558460

Martin, A.J. (2011). Prescriptive statements and educational practice: What can Structural Equation Modeling (SEM) offer? *Educational Psychology Review, 23,* 235-244. DOI: 10.1007/s10648-011-9160-0

Martin, A.J. & Liem, G.A.D. (2010). Academic personal bests (PBs), engagement, and achievement: A cross–lagged panel analysis. *Learning and Individual Differences, 20,* 265–270. doi:10.1016/j.lindif.2010.01.001

Martin, A., Green, J., Colmar, S., Liem, G., & Marsh, H. (2011). Quantitative modelling of correlational and multilevel data in educational research: A construct validity approach to exploring and testing theory. In L. Markauskaite, P. Freebody, & J. Irwin (ed.), *Methodological choices and research designs for educational and social change: Linking scholarship, policy and practice* (pp. 209–224). Dordrecht, The Netherlands: Springer.

Marton, F. (1976). What does it take to learn? Some implications of an alternative view of learning. In N. Entwistle (ed.), *Strategies for research and development in higher education* (pp. 32–42). Amsterdam: Swets & Zeitlinger.

Marton, F. & Säljö, R. (1976). On qualitative differences in learning, outcome and process I. *British Journal of Educational Psychology, 46,* 4–11.

Mayer, R.E. (2009). *Multimedia learning* (2nd Ed.). New York, NY: Cambridge University Press.

Mazur, E. (1992). Qualitative versus quantitative thinking: Are we teaching the right thing? *Optics and Photonics News, 3,* 38.

Mazur, E. (1997). *Peer instruction.* Upper Saddle River, NJ: Prentice Hall.

McCoach, D.B. (2010). Hierarchical linear modeling. In G.R. Hancock and R.O. Mueller (eds), *The reviewer's guide to quantitative methods in the social sciences* (pp. 123–140). New York: Routledge.

McDonald, R.P. (1981). The dimensionality of tests and items. *British Journal of Mathematical and Statistical Psychology, 34,* 100–117.

McInnis, C., Griffin, P., James, R., & Coates, H. (2001). *Development of the Course Experience Questionnaire (CEQ)*. Canberra, Australia: Australian Government Publishing Service.

McKay, J. & Kember, D. (1997). Spoonfeeding leads to regurgitation: A better diet can result in more digestible learning outcomes. *Higher Education Research and Development, 16*, 55–67. DOI: 10.1080/0729436970160105

McKeachie, W. (1997). Student ratings: The validity of use. *American Psychologist, 52*, 1218–1225.

McKernan, J. (1991). *Curriculum action research*. London: Kogan Page.

McKinnon, K.R., Walker, S.H., & Davis, D. (2000). *Benchmarking: A manual for Australian universities*. Canberra: Australian Department of Education, Training and Youth Affairs. Retrieved from http://www.dest.gov.au/sectors/higher_education/publications_resources/profiles/archives/benchmarking_a_manual_for_australian_universities.htm

McNiff, J. (1992). *Action research: Principles and practice*. London: Routledge.

Messick, S. (1989). Validity. In R.L. Linn, (ed.) *Educational measurement*, 3rd edition (pp. 13–103). Old Tappan, NJ: Macmillan.

Messick, S. (1992). The interplay of evidence and consequences in the validation of performance assessments. Paper presented at the Annual Meeting of the National Council on Measurements in Education, San Francisco, CA: April.

Messick, S. (1995). Validity of psychological assessment: validation of inferences from persons responses and performances as scientific inquiry into score meaning. *American Psychologist, 50*, 741–749.

Messick, S. (1996). Validity and washback in language testing. *Language Testing, 13*, 241–256. DOI: 10.1177/026553229601300302

Miller, M.B. (1995). Coefficient alpha: A basic introduction from the perspectives of classical test theory and structural equation modelling. *Structural Equation Modeling, 2*, 255–273. DOI: 10.1080/10705519509540013

Moon, J. (2008). *Critical Thinking, an exploration in theory and practice*. London: Routledge.

Morley, D.D. (2009). SPSS macros for assessing the reliability and agreement of student evaluations of teaching. *Assessment & Evaluation in Higher Education, 34*, 659–671. DOI: 10.1080/02602930802474151

Moser, C.A. & Kalton, G. (1979). *Survey methods in social investigation* (2nd Ed.). Aldershot, UK: Gower.

Mueller, R.O. & Hancock, G.R. (2010). Structural equation modeling. In G.R. Hancock and R.O. Mueller (eds), *The reviewer's guide to quantitative methods in the social sciences* (pp. 371–384). New York: Routledge.

Muthén, L.K. & Muthén, B.O. (1998–2010). *Mplus user's guide*. Los Angeles, CA: Muthén & Muthén.

Nelson Laird, T.F., Chen, D., & Kuh, G.D. (2008). Classroom practices at institutions with higher–than–expected persistence rates: What student engagement data tell us. *New Directions for Teaching and Learning, 115*, 85–99. DOI: 10.1002/tl.327

Noar, S.M. (2003). The role of structural equation modeling in scale development. *Structural Equation Modeling, 10*, 622–647. DOI: 10.1207/S15328007SEM1004_8

Northedge, A. (1976). Examining our implicit analogies for learning processes. *Programmed Learning and Educational Technology, 13*, 67–78.

Norusis, M. (2002) *SPSS11.0 Guide to Data*. Upper Saddle River, NJ: Prentice Hall.

Nunnally, J.C. (1978). *Psychometric theory* (2nd Ed.). New York, NY: McGraw–Hill.

O'Neill, J., Conzemius, A., with Commodore, C., & Pulsfus, C. (2006). *The power of SMART goals: Using goals to improve student learning*. Bloomington, IN: Solution Tree.

Onwuegbuzie, A.J., Daniel, L.J. & Collins, K.M.T. (2009). A meta–validation model for assessing the score–validity of student teaching evaluations. *Quality and Quantity, 43*, 197–209. DOI: 10.1007/s11135-007-9112-4

Osborne, J.W. (2010). Correlation and other measures of association. In G.R. Hancock and R.O. Mueller (eds), *The reviewer's guide to quantitative methods in the social sciences* (pp. 55–70). New York: Routledge.

Ouimet, J.A. & Smallwood, R.A. (2005). CLASSE – the Class–level Survey of Student Engagement. *Assessment Update, 17,* 13–15.

Pajares, F., Hartley, J., & Valiante, G. (2001). Response format in writing self–efficacy assessment: Greater discrimination increases prediction. *Measurement and Evaluation in Counseling and Development, 33,* 214–221.

Palermo, J. (2004). *Benchmarking student feedback across the ATN: A quality improvement group project 2003, Final Report.* Retrieved from http://www.atn.edu.au/docs/Benchmarking%20Student%20Feedback%20Accross%20the%20ATN.pdf

Pandey, P. & Zimitat, C. (2007). Medical students' learning of anatomy: Memorization, understanding and visualization. *Medical Education, 41,* 7–14. DOI: 10.1111/j.1365–2929.2006.02643.x

Pastor, D.A. (2010). Cluster analysis. In G.R. Hancock and R.O. Mueller (eds), *The reviewer's guide to quantitative methods in the social sciences* (pp. 41–54). New York: Routledge.

Patrick, K. (1999). Using CEQ results at RMIT. In T. Hand & K. Trembath (eds), *The Course Experience Symposium 1998.* Canberra, Australia: DETYA.

Pedhazur, E.J. (1997). *Multiple regression in behavioral research: Explanation and prediction* (3rd Ed.). Fort Worth, TX: Harcourt Brace.

Penny, A.R. & Coe, R. (2004). Effectiveness of consultation on student ratings feedback: A meta–analysis. *Review of Educational Research, 74,* 215–253. DOI: 10.3102/00346543074002215

Preacher, K.J. & MacCallum, R.C. (2003). Repairing Tom Swift's Electric Factor Analysis Machine. *Understanding Statistics, 2,* 13–43.

Prentice, D.A. & Miller, D.T. (1992). When small effects are impressive. *Psychological Bulletin, 112,* 160–164.

Private Universe Project in Science (1995). *Private Universe Project in Science.* Burlington: Annenberg/CPB. Retrieved from http://www.learner.org/resources/series29.html

Prosser, M. & Trigwell, K. (1999). *Understanding learning and teaching: The experience of higher education.* Buckingham, UK: SRHE & Open University Press.

Purdie, N.J. & Hattie, J. (2002). Assessing students' conceptions of learning. *Australian Journal of Educational and Developmental Psychology, 2,* 17–32.

Ramsden, P. (1979). Student learning and perceptions of the learning environment. *Higher Education, 8,* 411–427.

Ramsden, P. (1991). A performance indicator of teaching quality in higher education: The Course Experience Questionnaire. *Studies in Higher Education, 16,* 129–150. DOI: 10.1080/03075079112331382944

Ramsden, P. (2003). *Learning to teach in higher education.* London: Routledge.

Ramsden, P., & Entwistle, A. (1981). Effects of academic departments on students' approaches to studying. *British Journal of Educational Psychology, 51,* 368–383. DOI: 10.1111/j.2044–8279.1981.tb02493.x

Raykov, T. (2009). Evaluation of scale reliability for unidimensional measures using latent variable modeling. *Measurement and Evaluation in Counseling and Development, 42,* 223–232. DOI: 10.1177/0748175609344096

Raykov, T. & Shrout, P.E. (2002). Reliability of scales with general structure: Point and interval estimation using a structural equation modeling approach. *Structural Equation Modeling, 9,* 195–212. DOI: 10.1207/S15328007SEM0902_3

Richardson, J. (2005). Concept Inventories: Tools For Uncovering STEM Students' Misconceptions. In *Invention and Impact: Building Excellence in Undergraduate Science, Technology, Engineering and Mathematics (STEM) Education* (pp. 19–25). New York: American Association for the Advancement of Science.

Richardson, J.T.E. (2005). Instruments for obtaining student feedback: A review of the literature. *Assessment & Evaluation in Higher Education, 30,* 387–415. DOI: 10.1080/02602930500099193

Richardson, J.T.E. (2006). Investigating the relationship between variations in students' perceptions of their academic environment and variations in study behaviour in distance education. *British Journal of Educational Psychology, 76,* 867–893. DOI:10.1348/000709905X69690

Richardson, J.T.E., Slater, J.B., & Wilson, J. (2007). The National Student Survey: Development, findings and implications. *Studies in Higher Education, 32,* 557–580. DOI: 10.1080/03075070701573757

Rodgers, R. & Hunter, J. (1991). Impact of management by objectives on organizational productivity. *Journal of Applied Psychology, 76,* 322–336.

Rubio, D.M., Berg–Weger, M., & Tebb, S.S. (2001). Using structural equation modeling to test for multidimensionality. *Structural Equation Modeling, 8,* 613–626. DOI: 10.1207/S15328007SEM0804_06

Salmon, G. (2011). *E–moderating: The key to teaching and learning online.* Abingdon, UK: Routledge.

Samuelsen, K.M. & Dayton, C.M. (2010). Latent class analysis. In G.R. Hancock and R.O. Mueller (eds), *The reviewer's guide to quantitative methods in the social sciences* (pp. 173–184). New York: Routledge.

Savinainen, A. & Scott, P. (2002). Using the Force Concept Inventory to monitor learning and plan teaching. *Physics Education, 37,* 53–58. DOI:10.1088/0031-9120/37/1/307

Scheaffer, R.L., Mendenhall, W., & Ott, R.L. (1996). *Elementary survey sampling* (5th Ed.). Davis, CA: Duxbury Press.

Schmitt, M. (1996). Uses and abuses of coefficient alpha. *Psychological Assessment, 8,* 350–353.

Schneider, B., Carnoy, M., Kilpatrick, J., Schmidt, W., & Shavelson, R. (2007). *Estimating causal effects using experimental and observational designs.* Washington, DC: American Educational Research Association. Retrieved from http://www.aera.net/uploadedFiles/Publications/Books/Estimating_Causal_Effects/Causal%20Effects.pdf

Schratz, M. (1992). Researching while teaching: An action research approach in higher education. *Studies in Higher Education, 17,* 81–95. DOI: 10.1080/03075079212331382786

Scott, G. (2005). *Accessing the Student Voice: Using CEQuery to identify what retains students, and promotes engagement in productive learning in Australian higher education.* Canberra, Australia: DEST. http://www.dest.gov.au/sectors/higher_education/publications_resources/profiles/access_student_voice.htm

Scriven, M. (1994). Using student ratings in teacher evaluation: Evaluation perspective. *Newsletter of the Centre for Research and Educational Accountability and Teacher Evaluation, 4,* 1–4.

Shadish, W.R., Cook, T.D., & Campbell, D.T. (2002). *Experimental and quasi–experimental designs for generalized causal inference.* Boston, MA: Houghton–Mifflin.

Shavelson, R.J., Webb, N.M., & Rowley, G.L. (1989). Generalizability theory. *American Psychologist, 44,* 922–932.

Smallwood, R.A. (2011). CLASSE Overview. Retrieved from http://assessment.ua.edu/CLASSE/Overview.htm

Smallwood, R.A. & Ouimet, J.A. (2009). CLASSE: Measuring student engagement at the classroom level. In T. Banta, E. Jones and K. Black (eds), *Designing effective assessment: Principles and profiles of good practice.* San Francisco, CA: Jossey–Bass.

Smith, M.K., Wood, W.B., & Knight, J.K. (2008). The Genetics Concept Assessment: A new concept inventory for gauging student understanding of genetics. *CBE – Life Sciences Education, 7,* 422–430. DOI: 10.1187/cbe.08–08–0045

Snijders, T.A.B. & Bosker, R. (1999) *Multilevel analysis: An introduction to basic and advanced multilevel modelling.* London: Sage.

Strauss, A. & Corbin, J. (1990). *Basics of qualitative research: Grounded theory procedures and techniques*. Newbury Park, CA: Sage.

Streveler, R., Olds, B., Miller, R., & Nelson, M. (2003). Using a Delphi study to identify the most difficult concepts for students to master in thermal and transport science. *Proceedings of the 2003 ASEE Conference*. Washington, DC: ASEE. http://2020engineer.iss.utep.edu/world/Research%20Literature/ASEE03_delphi_paper.pdf

Taylor, R. & Canfield, P. (2007). Learning to be a scholarly teaching faculty: Cultural change through shared leadership. In A. Brew & J. Sachs (eds), *Transforming a university: The scholarship of teaching and learning in practice*. (pp. 233–247). Sydney: Sydney University Press.

Thompson, B. & Vacha–Haase, T. (2000). Psychometrics is datametrics: The test is not reliable. *Educational and Psychological Measurement, 60*, 174–195. DOI: 10.1177/ 0013164400602002

Tinto, V. (1975). Dropout from higher education: A theoretical synthesis of recent research. *Review of Educational Research, 45*, 89–125. http://www.jstor.org/stable/1170024

Tinto, V. (1987). *Leaving college: Rethinking the causes and cures of student attrition*. Chicago, IL: The University of Chicago Press.

Topping, K. (1998). Peer assessment between students in colleges and universities. *Review of Educational Research, 68*, 249–276. DOI: 10.3102/00346543068003249

Tucker, B., Jones, S., & Straker, L. (2008). Online student evaluation improves Course Experience Questionnaire results in a physiotherapy program. *Higher Education Research and Development, 27*, 281–296. DOI: 10.1080/07294360802259067

Tucker, B., Jones, S., Straker, L., & Cole J. (2003). Course evaluation on the web: Facilitating student and teacher reflection to improve learning. *New Directions for Teaching and Learning, 96*, 81–94. DOI: 10.1002/tl.125

USA Today (2010). How to make NSSE college scores work for you. Retrieved from http://www.usatoday.com/news/education/nsse.htm

Usher, E.L. & Pajares, F. (2008). Self–efficacy for self–regulated learning: A validation study. *Educational and Psychological Measurement, 68*, 443–463. DOI: 10.1177/ 0013164407308475

Vagias, W.M. (2006). *Likert–type scale response anchors*. Retrieved from http://www.hehd.clemson.edu/prtm/trmcenter/scale.pdf

van Merriënboer, J.J.G., & Sweller, J. (2010). Cognitive load theory in health professional education: Design principles and strategies. *Medical Education, 44*, 85–93. DOI: 10.1111/j.1365–2923.2009.03498.x

Vroom, V.H. (1964). *Work and motivation*. New York: Wiley.

Wage, K.E., Buck, J.R., Wright, C.H.G., & Welch, T.B. (2005). The Signals and Systems Concept Inventory. *IEEE Transactions on Education, 48*, 448–461. DOI: 10.1109/ TE.2005.849746

Watkins, D. & Hattie, J. (1985). A longitudinal study of the approaches to learning of Australian tertiary students. *Human Learning, 4*, 127–141.

Watson, S. (2003). Closing the feedback loop: Ensuring effective action from student feedback. *Tertiary Education and Management, 9*, 145–157. DOI: 10.1080/13583883.2003.9967099

Wilson, K., Lizzio, A. & Ramsden, P. (1997). The development, validation and application of the Course Experience Questionnaire. *Studies in Higher Education, 22*, 33–53. DOI: 10.1080/03075079712331381121

Winer, B.J., Brown, D.R., & Michels, K.M. (1991). *Statistical principles in experimental design* (3rd Ed.). New York: McGraw–Hill.

Wright, T. & Hamilton, S. (2008). Assessing student understanding in the molecular life sciences using a concept inventory. In A. Duff, M. Green, & D. Quinn (Chairs), *Proceedings of ATN Assessment 08: Engaging Students with Assessment* (pp. 216–224). Adelaide, Australia.

Zuber–Skerrit, O. (1992). *Action research in higher education: Examples and reflections*. London: Kogan Page.

Index